TALES OF PSYCHOTHERAPY

To Chris and Fred

TALES OF PSYCHOTHERAPY

Edited and introduced by
Jane Ryan

KARNAC

First published in 2007 by
Karnac Books Ltd
118 Finchley Road
London NW3 5HT

British Library Cataloguing in Publication Data

A C.I.P for this book is available from the British Library

ISBN-13: 978–1–85575–492–8

Edited, designed, and produced by
Florence Production Ltd, Stoodleigh, Devon
www.florenceproduction.co.uk

Printed in Great Britain by Biddles Ltd,. King's Lynn, Norfolk

www.karnacbooks.com

Cover design: Gubert Courbanally

CONTENTS

ABOUT THE CONTRIBUTORS

The Editor

Jane Ryan initially went to art school in Canterbury, and then followed a career in community development. She founded an intercultural community centre in St Paul's, Bristol, now known as Kuumba. She trained in psychoanalytic psychotherapy in the early 1990s and then set up Confer, an independent organisation that offers a platform for leading thinkers in mental health and an inclusive space for the exchange of views between theoretical approaches within mental health and medical disciplines. She is the editor of *How Does Psychotherapy Work?* (Karnac 2005).

The Authors

Helen Alexander has a professional background in social work, the Christian ministry and psychoanalytical psychotherapy. Lately she has rediscovered a delight in writing. She lives and works in Edinburgh.

William Bedford has published essays, short stories and poetry in *The Critical Quarterly, The Daily Telegraph, The Dalhousie Review, Encounter, Essays in Criticism, The Independent, London Magazine, London Review of Books, The Malahat Review, The Nation, The Poetry Review, Punch, The Southern Review, Tribune, Wascana Review, The Washington Times* and many others. His first novel *Happiland* was shortlisted for the Guardian Fiction Prize, and he has received Arts

Council, Society of Authors and Yorkshire Arts Council Awards. He is founding editor of *Enigma*, editor of *Delta*, editor of three special editions of *Agenda* on Robert Lowell, Peter Dale and Seamus Heaney. He is currently working on a radio drama about Simone Weil.

Bernardine Bishop has a background in academic English, writing and teaching. She is a member of the London Centre for Psychotherapy and of the Lincoln Clinic. She is the editor of several books on psychotherapy and works in private practice as a psychoanalytic psychotherapist in London.

Sandra Black has worked as a psychoanalytic psychotherapist since qualifying at IPSS, London when R.D. Laing was supervisor. Born in India of Scots parents, with schooling in both countries she finally chose to train at the Royal Scottish Academy as a drama teacher—a good grounding in conflict, struggle and passion. She is interested in dreams; curious about synchronicity, destiny versus fate, and life's karmic happenings. She has one daughter (and three cats.)

Dr A. H. Brafman is a psychoanalyst of adults and children. He worked in the NHS as a Consultant Child and Adolescent Psychiatrist. He has been involved in teaching programmes for analysts, psychotherapists and medical students. He was a member of the Child Analysis committee of the Institute of Psychoanalysis and of the BAP Ethics Committee.

Alice Bree is a psychoanalytic psychotherapist who also has a BA(Hons) in Ceramics. She taught part time at Eton College and the University of Hertfordshire for ten years, but now works in Private Practice and at Marylebone Healing and Counselling Centre as well as supervising trainee counsellors at Highgate Counselling Centre. She is particularly interested in the creative process, and is currently working with music therapists.

Barry Christie is a United Kingdom Council for Psychotherapy registered psychotherapist who trained at the Centre for Attachment-Based Psychoanalytic Psychotherapy. Since graduating from the London School of Economics in 1983 he has maintained a strong interest in psychoanalytic theory and practice. He has worked as a therapist within the NHS and voluntary sector and also held public sector policy and project management positions within social services, urban regeneration, community safety, education and healthcare.

Stephanie Elliott is a Senior Mental Health Nurse in an in-patient setting, a counsellor/psychotherapist in HM Prisons and in private practice. She obtained an MSc in Psychotherapy and Counselling as a Means to Health at the University of Surrey and is accredited with the BACP. She is currently training in Forensic Psychotherapeutic Studies at the Portman Clinic in London.

Ella Landauer is an integrative psychotherapist and a writer, working in Oxford and Windsor. She has a particular interest in the use of written narratives in working with clients. Brought-up in London, in the 1980s she lived and worked in Vienna and Graz and now lives near London with her husband, daughter and son.

Zoë Fairbairns' short story collection *How do You Pronounce Nulliparous?* is published by Five Leaves. She is currently writing a radio play about the lives of the writer Karthryn Hulme and her partner Marie Louise Habets. Her published novels include *Live as Family* (1968), *Down: An Explanation* (1969), *Benefits* (1979), *Stand We At Last* (1983), *Here Today* (1984), which was awarded the 1985 Fawcett Society Book Prize; *Closing* (1987), *Daddy's Girls* (1992) and *Other Names* (1998). She lives in London and teaches short story writing at the City Lit.

Anna Fodorova works as a psychoanalytic psychotherapist in private practice and also as a senior lecturer in audiovisual studies at Central Saint Martin's College of Art and Design. She originally trained as an illustrator and filmmaker at the Royal College of Art. She has made animated films for TV programmes, written live action feature length TV scripts, published children's fiction and contributed papers to Psychodynamic Practice.

Judith Harris is the author of the poetry collection *Atonement* and the critical work *Signifying Pain: Construction and Healing the Self through Writing*. Her latest collection of poetry *The Bad Secret* has been nominated for the Pulitzer Prize for poetry. She teaches creative writing, literature and psychoanalytic theory at Catholic University and George Mason University and lives in Washington DC with her husband and daughter.

Peter Heinl is a psychiatrist, psychotherapist and family therapist practicing in London, Germany and Austria. He is director of the psychosomatic training course at the Centre for Science and Higher Eduation in Schloss Hofen, Austria. Peter Heinl is author of the book *Splintered Innocence: An Intuitive Approach to Treating War Trauma* (2001) and many other writings in the fields of physiology, psychotherapy and family therapy.

Diane Helliker was born in Ottawa, Canada and lived for many years in Toronto. She now resides in Quebec City with husband Douglas and her cat Molly. She has a degree in Drama and History from the University of Toronto and is currently working on a full length play about two young women sharing a room in a psychiatric hospital in the 1960s. Her publications include *Mother, We Never Knew You*, a play performed for the Wells One Minute Playwrighting Festival, Wells, British Columbia (2002), and 'Serendipity', a short story published in *Cat Tales: The Meaning of Cats in Women's Lives*, Spinifex Press, Australia (2003).

Marika Henriques is a Jungian psychotherapist in private practice. She is a Member of the Guild of Psychotherapists and the Foundation for Psychotherapy and Counselling. She is an active Member of the C.G. Jung Analytical Psychology Club, where she has given several talks. She has published in various psychotherapy journals. Her last paper 'The Lions Are Coming': The Healing Image in Jungian Dreamwork was published in the British Journal of Psychotherapy in 2004.

David Herbert has a background in the theatre, acting and writing for the stage. The bridge across to a seemingly new profession, psychotherapy ('Theatre of the Mind'), was a natural route to take, initially through Psychodrama. He now practices Jungian dream analysis with a down-to-earth Adlerian application. The change of profession has not deflected his need to write.

Barbara Hillman was born in South Africa of English parents in 1947, where she lived for 18 years. She has three children and a stepson. Fascinated by her youngest daughter's speech development, she began a daily journal, unwittingly finding her own voice. She writes poetry, short stories and currently a memoir. A pianist and teacher, she lives with her husband in Oxfordshire.

Katherine Justesen was born in Plymouth and spent her early childhood in South Africa before returning to the UK. She worked for many years in IT Marketing and Formula One sponsorship until her own experiences in therapy led her to start training to be a psychotherapist. She has recently completed an Advanced Diploma in Integrative Counselling & Psychotherapy. She holds a clinic for a charitable organisation and also sees clients privately.

Brett Kahr is a psychotherapist who has worked in mental health for twenty-five years. He is the Senior Clinical Research Fellow in Psychotherapy and Mental Health at the Centre for Child Mental Health in London. He is also Visiting Clinician at the Tavistock Centre for Couple Relationships. He is a prolific author of several mental health publications on topics from schizophrenia to sexual fantasy, and his book *D.W. Winnicott: A Biographical Portrait* was winner of the Gradiva Prize for Biography. He can be heard in regular slots on BBC Radio 2's as their Resident Psychotherapist.

Phil Lapworth lives and works as a psychotherapist and supervisor in the Avon Valley near Bath. He is the author and co-author of several publications in the field of counselling and psychotherapy, most recently *Integration in Counselling & Psychotherapy—Developing a Personal Approach*. He has had a longstanding wish to see some of his fictional writings published, so he is more than delighted that his work is appearing in this volume.

Phil Leask is a writer of novels and short stories. Originally from Australia, he now lives in London. His three novels—*Olhovsky, Prince of Hamburg*; *The Slow Death of Patrick O'Reilly*; and *By Way of Water*—have been published by Black Pepper (Melbourne). His short stories have appeared in the UK and in Australia.

With an early background in psychology and in teaching, **Annie Macdonald** then had a career as a writer and as a television producer, culminating in an eighteen year study in child development filmed for Channel Four. She continued her training in psychotherapy, taking an MSc at Birkbeck, and is now in private practice in London and Wales.

Before undertaking psychoanalytic psychotherapy training, **Annie McMillan** worked as a mental health social worker specialising in para-suicide and community mental health. For the past fourteen years, she has been in private practice as a psychoanalytic psychotherapist. She is interested in developing a broader understanding of mental health issues through a psychoanalytic psychotherapy-informed approach. She is a Member of the United Kingdom Council for Psychotherapy and a Member of the College of Psychoanalysts.

Antoinette Marshall was born in France and came to live in England after graduating in English from the University of Lyon. She married and studied for a PGCE at the University of Durham. She taught French for many years then qualified as a psychotherapist at the Institute for Psychotherapy and Social Studies, London, in 1984. Meanwhile she brought up three children and carried on writing, mainly short stories and poems. She practices as an analytical psychotherapist in North London.

Maggie Murray is a psychoanalytic psychotherapist trained in London at the Westminster Pastoral Foundation and at the Foundation for Psychotherapy and Counselling. She works in private practice in North London. In an earlier life she was a documentary photographer.

Deborah Oilman grew up in Jerusalem in the post War of Independence years of shortages, and witnessed the ebb and flow of despair and hope in this diverse, multi layered city. After studying at the Hebrew University of Jerusalem she moved to England where she worked for many years in the field of mental health, as well as involving herself in literary activities. She is the author of a number of short stories.

After bringing up her children, **Sandra Primack** became a sign language communicator while embarking on a part time psychodynamic counselling course. After four and a half years she was awarded an Advanced Diploma. She has been a student counsellor at Middlesex University for the past twelve years and works in a doctor's surgery. She rediscovered writing after she became a widow, and is delighted to have merged her career and her hobby in this short story.

Carole Smith was born and educated in Sydney, Australia where she took a degree in Arts, before travelling to England in 1962. After teaching, she became involved with film production, and produced documentaries and children's feature films. Following the birth of her children, she trained as a psychoanalytical psychotherapist, and worked in private practice, after further training with R.D. Laing. She is an outspoken critic of government policy, which increasingly diagnoses human unhappiness as mental disorder. She has been a contributor to the psychoanalytical journals, *Free Associations*, and the *Journal of Psycho-Social Studies*.

Valerie Sinason is a poet, child and adult psychotherapist and adult psychoanalyst specialising in trauma and disability. A post consultant psychotherapist at the Tavistock and Portman Clinics, Anna Freud Clinic and St Georges Hospital Medical School, she is now director of the Clinic for Dissociative Studies. Her most recent book is *Attachment, Trauma and Multiplicity: Working with Dissociative Identity Disorder*. Her latest poetry collection is *Night Shift*. She lives and works in London.

Melanie Skye is a visual artist who has had many experiences of different therapists. She has also completed a counselling course. She is a parent and lives in London.

Mary Steel is an Art Therapist working in Adolescent Psychiatry. At the time of writing 'The Process of Healing the Fish', she had recently left a specialist school after four years of individual work with children and adolescents who had a variety of behavioural and emotional difficulties. This piece is a synthesis of some of her experiences which focuses on the process of one session, and it is dedicated to all of the children who inspired its writing.

Rosemary Stones is a psychoanalytic psychotherapist in private practice and a writer. She has written a number of self-help and situation books for children and young people including *Don't Pick on Me: How to Handle Bullying*, now in its fifth edition. She is also the editor of the children's book review journal *Books for Keeps*.

Paul Thompson originally qualified in social work and then in psychoanalytic psychotherapy. He was a principal psychiatric social worker and then a mental health team manager until heading the course in Social Work at the University of East London. Since 2002 he has been Director of Social Work for the West London Mission. He has published papers in the European Journal for Counselling, Psychotherapy and Health, and Psychoanalytic Studies, together with a modest output of poems in various anthologies.

Jan Waterson has worked in health and social care and in higher education. Although she has a longstanding interest in narrative research, it is only by chance and relatively recently that she started writing reflective autobiographical pieces. These have offered an antidote to academic writing and, although unanticipated, have themselves become part of her therapeutic process.

Born in 1942, **John Welch** lives in London. He has published four collections of poetry, the latest being *The Eastern Boroughs* (Shearsman 2004) He contributed an article 'Dream and Restoration', on the subject of poetry and psychoanalysis to *Poets on Writing: Britain 1970–1991* edited by Denise Riley (Macmillan 1992) while other writings touching on his personal experience of psychoanalysis have appeared in *The London Review of Books*, *The PN Review*, *The Reader*, *Scintilla* and elsewhere.

Alexandra Wilson is a member of the Severnside Institute for Psychotherapy and works in private practice. She is a founding member of the Analytic Network in Bath. She has a particular interest in the therapeutic potential of creative writing and runs a writing group for counsellors as well as facilitating workshops for counsellors and psychotherapists using writing for self development. She has had short stories published and won several prizes.

John Woods is a child and adolescent psychotherapist at the Portman Clinic, London. He is the author of *The End of Abuse; A Play Reading in Three Parts*, Open Gate Press 2002, *Boys Who Have Abused; Psychoanalytic Psychotherapy with Young Victims/perpetrators of Sexual Abuse*, Jessica Kingsley Publishers 2003, 'The Self Report of Andi; a fictional account of an adolescent's inpatient treatment' in *Clinical Child Psychology and Psychiatry* (2006), and the play *Compromise* performed at the Cockpit Theatre Nov 2005.

Anne Zachary trained in medicine and psychiatry at the Royal Free Hospital. She specialised in psychotherapy at the Cassel Hospital, trained concurrently as a psychoanalyst and worked briefly at the Maudsley before obtaining a consultant post at the Portman clinic where she has been for nearly twenty years. The Portman Clinic assesses and treats patients in the community with problems of violence, sexual perversion and delinquency. She currently spends two days a week seconded to the High Security Hospital, Broadmoor and has a half time private psychoanalytic practice.

Introduction

Psychotherapy is a unique relationship—as private as confession, as intimate as love, and as profound as can be borne—
not least because of the specific and unusual boundaries that
are placed around the encounter. Unlike friendship, marriage or
pastoral care, therapy occurs in a regular and repeated pattern of
meetings in which the therapist will strive to be consistent, authentic,
and offer an exceptional quality of listening to the intricate tales of
everyday life that tell of inner conflict and buried desires. That
back and forth between narrator and listener goes on at many levels
of consciousness—and hopefully with an exceptional degree of
awareness.

In good psychotherapy these countless stories are explored,
elaborated and reconfigured until fresh and empowering per-
spectives are discovered that enable the client to approach life with
greater confidence; out of these detailed exchanges new senses of
self are born and lives re-shaped. Being made up of many short
stories, psychotherapy effortlessly lends itself to a book of tales. The
therapeutic process itself is structured like the short story, designed
to enable a movement forwards and towards resolution, no matter
how open-ended each session might appear. It has its own special
vocabularies and concepts to describe experience, giving us access
to the subtleties and complexities of human existence. It transfers
elegantly and organically to a literary form.

When we invited people to send in their short stories we asked
them to submit either fictional or true pieces, and to be specific. Tales

1

that were written by therapists were clearly fictionalized to conceal the identity of patients or therapist authors. Others that were presented as fiction were obviously autobiographical in essence. Pseudonyms were being used—fact and fiction were simply melting into each other. Simultaneously, it was clear that many authors had taken great trouble to be honest and very specific about real events, even though details are disguised. It soon became clear that this distinction was not sustainable. Rather than dividing the book into fact or fiction, therefore, the chapters have been organized around unifying themes: boundaries, coincidence, healing, the psychotherapy relationship itself, childhood and love.

Many pieces were submitted. All had merit, either because they were so personal, so heartfelt or illuminating of human nature. The most difficult part of editing the book was drawing up the short list. Finally, the stories chosen were the ones found to be most enlightening, or tender.

Sadly, there are two or three stories that will reinforce the perception that psychotherapy is a precarious relationship because of the combination of power and frailty that is sometimes found in the therapist. It would have been enjoyable to create a collection that would only uplift the reader but it has been felt essential to allow space for the shadow of the profession within the book. Nonetheless, the reader can be hopeful of finding inspiration in the stories, as well as much gratification as a detective of the truth. They each have an immediacy, and accessibility that allows us to find our own resonance with each character or situation with ease. I would recommend reading with openness in order to capture the essence of what is sometimes transforming between people, but more often a painful struggle to shift one's experience of self and other. This book neither attempts to glamorise, disparage or purify the psychotherapy process. It attempts to show it in its full complexity, giving us an unguarded insight into the consulting room so that its strengths can be celebrated and its vulnerabilities better understood.

Jane Ryan, June 2007

Thanks to Brett Kahr, Phil Leask and Judith Harris for their helpful contributions to the editorial task.

BOUNDARIES

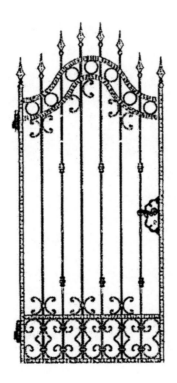

Why Freud Turned Down $25,000

Brett Kahr

On 21st May 1924 two wealthy, academically precocious Jewish-American teenagers attempted to commit the "perfect crime". Nathan Leopold, Jr (1904–1971), aged nineteen, son of multi-millionaire box manufacturer Nathan F. Leopold, Sr, and Richard Loeb (1905–1936), aged eighteen, son of Albert H. Loeb, a multi-millionaire Vice-President of Sears, Roebuck and Company, kidnapped Robert "Bobby" Franks, a younger boy of fourteen years of age, as he journeyed home from the Harvard School for Boys in the exclusive Hyde Park district of Chicago, Illinois. The following morning, Bobby Franks's father, Jacob Franks, a Chicago property tycoon, received a ransom letter by special delivery, demanding $10,000 in unmarked twenty dollar bills and fifty dollar bills; but before Franks could respond, the police had already located the naked body of Bobby Franks, soaked in blood, its skull bludgeoned by a chisel blow, abandoned in a marsh on the South Side of Chicago.

Although intent on committing the perfect crime, Nathan Leopold had nevertheless dropped his specially manufactured horn-rimmed spectacles at the scene of the crime, a symptomatic gesture perhaps indicative of the wish to be apprehended and treated. After consulting with Almer Coe and Company, the oculist who made the eyeglasses, the Cook County police eventually captured the killers. Both scions of wealthy Jewish families whose joint estimated wealth amounted to $15,000,000, the case of Leopold and Loeb excited tremendous anti-semitic bloodlust among the American populace, who clamoured for the execution of the two young culprits. Both fiercely intelligent, Loeb had become the youngest person ever to graduate from the University of Michigan, and Leopold held a similar distinction as the youngest ever baccalaureate from the

5

University of Chicago, graduating with Phi Beta Kappa honours, who had already commenced his postgraduate studies at the University of Chicago Law School. Leopold in particular shone as an academic, having studied fourteen languages, both classical and modern, as well as philosophy, enjoying a particular penchant for the works of Friedrich Nietzsche. He also delivered regular addresses to ornithological organisations based on his encyclopaedic knowledge of birds, as well as being an "advanced botanist". The press had a field day with such unusual and colourful brainy murderers.

In desperation, the family of Richard "Dickie" Loeb approached the famous lawyer, Clarence Seward Darrow (1857–1938), then sixty-seven years of age, suffering from neuralgia and rheumatism, in the hope that he would represent the boys, and save them from a death sentence by hanging. Though physically weary, and wary of the tide of public opinion against Leopold and Loeb, Darrow agreed to handle the case; and of course, he proved to be the perfect lawyer to represent them. A vocal opponent of capital punishment, Darrow (1922) had only recently published a pioneering and compas-sionate book *Crime: Its Cause and Treatment*, a hitherto unappreciated classic which anticipates many of the philosophical tenets of contemporary psychoanalytical forensic psychotherapy by insisting on compassionate treatment for offenders, recognising that criminals will be victims of their own histories. In his feisty polemic, Darrow spoke about the causal role of poverty and disadvantage in the genesis of criminal behaviour. He also argued strenuously for prison reform, and he believed passionately that the general public must also take responsibility for criminals. As a trial lawyer, Darrow endeavoured to introduce the psychological-motivational dimension into the courtroom itself.

Expert psychiatric testimony would be needed before the com-mencement of the trial in July 1924, and Darrow sought out his preferred experts, as did other progressive individuals who attempted to embroil themselves in this spectacularly public case. The prosecution had already secured the services of several eminent Chicago psychiatrists, so Darrow sent his colleague Mr Walter Bachrach, a relation of the Loeb family, to the annual meeting of the American Psychiatric Association in Atlantic City, New Jersey, who enlisted the support of Dr Bernard Glueck, Sr, Dr William Healy and Dr William Alanson White, three titans of American psychoanalytical psychiatry, all of whom had already established a specialisation in forensic work.

In view of the sensational scandal surrounding the case, and in view of pleas from the families of both Nathan Leopold and Richard Loeb, Colonel Robert Rutherford McCormick (1880–1955), the libertarian co-editor and co-publisher of the *Chicago Tribune* newspaper, instructed his staff reporter George Seldes to contact Professor Sigmund Freud in Vienna, inviting him to come to Chicago to serve as an expert witness in the infamous murder trial of the two young, privileged boys. A relation of Medill McCormick, a devotee of Carl Gustav Jung, and therefore, perhaps, sympathetic to the depth psychologies, Robert McCormick had instructed George Seldes to "Offer Freud 25,000 dollars or anything he names to come to Chicago psychoanalyze [the murderers]." Although Freud could have used the money fruitfully to sponsor the growing psychoanalytical movement, he refused the invitation of the *Chicago Tribune*. Newly diagnosed with carcinoma of the jaw one year earlier, and never a great fan of the United States of America, Freud remained in Vienna, having replied to Seldes by letter on 29th June 1924: "Your telegram reached me belatedly because of being wrongly addressed. In reply I would say that I cannot be supposed to be prepared to provide an expert opinion about persons and a deed when I have only newspaper reports to go on and have no opportunity to make a personal examination. An invitation from the Hearst Press to come to New York for the duration of the trial I have had to decline for reasons of health." It seems that William Randolph Hearst (1863–1951), the phenomenally wealthy newspaper tycoon whose life inspired the character of Charles Foster Kane in Orson Welles's acclaimed film *Citizen Kane*, had already invited Freud to come to New York for the same purpose. Hearst had told Freud that he could claim whatever fee he desired, and that Hearst would also charter a special ocean liner for Freud's express use.

Of course, Freud may have had other reasons apart from illness and anti-American prejudice which prevented him from travelling to the United States. We do not know whether he regarded the invitations of McCormick and Hearst as genuine, or rather as callous publicity stunts, because to the best of our knowledge, no surviving documentation exists which fleshes out the reason or reasons for

Freud's refusal. At the time of the trial, the *Chicago Tribune* had offered to arrange for a radio broadcast of the trial, whereas the *Evening American* had hoped to turn Comiskey Park, the local baseball stadium and home of the Chicago White Sox into an open-air courtroom. Thus, Freud may have worried that he would become embroiled in a media circus.

Fortunately Darrow, known in the press as the "Old Lion", managed very well indeed without Freud's intervention. Dr Glueck, Sr, a New York prison psychiatrist, Dr Healy, an expert in juvenile delinquency, and Dr White, the director of St Elizabeth's Hospital for the Insane in the District of Columbia (Washington, D.C.), testified successfully, albeit for the rather more modest fee of $250 per doctor, per day. The London-born judge, the Honorable John Caverly, capitulated to Darrow's pleading, and although entitled to insist upon death by hanging, Caverly sentenced Leopold and Loeb to life imprisonment, after having listened to Darrow's masterful twelve hour summation, delivered over the course of three days.

Freud's refusal to become an expert witness for the defence did not prevent Clarence Darrow from participating as one of the speakers in the special banquet for two hundred guests, organised by the Ritz-Carlton Hotel in New York City, in honour of Freud's seventy-fifth birthday in 1931. Dr William Alanson White delivered the principal address, and other speakers included Darrow and the noted novelist Theodore Dreiser.

One wonders, of course, what Freud might have had to say about Leopold and Loeb, and whether his insights on the case would have helped to facilitate the development of the field of forensic psychotherapy—the psychoanalytically-orientated treatment of patients who commit offences. Naturally, we cannot know. We also remain mystified as to the full extent of Freud's refusal of the blank cheque to come to the United States in a private ocean liner. Naturally, his cancer would have deterred him from making a long journey, but the cancer at that time did not confine him to his bed—he continued to work devastatingly lengthy days and nights treating patients, writing books and papers, and administering to the increasing complexities of the international psychoanalytical movement. Did cancer deter Freud from testifying for Clarence Darrow, or could anti-American feeling be blamed? Or did Freud fear the prospect of dealing with a case of murder, perhaps for countertransferential reasons? Or did he simply worry about the impact of collaborating with the mass media?

Several months after the completion of the Leopold-Loeb trial, the American film mogul Samuel Goldwyn travelled to Europe to meet with Sigmund Freud, to offer him the even more princely sum of $100,000 to serve as a consultant to proposed film on great love stories from history, beginning with Antony and Cleopatra. Not only did Freud turn down the offer of consultancy, as well as the gargantuan fee, but he refused even to meet with Goldwyn in person, in spite of the latter's long journey to Europe. According to Freud's colleague Hanns Sachs, Freud's treatment of Goldwyn created a greater stir in New York than had the original publication of the English translation of *The Interpretation of Dreams*.

Shortly thereafter, Freud expressed deeper concern still, when he discovered that two close disciples and collaborators—the afore-mentioned Hanns Sachs, and his beloved colleague Karl Abraham—had begun to offer their advisory services to the German film company, Universum Film Aktiengesellschaft (U.F.A.), for a film about psychoanalysis, eventually entitled *Geheimnisse einer Seele* [Secrets of a Soul], directed by the noted Austrian film-maker Georg W. Pabst. Though ultimately well-made and favourable towards psychoanalysis, Freud remained wary. Clearly his reluctance to participate in the Leopold-Loeb trial, the Samuel Goldwyn film project, and the U.F.A. film project betoken someone with a reluctance to engage with the popular media.

Naturally, Freud did not have the luxury to explore the media in the way that we do today—after all, psychoanalysis and psycho-therapy have become such well-established fixtures of both the clinical and the cultural landscapes that one injudicious piece of consultancy will hardly cause the edifice of modern psychology to crumble. Freud, by contrast, had to protect the scientific integrity of psychoanalysis in its early days to prevent its dilution. But ... did he protect the integrity of psychoanalysis too much?

French Leave

Rosemary Stones

"Kirsty's so bloody depressed!" says Joan, "to be honest, I dread her turning up. It's like a cloud arriving."

"She will be depressed," Alice replies. "Now she's managed to leave Dave there's space for the depression to come out. I talk to her on the phone quite a bit but she needs some proper help, not someone calling from England."

As she puts the phone down in her Birmingham flat, Alice pictures Joan, warm capable Joan, hurrying to open the gates of her Perigeux town house in response to Kirsty's ring, ushering the young woman through the limestone passage into the sunny courtyard with its wisteria and its bay tree. The swallows will still be swooping confidently overhead, back and forth to feed their young whose serious little faces will be peeping over the edge of their nests. Joan will offer tea and perhaps a slice of cake. She is one of those women whose cake tin always has a cake in it. Cake making is something I can't do without following a recipe, reflects Alice. And I don't have a cake tin.

Alice is a psychotherapist. These last weeks before her summer holiday she is experiencing each day as a series of obstacles that must be confronted or negotiated. Today is Tuesday and she has nine patients. She counts them off one by one. One done, eight to go. Another done, seven to go. And so on. Soon Alice will be going to the Dordogne to stay with Joan but at the moment that trip seems far away and unattainable. This week is never ending. Alice can't remember a more difficult time with patients just before a holiday. So far three have described suicidal thoughts, one has stormed out telling Alice that she is 'frigging useless' and another has announced that he is not planning to return after the break as he is not sure what the sessions are for any more. Alice reminds herself that this is to do with her going away and the separation and loss that her patients are experiencing but she wishes that they didn't have to let her know about their feelings quite so forcefully.

But now there is some light relief: today is the final session before the summer break with Roberto, a patient of whom Alice is fond— a pale, thin young man who curls up on the couch and pulls Alice's tartan rug up and over his head. He carefully leaves his feet hanging off the edge of the couch to protect its cover and his fragile, fine boned ankles are immensely poignant. This is why I do this work, Alice thinks to herself as she looks at the tartan shape on the couch. Roberto had a violent father who left when he was twelve and a mother who made him the man in her life—until a new boyfriend came along who also turned out to be violent. Earlier in the session he has reminded her how unsure he is that his life has meaning, that he matters to anyone. And do you matter to me? she had countered, partly on automatic pilot, partly from some profound and genuine response from within herself, mindful of how impossible it used to feel to her that she might be anything other than superfluous to requirements. How many years of therapy did it take for me to envisage even the possibility that I might be offered cake, she thinks, suddenly envious of Kirsty's ability to provoke concern.

It was five years ago. Outside the newsagent's window in the Grande Rue in Thiviers, Joan and Alice were scanning the cards pinned to a board advertising kittens, tractors and cars for sale. Joan was hoping to find a wood burning stove for her outhouse. The card was written in blue biro: *Dame anglaise sérieuse recherche travaux ménagers. Chèque emploi service.* Joan needed a cleaner and so it was that Joan contacted Kirsty, the dame anglaise.

Kirsty arrived punctually in a maroon estate car with English number plates driven by her husband, Dave. She was a heavily built, rather stolid young woman in her late thirties with short dark hair who said little. She and Dave, so the story went, tired of doing nothing but work (classroom assistant and supermarket manager respectively) in order to pay their mortgage, had recently arrived from England to make a new life in France. They had bought a house outright with their savings in a small hamlet outside Perigeux. They were available for any kind of work. Dave was chatty and deferential.

He admired Joan's splendid maison bourgeoise with its elegant windows, grand fireplaces, tommettes and spiral stone staircase. He talked convincingly about solutions for her outhouse conversion. He had a rather small, moist mouth and ate several of Joan's home made Langues de Chat.

It was agreed: Kirsty would come and clean for four hours, twice a week. She was unexpectedly fierce in her negotiations over the hourly rate, pointing out how far she would have to travel to get to Perigeux. Joan compromised, offering more than she had intended.

Reflecting on that first meeting, Alice wonders if there were clues she should have picked up. She remembers, guiltily, finding Kirsty a bit of a pudding. Then there was Kirsty's flustered concern that she and Dave might be overstaying their welcome; her embarrass-ment at Dave's acceptance of a second glass of wine; her own adamant refusal.

On a subsequent visit to Joan's house, Alice had encountered Kirsty, vacuum cleaner in hand. Later in the day the three women had sat together in the sunny courtyard, the bees meandering from one lavender bush to another.

"How is it working out for you in France?" Alice asked Kirsty.

"Oh, fine."

"And how's your French?"

"I get by."

"She managed to get her car registered as a French car", said Joan. "If you can manage that you can manage anything. It even had to go to the Inspector of Mines. When she told me that I thought she was joking."

"It's true though," murmured Kirsty.

"More tea? Alice? Kirsty?"

"No, really," said Kirsty. "I don't feel right sitting here when you're paying me. I should be working."

"But it's nice to have a chance to chat," Joan replied encouragingly. She filled Kirsty's cup. Kirsty sat uncomfortably.

"Do you have family in England?" Alice asked. "How do they feel about you being here?"

"There's my mum. I'm adopted and she remarried recently. Her new husband doesn't see that I'm anything to do with her because I'm not her real daughter."

"You feel you've lost her," said Alice.

"We were never very close. I don't think she liked me. Perhaps I wasn't what she wanted."

Not so surprising then, Alice reflects, to hear from Joan that Dave has been mistreating Kirsty for years and she has been on the point of killing herself. She must have been desperate for love when she met him. And now, in her mind, no one would miss her. How to get her some help? Even if she and Joan manage to find a therapist, Kirsty's limited French will be a problem. No wonder she's had trouble picking it up, thinks Alice, picturing Kirsty's awkward wariness and diffidence. She's been afraid all this time. And there are the financial problems now that she has moved out and is renting a room. Dave isn't offering her any money.

Alice imagines herself offering Kirsty sessions. There would be boundary issues of course, but some of Freud's patients went on holiday with him so that sessions could continue. There would have to be a regular time and should it be every day? An intense therapeutic encounter for the duration of her stay in Perigeux? Alice pictures Kirsty arriving for sessions in a room that she would have prepared. Perhaps in Joan's outhouse? That has its own separate entrance. How strange it would be to be working in such surroundings. She imagines a spartan yet beautiful room with the sounds of the birds outside the open windows and a glimpse of blue sky. This pleasant picture is gradually replaced by one where Alice dreads Kirsty's arrival and the interruption of her holiday. Resentment and irritation swirl up and the outhouse consulting room fantasy is consigned to oblivion. A French therapist must be found.

On the phone Kirsty is sceptical about the possibility of help. "I once told a friend at work how I felt and after a bit she said, why don't you have a cup of tea and a biscuit. So I learnt. Nobody wants to know. And it's understandable. People have their own problems and lives to lead. I have to sort this out for myself. I mean a therapist can't do anything. They just listen." Alice is persuasive: "If I can find a name, would you allow me to make contact on your behalf? I could explain the situation and we could find out what's possible."

"I suppose it won't hurt."

Should she put Cher Colleague or Cher Confrère? Alice is pleased with her letter to the social worker Joan met at her friend Pierre's house. She has little occasion to write in French these days but she has put together a good letter setting out Kirsty's situation and requesting advice on what therapeutic help might be available.

When the phone rings and it is Kirsty's voice, Alice is surprised. "Everyone knows about me," says Kirsty. "I can't go anywhere without people knowing."

"What do you mean?"

"Your letter. The man you sent it to must know people in my village because the mayor said to me, You're the English woman with the friend in Birmingham. But I can't help you. It's not my job. But I didn't ask him for help. I didn't ask anyone for help."

"How awful," says Alice. "That shouldn't have happened. The letter was confidential . . ."

"I've had sleepless nights," Kirsty interrupts, "because of this. I've had to decide, so what if they're talking about you. It will be a one-day wonder."

"You feel exposed," says Alice.

"I have been exposed by your letter," says Kirsty. "It was kind of you to try and help me but please don't do any more. I have to look after myself. No one else is going to."

There is a forceful confidence in her voice that Alice has never heard before.

"I'm sure you meant well," Kirsty continues, "but I'm fine. Really."

She's angry, thinks Alice. What happened has made her angry.

As the TGV leaves the Gare d'Austerlitz on its journey to Bordeaux [a year later,] Alice settles into her seat. She is not sure that she will like the new forceful Kirsty but she is looking forward to a holiday.

The Complaint

John Woods

The Patient's Account

I bring my case before you, without expecting that you will be particularly sympathetic. I am used to being treated as someone who has no rights; maybe it's true I have lost them. But my therapist ended the treatment, without explanation. I turned up at the Unit at the usual time and found a message to say he would not be able to see me anymore. I first thought at last it's got to him that I am a paedophile. I mean he knew it—it was the reason I was in therapy—but suddenly something happened. I don't know what, and I don't know if I will get a fair hearing here. People like me are treated with contempt. Rightly so. No-one hates them more than I do.

I have been abstinent for years. At this stage in my life (for I am now in my seventies) I was finally beginning to develop some self-respect. I don't understand why I was told not to come to sessions any more, with no reason, out of the blue. I protested to the Head of the Unit and was eventually offered an appointment. However he could say nothing about the abrupt ending of my therapy, instead that he would find me another therapist when the waiting list permitted. For nearly two years I had been seeing Mr Fisher. He hasn't answered my calls, nor my letters. I have had to make this complaint in order to get at least a hearing.

I want to say something about my past. I was a Catholic priest, and that was because I had hopes that the sexual feelings that were perturbing me, could be neutralised, as it were. I would devote myself to God, and do good, instead of what I knew was wrong. You see, right from when I was younger I had been tormented by impure and corrupt thoughts—about younger boys, younger than me I mean. I knew it was abnormal and I thought I could have no place in society. I wondered, still do: why did God afflict me like this? My only choices were suicide or relinquishing all hope of a sexual life.

The Church offered me a solution. Confession was the only place where I could confide my shame and fear. I was accepted. I studied hard and created a place for myself that seemed safe. The sexual desires, so unwelcome to me, were at least curtailed. I got solace from things like the boys' choir. It was innocent. No-one thought it strange that a priest was enraptured by these heavenly voices, raised to the greater glory of God. But the old feelings came back. There was always one who was special, who had the best voice, or was more fine, more sensitive than the rest, and I wanted to . . . well, I told myself that I wanted to be closer only to reward his hard work. Now I know it was really my own desire to relish his beauty. I felt safe in my role, so I was led into a false sense of security—and on occasions I lapsed.

It was not how it is portrayed by the law, by those words "indecent assault". There was never any coercion. It was just . . . touching. I know that's no defence. I'm not denying my wrongdoing, but I want to say that I should not be seen as some kind of violent rapist. I do know that it is always damaging to the child, but I want certain things to be clear.

I went to confession all the time. It was not enough. I had to evolve my own penances. There is no need to go into those here. I made my own Stations of the Cross. I have wondered if it was that which my therapist could not stand. If I suffered enough perhaps I would find absolution. At times I think it was granted me, but at others I felt abandoned by God. Remorseful? I was close to despair. I could go on living only by my determination each time not to slip again. For a while this would work, and I would think I was free of it, but then I would succumb . . . .

Since everything that has happened—a disclosure the Church could not conceal, my disgrace, the conviction, departure from holy orders, and going to prison—I have wondered if perhaps the Church did me a disservice by its forgiveness. Not that I am blaming them. How could my sin be understood as anything but the temptation of the flesh, the evil of Satan, getting me to turn away from God? But you see things differently in prison. I took part in the group treatment. Just as with religious studies, I devoted myself to the work.

I learned about the cycle of abuse, justifications, the cognitive distortions, victim empathy. I was absolutely committed to my relapse prevention plan, which was watertight in all but one respect. I yearned for affection and physical contact. I was advised to seek further therapy because I could only conceive of the love of a young boy. I knew from my life-script work that this had something to do with my childhood. It was emotionally bleak, as my therapist said, especially following my mother's long illness and death by the time I was ten years old. I was afraid of my father, and it was not difficult to take over the care of my younger brother, until that is I was sent away to boarding school, which was . . . just awful, indescribable.

So I sought long term psychotherapy to try and undo or at least modify the emotional side of my sexual problem. I had not touched a child for fifteen years, that is eleven spent inside, and the four years since. But I could not go on as I was, preoccupied still with thoughts of looking—only *looking* at boys, on the street, on public transport. They seemed so carefree, full of energy and delight, unpolluted by adult life. Of course I avoided playgrounds, school gates, swimming pools. It was only in the public library, one where the children's section was well away, that I found peace. And that was what my life consisted of, reading theology and philosophy. My doctorate was on Theories of the Meaning of Suffering; I considered myself already something of an expert. But away from the library, alone in my bedsit, I was living an empty shell of an existence. Probably I could have kept going. I could not commit the ultimate sin of self-murder, but I knew I needed help. Sometimes it seemed that God must hate me, or at least cared nothing, as indifferent as my father now, whose mind is completely clouded by Alzheimer's. What hell, to think that God has no compassion. And then I think of how little my suffering is compared to the millions tortured and starved to death.

And so I commenced therapy. Mr Fisher seemed sympathetic, though he made no promises. He said that psychotherapy would offer an additional dimension to the work I had already done. He agreed that maybe I could, by this means, get to the root of the problem—understand why I was trapped in the prison of impossible desires, tortured by the knowledge that if I were ever to reach, or even get near the pleasure and warmth of physical contact, I would be guilty of destroying that which I loved. All I should do was to tell him what came to mind, without editing or concealment.

I did so, and discovered that there was a great pool of anger beneath my self-loathing. I found this disturbing, but somehow went on to speak about all the things that had happened to me, the things I had done—there had never been space for such detail in the group sessions. The strange thing is that it was he who encouraged me to give up the victim role, to be aware of the bitterness in me. Perhaps it is only since the sessions have stopped that I have thought over what he used to say. At the time I hardly understood what he said and was sometimes a bit mystified by his comments about feeling dependent on him. I think I did have a therapeutic relationship, but when I spoke of my loneliness and isolation I did not think, as he seemed to be suggesting, that it was really him that I was missing when he went away. Of course I would struggle without my therapy, and the emptiness would come back, the sense of being spurned by everyone I have ever met. Apart that is from my mother, who was the sweetest, kindest, most beautiful person, more than a person, my world, until everything became dark when she fell ill.

It seems now that everything has gone back to that strange disjointed time when I did not know where to put myself, before I found the Church, although it found me, at boarding school. I had been really lost until then, and now I feel lost again, confused, and bewildered that maybe I did something to drive my therapist away. In bringing this complaint, I do not want him sacked, struck off, or sued for damages or anything like that, I just want to make sense of what has happened. Since he will not communicate with me I must do this, and what I am really hoping for is that you could do something—I don't know what—to resolve this. I felt he did really understand me. I was beginning to develop some hope. I don't know why the sessions were having this effect on me, but it was so, there was something about the way he listened. He was not judging, he seemed to accept what I was saying and the impossibility of love for me. I felt I had his sympathy though I also knew that professionally he would not say so exactly, because of course he is supposed to be impartial. But now I am wondering if maybe I was just imagining it. Perhaps he came to hate me, as he knew me better? In a way that would be preferable than being left hanging like this.

What I am left with is guilt. I thought I had more of a connection with him than with the group therapists who saw me when I was in prison. I fear I have caused some harm to him, and as I write this

I realise yes, he is still my therapist, and will always be, even though he wants nothing to do with me.

The Therapist's Response

I am told this is completely confidential, and I want to clarify that we are agreed on that. Specifically I do not want this letter nor the details of what is discussed here to be shared with my former patient, whom I shall call Mr Y. Although of course you have the names, I would request that in written submissions the privacy of everyone be respected. I have read the complaint that has been brought against me. I would like here to make my response, and though I accept that my behaviour has fallen short of professional standards, I want to present the circumstances, which I think do mitigate my fault.

Although only recently qualified as a psychologist I have worked with some complex and difficult cases in the forensic field. Mr Y, a convicted paedophile, did not seem particularly challenging because his assessment showed him to be well motivated for treatment, intelligent and articulate, and not highly disturbed emotionally. Although mild to moderately depressed there did not seem to be a suicidal risk. Previous reports from his group therapy reported him to be at low risk of re-offending. Furthermore I had been doing some research into the effects of child sexual abuse, had interviewed perpetrators, and wanted to get some direct experience of working therapeutically in depth with one. However I was not prepared for what was to transpire in the course of my working with Mr Y.

For about a year of therapy I found him to be preoccupied with his paedophilia in a narcissistic, self-pitying way. I admit it was difficult for me to maintain a professional stance from the beginning. He had a kind of intimacy in his manner that presumed familiarity and which grated. He could be almost self-righteous in the acknowledgement of his own fault. The bleating on about God was driving me nuts. He would induce boredom, irritation and revulsion. I took this problem to my supervisor, Miss Z, who helped me deal with the counter-transference. I understand that she has been asked to submit a report for this enquiry.

Respect for the patient, and the quest for new meaning in their life has always been my guiding principle. I was aiming to engage in a kind of therapeutic dialogue in order to find a new structure by which Mr Y could order his life. I tried as hard as I could to avoid judging him on the basis of his history of offences against children. You see, I believe that some perpetrators, not all perhaps, but many, do not have sufficient choice in their lives to adapt to the expectations of society. It is a fundamental misunderstanding that punishment, or treatment, will "correct" their wrongdoing. The label "abuser" is applied because society needs scapegoats. We have guilt, largely unconscious, about our own abuse of power, and the inequality of social structures. His discourse as a victim was a mirror of our discourse of power that needs victims like him who can be identified as an abuser/victim. I tried to show him how by adopting the punished abuser/victim he was playing into society's exploitation of his guilt. But perhaps because of the legacy of Mr Y's religious beliefs, we could not achieve an understanding on this basis. He seemed locked into his subjectivity. Clearly he had suffered as a result of his sexual orientation, and I never thought there would be a "cure" for that. However it felt as though we were getting nowhere. My supervisor at that time advised me to drop all preconceptions and listen more to Mr Y's own version of his experiences.

This is where things started to come apart. I found I did not want to hear about his idealisation of young boys. His romantic notions of their beauty started to make me feel sick. Subtly he was trying to induce in me some similar perverse pleasure in spoiling the innocence of a child. Despite myself, I was reminded of times in my own childhood when everything did seem simple and straight-forward. I was having dreams that took me back. I knew there had been a great change at some point, but had no idea why. Up until I was about eight years old I was part of the well-ordered world of my conventional Catholic family, the predictability of the Church, and the choir. It was said I had a fine soprano voice, and was happy enough in my small provincial city with no thoughts of the grandeur of Rome. But I was chosen to go to St Peter's along with the pick of other English boys' choirs. My mother was excited and proud but would always say how sad and mystified she was that I suddenly stopped singing after that trip. When asked why again and again, I pleaded with her to forget about it, I was not going back to the choir. At school and at Mass I clammed up. My father, who had always been distant, said it was up to me. A non-religious boarding school after that suited me fine, but photographs show a glowering and suspicious face. I didn't really know what it was but there was something I desperately needed to forget about Rome. No-one ever knew what had happened, nor did I know myself.

It started when Mr Y began to intrude into my dreams. I would wake up in a panic, shouting at him to get off, go away. I could not explain it to my wife, because I still did not understand. I knew that Mr Y had been a priest, but did not put it together until in one session, he mentioned Rome, and a particular boy whose charming voice was matched only by his open and free personality. This boy was so generous and lacking in vanity or self importance, he seemed to be unaware of the specialness of his gift. As I listened I thought: he is feeding off the boy's *unself-consciousness*. Still I could not see what was in front of me. Mr Y. spoke about the boy's clear, almost translucent skin, and I became aware of his pock-marked liver stained hand, dirty nails, grey straggly hair around his head, growing from ears, nostrils. And though I was always careful not to sit too close, I felt overwhelmed by a bitter smell that was unidentifiable, yet familiar. I became dizzy, nauseous, and hot. I was sweating, there was ringing in my ears, I could not breathe, I feared I would collapse. I thought of his creased and hairy body with which he would pollute the child's, and the smell came back to me, of an old sacristy, the same mustiness as in any church of the world, stale incense and rotting wood, and the smell of him, the grunting and furtive fumbling under black priestly garments. Him grabbing under my own white and red cassock that I would never wear again. There was an urgency in his talk I was not imagining because as it subsided I felt my own panic reduce into a dull fear of being there and an urgent wish to escape. I did not run from that session though I think I may have from the back room of the church. As I listened to his mournful ramblings I could not believe I had been so stupid. Of course he no longer had his priest's name, and I had so effectively forgotten the incident. I could hardly connect the living wreck of a patient I now had before me with the shadowy figure that threatened my dreams. Was he the same? Both yes and no. All I knew was that nothing would be the same for me again. Like the murder of a child this was final, irreversible, a life sentence.

I cancelled his sessions, mainly to give myself time to think. I struggled with feelings of revenge, when I should have been thinking what should be done from a professional point of view. I fantasised how I would have launched myself across the room and struck him down, but it would not have been him destroyed, or if it were he would love it. He would have won then, and my life damaged beyond repair. But the life I had lived was already in ruins. Who was I? The psychologist? The helper? The expert? Like a doctor in an epidemic I thought I was immune. Nothing could go back to how it was. This time there was no denial. Vengeance burned within me. I was nurturing plans for killing him in ways that could not be detected, of preparing the perfect alibi. My wife could be convinced I had been sleeping beside her instead of disposing his body in some clean quick fashion. But then there would be no forgetting. I guess I killed him symbolically, by killing off the therapy. Perhaps I should not go on being a psychologist, but cannot think of what else I can do.

After some weeks I brought myself to speak to my supervisor, and was astonished that she was not horrified but said yes, an extraordinary coincidence but essentially not surprising. After all people are drawn into this work for all sorts of reasons of their own.

"The first thing we need to do", she said, "is to make some arrangements for your patient. Then we have to think about therapy for you."

But I have been in a state of paralysis. I know she is right, but I resist going to someone because my whole professional development is going to be overshadowed by this. It won't be easy for me to let go of my anger—that's too mild a word—let go of my hatred and rage against Mr Y. I can see also how I repeated something of the abuse, by turning the tables and taking away his rights.

Then came the complaint, and after my initial panic at having to tell someone, and fear of the consequences, I welcome the chance to tell the story. Perhaps this hearing might help me resolve something. I have told my wife who says that now she knows now why I can be so cut off, obsessed with work. Sometimes she says there is a terrible anger in me that she does not understand. She used to feel it must somehow be her fault, but has learned to give up trying to get close when I am taken over by the "massive sulk", as she calls it. At least I now know where the feelings of hurt come from, and the impossibility of retribution.

I want to say how sorry I am to have brought such a problem upon the Unit. I realise I have behaved badly and may have brought the service into disrepute. My supervisor has suggested that I restrict my work in this area, until such a time when I can feel I have sufficiently dealt with my personal experiences, if ever.

The Supervisor's Report

I have been asked to give a professional opinion of Mr Fisher's work, which might help account for the complaint he is facing. I understand the question here is whether there has been a breach of the code of ethics, which may have caused emotional harm to the patient. And, that the consequences of such unprofessional behaviour may range from a reprimand to a termination of employment. Firstly however, with your permission, I would like to make some remarks of a more general nature. What I have to say refers not only to forensic work, but to many settings in the wider mental health field.

Although officially qualified to practice, many mental health workers are unprepared for the emotional impact of the traumatic lives of their patients. Everyone in the "helping" professions wants to help others. But when, for example, a psychologist moves from assessments, evaluations, and structured group work programmes into psychodynamic treatment he or she is exposed to the toxic effects of psychopathology. From one point of view, the professional is simply performing a function for an institution, which is providing containment as constructively as possible, protecting society and individuals from the harm that they may do or have done to them. But that harm is not just the consequence of specific acts or crimes that may have taken place years before. The harm is real and present, lodged in the mind of the victim even though he may have trans-formed himself into a perpetrator. Just hearing about destroyed lives should cause us pain, but when we change our way of working and engage with the inner world of such a person we cannot but be affected in all sorts of ways. We have a peculiar language for these effects, projections, counter-transference, empathy, identification, mentalisation, introjection, re-introjection, and so on, but the human side of this is that a potential for trauma is awakened in ourselves. We become part of the nightmarish world of abuse. I'm not going to give a lecture here, but must point out how my supervisee, like many others, was working in a context where there is minimal preparation or awareness of what he was getting into. It is a general characteristic of institutions of this kind; there is an abandonment of anyone who steps a little closer to the client, service user, inmate, patient, prisoner, whatever they are called. We should recognise, I believe, that our institutions do harm to those working for them as well as to the so-called "client" group.

Now there was a very specific vulnerability of this therapist. I understand from Mr Fisher that certain long suppressed childhood memories have come to mind as a result of working with his patient. This brings me on to a point that may have made me somewhat unpopular in the Unit, my belief that anyone working with severe psychopathology needs their own personal therapy. I hope it is clear now that this is not simply being precious. I have become accustomed to the fact that my role as a supervisor/consultant is more like an adviser, one who can be ignored. This particular situation, though unusual and possibly unique, nevertheless highlights certain features of our whole professional purpose. If we are to do any more than serve as a holding tank for vulnerable people, in order to ship them off to whatever provision can be found, if we are to have any therapeutic aims, then we have to rethink our whole ethos and consider the importance of training, whether it be in service, or seconded. We cannot afford to ignore the emotional strain of our work.

To come to the charge against Mr Fisher: that he behaved unprofessionally. The fact is that his work up until suddenly he stopped seeing his patient was fine, conscientious and responsible. With the benefit of hindsight one might say that a certain slowness in the development of a therapeutic process may have been due to interferences from the therapist's own personal history, but how often this happens in so many cases is incalculable, and cannot be the grounds for alleging unprofessional behaviour. Without doubt he could have handled the situation better. I could well have wished to be informed of the situation earlier myself. In this sense we all failed. The therapist should have ended "properly", but because of his personal dilemma was not able to do so. It is most unfortunate that the patient had yet another rejection in his life. The abused/ abuser dynamic was being repeated, and in breaking off the treatment, it seems to me that Mr Fisher was doing the best that he could, at the time.

In this scientific era, where clinical facts have to be proved, we are in danger of ignoring that which cannot be measured or objectified. I mean the personal authenticity without which real therapeutic work cannot take place. I believe that Mr Fisher has used this experience to learn much about himself, and has shown the potential to become an effective psychotherapist.

Codes of ethics should not be applied, I believe, in an unthinking way. If a therapist has behaved questionably he should account for himself. We need to consider whether that account demonstrates an ethical attitude in the therapist or not. I would respectfully suggest that the appropriate action in this case should be not to punish or reprimand, but to recommend that Mr Fisher undertake personal therapy as well as additional training and supervision before engaging in work of this kind again.

Then and There

Deborah Oilman

His name was Dr Kauff. He was an American psychoanalyst who lived in Jerusalem. A friend at university gave Dina his name and telephone number. She has held a fascination for anything American since childhood, when she learnt from her mother that her grandfather left his little hometown in Palestine around the turn of the century to go to America to earn a living. Palestine under the rule of the dying Ottoman Empire was not a good place to be. The tired Turkish administration cared little for subjects in those far reaches of its territories and basic amenities had collapsed under the strain of military occupations. For the small communities of Jews then living in the Holy Land *baksheesh*, a little present of gratitude, went a long way. So her grandfather bribed the officials responsible for travel documents and left his wife and small daughter—her mother—to go for a job in America.

His travels were a source of intense interest for the young Dina. She thought of him as very brave. He was the only man in the family who had dared to go and live outside the Holy Land. His life was amazing, she thought. He had two wives, both sisters of the same family. When the first died at a young age leaving her mother an orphan at the tender age of five, they swiftly arranged for her sister to replace her. His profession was extraordinary. He was a kosher slaughterer. He knew all the intricate rules by which animals' lives could be put to an end, because he did it according to The Law, he was seen as a holy man in service of a holy cause. For Dina's family living with post-war shortages, American aunts and uncles were a link to an affluent, glamorous world, which was treated with awe and suspicion. There were packages of old clothes; nylon nightdresses and fox fur collars that were handled with excitement and a tinge of ridicule. 'Guilt packages' her mother called them. But Dina, aged ten, had an American dream all of her own. She had wished she had not been her parents' child and longed for it—that is her place in the family—to have all been a dreadful mistake. She was occupied with daydreams in which another family would adopt her, and with whom she would start a new life. When her Aunt Sally came to visit and showed her a photograph of her house in Brooklyn with her two young boys smiling broadly, comfortably, in front of it, she decided that Sally's would be the new home for her. Why not? It had been done before, in the family, a child moving from one mother to another. Though her own mother was still alive, she concluded that having five other children would be more than enough compensation for the removal of one. But it would be a long time before any American would take her in and when Dina went to see Dr Kauff for a consultation she was already in her twenties. She was studying at the Hebrew University in Jerusalem. She had never left Israel.

Dr Kauff had a consulting room on top of a house in Ishayahu Street, the name of one of the Prophets. Streets had been given Biblical names in that area of Jerusalem, where many orthodox people lived. Nearby was the old Cinema Edison, a landmark in that part of God-fearing Jerusalem, which showed the tensions and collisions between the secular and religious in the city. Dina had his name written on a piece of paper given to her by a friend at the university. Aviva told her she was seeing this brilliant psycho-analyst who was warm, professional and not at all critical. Dina took the precaution of checking that he was a proper member of the Psychoanalytic Society. Aviva assured her he was. As she climbed up the three flights of narrow stairs to meet the American psychoanalyst, questions hung in the dark staircase. Where was she ascending to; what would she find at the top? She negotiated the steps laboriously, intently; she knew about cloying her way up—out of helplessness, and out of despair. For a long while now she had been attempting to unstitch her destiny from what she called her 'background'. She was exhausted. There were so many things she could tell Dr Kauff, if she could find a voice with which to tell him. He had sounded pleasant and patient on the phone.

At the top she saw a door to a flat and a small landing leading to the flat roof outside. On the roof, near the water tanks and pipes was a small built-on shack-like room. She assumed this was his consulting room. It was common at the time for people to put extra living spaces on balconies, on roofs. In the late sixties, after the wall between East and West Jerusalem had been removed the city attracted many new immigrants who fell in love with its mixture of ethnicity, Eastern bazaars and the new hope for peace. The intellectuals of the Left, quite a sizeable and influential group at the time, enjoyed mixing with Arabs in the cafés of East Jerusalem, trying *narghiles* and the occasional *hashish*. People strolled freely in the markets of the Old City, buying carpets, ornate jewellery, long cotton dresses embroidered by Bedouin girls, adorned with little coins and mirror fragments.

There was no one at the top. She wondered where she should wait. She hovered between the flat and the supposed consulting room on the top platform that was partially lit by the sun peering from the roof. Then the door of the room on the roof flung open and Dr Kauff appeared with a patient. There was an air of friendliness about him. The patient looked calm. Dr Kauff had the look of someone assured and satisfied. They turned to each other and Dr Kauff threw his arms around this woman. They stood in bonded silence, as though performing a ritual. Without a word, just throwing a half-knowing, half-assuring glance at the psychoanalyst, the patient left. Dina felt alarmed, shocked. This was not a sign of the professional distance and neutrality that she expected. But her life was full of the unexpected, confusions, and compromises. One always had to tolerate some unpleasantness to get something. Maybe what he did was part of some new form of psychotherapy from America, she tried to reason with herself.

Dr Kauff was shorter than she had pictured him, shorter than her. He wore a benign smile. He had straight dark hair and small warm eyes. There was the look of confidence on his face, like a man pleased with his work. He turned to Dina and gestured to the door with a wide sweep of his hand, and she entered. Small but warm, the room contained just a few pieces of furniture, and there was evidence of visits to the bazaars of East Jerusalem in the little rug, and the few ornaments. He lowered himself into the chair in the corner opposite the door, behind the couch that occupied the length of the room, and calmly looked at her. A small window with a net curtain let in the sun. It is a proper psychoanalyst's room in here, she assured herself, trying to leave the memory of the cuddle outside.

She sat on the couch, crouching forward, hugging herself with her arms. She knew what was expected; after all she was a student, in her last year. She started telling him, in a low voice, her lips pressed, about herself, her life. Background, one always started with background. That was simple enough, the facts of her life: mother, father, three brothers and two sisters; going to the House of Jacob School for orthodox girls in the neighbourhood nearby—the cramped school that was only a five minutes walk from where she sat.

She did not know what she wanted of this new American, except that she needed help, and a lot of it. It was her first ever psychoanalytic session—there would be many more to follow in later years. He seemed so understanding, such a good listener, and being listened to was a new and wonderful experience—and by a man. But there was that other nagging thought: the hug she saw outside. She tried to put it out of her mind.

There followed other wonderful sessions of talking about herself. This experience was new. She could not remember what he said; it did not matter. It was his presence that mattered. She doubted if he could really appreciate what her life had been, coming from another country, being affluent, while she came from a family that had been native to the Holy Land for several generations, and very poor. He was a man of the post Six-Day War-unified, optimistic Jerusalem of the late sixties, while she knew about the city from birth. She knew about the wars and the wall and the clashing aspirations of city's inhabitants that fermented underneath the surface, dangerously. But evidently he was interested in what she had to say about her life, its complications and difficulties, her branching out on her own, leaving her family behind, the hostility that followed, the utter rejection. The sessions with him soon filled Dina with anticipation. She thought of Dr Kauff as her new friend and confidant. The image of his attentive face when she spoke followed her. He nodded, he affirmed, never judging or criticising, never putting forward another view. He was paying close attention. She was grateful, so grateful.

But, always, there was this hurdle of the ritual hugs to be overcome. Waiting outside the consulting room—he was always a few minutes late—she first had to witness him hugging the previous patient, always a woman. She wondered if he had any male patients. Then there was a hug to her, which she handled with frozen acceptance. He would fling his arms around her and, looking directly at her, put a shine in his eyes and a smile on his face. She would stand there, rigid, her hands folded across her chest for protection, her eyes lowered, waiting for it to be over. Lastly there would be the hug at the end, but this could be dispensed with quickly on grounds of being late for the next thing or other.

Leaving the hugs to one side, she thought in later years, she really loved the attention. An intelligent man being with her in one room, listening to her talk, being sympathetic was so new and utterly wonderful. She could hardly wait from one session to the other, and soon requested two sessions a week. She became increasingly engrossed with the meetings on the roof of the third floor of a certain house near the old Cinema Edison, where the relentless condemnation of her life was silenced, at least for two hours a week.

Dina did not lie on the couch. Kauff did not talk about it. A short while into the treatment, she sensed this would not be her definitive 'analysis'. There was something wrong with it, improper and shallow. There would have to be another, proper analysis, some other time, the present one being spoilt, corrupted somehow. Still, her absorption in the appointments with Dr Kauff was complete. Her need for this attention, for his listening to her outpourings, nearly overwhelmed her. It was like a dam had vanished in a haze of warmth, and let the floodwater in.

Never clear quite how it began, one day she found herself sitting on the floor in the space between the couch and his chair. Could it be gratitude that made her sit at his feet, like a disciple? He created that allowing atmosphere. Non-judgementally he continued in the same vein, with no comment about her shift of place. Self-satisfaction exuded from him. She felt amazement for his acceptance, for his delight in her becoming more relaxed with him, so she continued to sit on the floor. It was freedom. Students did it all the time; on rugs and scattered cushions; in post Six-Day War Jerusalem, people were emulating Bedouins and Arabs.

Soon something in her transformed. She began to feel like a small child, a girl at her father's knee. Kauff smoked a pipe. He was engrossed in the details of cleaning, stuffing, lighting it. She gazed at his activities, intently, as she quietly recounted her life, her troubles, the daily challenges. Strangely he did resemble her father. He had a similar short, stout frame, and a protruding paunch, the same small round eyes that seemed to glisten and dance as they looked at you.

Longings tore and pulled at her. How she wished she had had him for a father. This could have been the next best thing to having Aunt Sally as her mother. In a mist of obscure yet intense emotion, past and present mingled and converged. She was at once herself and his little daughter playing at his knees, while he relaxed in his chair after a long day with patients, pondering over the day's work, smoking his pipe, looking at his little girl approvingly. She wanted so much to rest her tired, conflict-worn head on his knees. Of course she could not speak of it; there wasn't that sort of language between them. They never discussed their relationship; he made no reference to it (there certainly was no hint of talk about the ritual cuddles). It was as though he was above personalising anything that went on; it would interfere with the guru-like stance he adopted and the atmosphere of universal love and acceptance that he sought to create.

One day she drew a bit nearer him. He watched her with an expectant look, and said nothing. She drew a bit nearer. Tentatively, slowly, slowly, she raised her hand to touch his knee and checked to see his reaction. He smiled his shiny smile and reached his hand to hold hers. Did he want them to hold hands? He held her hand decisively in his, pulled it towards him, towards the middle of his body, and laid it on his penis. Then he looked away, his hand firmly cupping hers, giving himself up to the sensation.

Her hand froze there. She looked down to the floor, wishing it would detach itself from her body and stop belonging to her. Let him have the hand if that is what he needed, for she could not refuse him; she dare not withhold from him; he was the subject of her adoration. But if she could only run away, minus one hand . . . If she could only not be there. After a few seconds, maybe minutes, when the hand that held hers on his penis relaxed, she slowly withdrew hers. A new, shocking, numbing reality entered her relationship with her psychoanalyst. An ugly twist was added to her already turbulent life. It would take a long while for the shock that went through her to subside. Lengthy, silent, Edvard Munch-like screeches of rage emanated from within her in wave upon wave, for a very long time, and she could find no solace for his betrayal.

Thirty years later Dina came back to Jerusalem for a visit. She called her friend Ruth, a psychoanalyst she had met, and went for dinner at her house. Somehow Dr Kauff's name was mentioned. Dina learnt that he had been dead for many years, and that he had been ill for a long while before he died. There had been rumours about sexual meddling with patients, but nobody did anything about it because he was very ill at the time it was raised.

Dina invited Ruth to her hotel the following evening. They met at the lobby of the David Citadel hotel, near the old city, and looked for a quiet area where they could talk. Ruth noticed the piped music. "They are trying to entertain us," she said.

Dina, feeling anxious for her guest's comfort, suggested that the sushi bar might be quiet, and they settled there. Ruth sat on the sofa edge, and Dina on the armchair nearby, alert to her friend. She had made up her mind to try and find out more about Dr Kauff. She also longed to confide in Ruth about her being part of the rumours, the stories about Kauff's meddling and whether there was anything that could be done about it now. They talked about their lives, their work, their plans for the summer holidays. Then Dina decided to do it, to tell Ruth. She had wanted to tell for a long time. "Do you remember we talked in your house, yesterday, about the psychoanalytic scene in Jerusalem, many years ago when I was at the university?"

"Yes" Ruth said, perhaps surprised at the change of subject, perhaps curious.

"Do you remember you mentioned Dr Kauff? You said he had died, that there had been rumours circulating about sexual goings-on with his female patients?"

"Yes, I heard the rumours, and that they were thinking of doing something about it. I was in my training at the time. But he was very ill then, so they left it. He died a long time ago."

"You know," Dina said, "I was one of those patients he meddled with".

There it was. It was out. She said it, in Jerusalem,where it had happened, for the first time. She described some details, as though she still needed to substantiate her story, to assure the listener of its authenticity. Ruth listened. "What a difficult life you have had, and to come out like that," she sympathised. Dina knew she did not want sympathy. She pressed on.

"Do you think something could be done about it, now, in the Society? He was a very respectable member after all. At least there should be some record of this somewhere. I mean from the professional ethics point of view, you know. These things have got to be exposed, don't you think? It doesn't matter how many years ago, it has to be exposed, and righted, in some way, somehow! People have been affected—badly affected."

"Yes, but who is going to do it? All the people who were with him at the time are dead," Ruth said. "And what will it do to you if there is such a record somewhere in the archives, gathering dust? It would do you a lot more good if you used your experience to write about it, to use it, to help others learn from it somehow, do something with it. There is a lot written about it in psychoanalytic literature now, you know; you should read it."

"Really?"

"Really, you should read, and write about it."

Dina travelled back home and mulled it over and over again in her mind, through that whole ponderous, heavy summer. In the end she knew it had to be done then, before that summer's end, or never. Like the proverb that says 'Every man has their place and their hour'. Hers had come. She sat down in the garden and wrote her story, then and there.

Silence is for Listening

Anne Zachary

Newcomers to psychoanalytic technique find the idea of the therapist remaining silent at the beginning of an interview, allowing the patient to lead the way, most anxiety-provoking. That this could be possible, let alone therapeutic, is hard to grasp and I say this after much experience of teaching on courses that introduce other professionals to psychodynamic work. They will always want to say at least something at a social level such as "Tell me why you are here" or "This is an assessment . . ."

One particular assessment interview at the Maudsley Hospital many years ago, sticks in my mind and illustrates the benefit of just remaining silent. A rather belligerent-looking eighteen year old girl, who was diabetic, was referred for assessment for psychotherapy. She had a disastrously negative relationship with her mother that obviously stemmed at a somatic level from the early feeding relationship.

We sat together in silence and I noted that, despite the hostility of her body language, I did not feel too uncomfortable. Fifteen minutes went by. Then she spoke. She said, "You are the first doctor I have ever met who did not want to stick needles in me from the word go." A constructive assessment then proceeded, connecting her relationship with her mother to her illness, which meant that she could not process food normally.

The Bike

Barry Christie

Paul and I had been working together for over five years. We
met once a week in the same room and at the same time on a
Wednesday evening. He was my first ever referral and we
have remained as a pair through thick and thin: a strong bond has
grown between us. Paul is a married man in his late twenties. He is
sociable but lacks self-esteem following incidents of abuse and
mistreatment as a child. He has also spent much of his adolescence
in local authority care, having been moved away from a violent father
and a mother who was struggling with chronic mental health
problems that required periods of hospitalisation. Paul's commitment
to therapy has been courageous, although his daily use of marijuana,
regular visits to the local pub and gambling on the fruit machine
could be seen as alternative strategies for dealing with depression
and the hidden rage and shame that he has felt.

This story actually began six months earlier during the spring of
2005. The crowds and delays on the trains, tubes and buses in
London were becoming insufferable, so I decided to trade-in my old
bicycle for a new mountain bike, in anticipation of the warm summer
days that lay ahead. Over the following months, a regime of daily
cycling had improved my fitness and allowed me to travel to my
appointments with relative ease. I felt free and independent as I
scurried in-between the traffic; cycling was fun and had given me a
real sense of freedom. One evening I arrived at the therapy centre
with twenty-five minutes to spare before the start of my session with
Paul. I locked my bike up, with two high security padlocks, against
a twelve-foot high traffic signpost in a secluded spot that was visible
from my first floor consulting room window.

Paul arrived a few minutes late for his session and launched into a vignette that demonstrated how the bitter conflict he had witnessed as a child between his mother and father was now being replayed in his own marriage. After thirty-five minutes of our session, I heard a loud rattling sound outside in the street and I immediately sensed that somebody might be tampering with my bike. I jumped up from my chair and went over to the large window behind Paul; to my horror a group of three boys had somehow managed to lift the cycle, which was still locked, over the signpost. They appeared to be making a quick getaway, although carrying such a large item could not have been easy.

Quite spontaneously I said to Paul, "Someone's stealing my bike!" I then, instinctively, opened the consulting room door to dash out and try and catch the thieves. To my surprise Paul leapt up and said, "Let me go ahead, I'm quicker". We left the room together, and ran across the busy reception area where clients, students and fellow therapists looked at us in open-mouthed amazement. We scurried down two flights of stairs; the front door to the centre was quickly opened and then firmly shut behind us. Outside, Paul turned a sharp left and rushed ahead down the street leaving me yards behind. Ahead I could hear him shout "Stop!" When I arrived on the scene the boys had scattered into an adjacent housing estate and left the locked bike undamaged against a wall. A resident then came out from a nearby mansion block and said that he had seen two boys acrobatically supporting a third boy as he lifted the padlocked bike over the signpost, in what seemed like an audacious act in broad daylight. He had summoned the police twenty minutes before but they had not yet arrived.

After the bike was recovered, and we returned together to the centre, I was left with a number of questions. How would other therapists have responded to this unexpected event? How common-place were such disruptions to the therapeutic frame? Would I have done the same for my own therapist if a similar external threat had arisen? I also wondered how our work would have progressed if the boys had been caught or wanted to confront Paul and me in the street? Thankfully, we were able to get started again, albeit a little bit out of breath.

When we returned to the room I realised that nearly ten minutes of Paul's session had been absorbed by my problem: our roles had been reversed. In my panic to retrieve the bike, the session's boundaries had been broken, and I was left with a mixture of guilt and gratitude. I thought "If only the bike had been put in a safer place". Only five of the fifty minutes remained of our session and I wondered what could profitably be said following such an abrupt interruption in our work?

Just before the bike incident, Paul had been talking about how his wife, family and work colleagues had taken him for granted. Upon our return, we were able to make a connection between the feelings present in both of us following the attempted seizure of the bike and the emotions aroused earlier in the session by the much more damaging emotional and social thefts that had taken place in Paul's life since childhood. Thus an attempted theft in the present had provided a useful metaphor for us to explore what had been stolen from him in the past, and the subsequent feelings of loss that had arisen.

Paul's courageous act of helping me to confront the thieves was a testimony to the bond that had developed between us. He was now returning something back to me for the years of support I had given him. Paul had a history of petty crime, having been in trouble with the police for handling stolen goods, so perhaps this incident also provided him with a source of new identity, as he boldly intervened to help. By supporting me, Paul was able to act as a rescuer and also, at the same time, re-live some of the excitement of his delinquent teens.

We should always be grateful for what we learn about ourselves from our clients during therapy, but what is the place for more overt feelings of gratitude within the clinical space? Paul had behaved in an assertive and positive way and no doubt knew that I valued him for his actions. This attempted theft shook me up and it reminded me that the therapeutic frame is not a space cocooned away from external reality. Yes, it must remain as a special place where the internal world can take centre stage, but external reality is always waiting to impinge at any moment upon the private relational work that takes place in psychotherapy.

Following this incident, Paul has continued on his journey of self-discovery in therapy, whilst I still cycle between appointments on my trusted bike.

COINCIDENCE

Coincidence or Fate?

Sandra Black

When Tina first came to see me it was to tell me a story that is so remarkable in its twists of fate that I could not have imagined such a sequence of events. I cannot say that this is a case that I would have chosen—it has taken me to the brink of what I could bear to hear. But as I sit down to tell this true story, I believe that together Tina and I began a journey of transformation that we will not regret.

Our first meeting took place one Thursday in spring. Unwanted apprehension filled me as I sat before her, waiting for her to begin. She was slight, nervous, Cockney, with auburn hair and pale skin. She looked down at her hands and picked at a nail. The silence grew. My room felt oppressive, airless. I began to feel hot and dizzy and anxious. Then she said, "I've been having flashbacks. It was five years ago now. My sister—she was nineteen. I witnessed, I saw her," she faltered, "She was murdered in our flat. Number fifty-two. I couldn't stop him." She took a breath.

"She died in the ambulance. Fifteen stab wounds—didn't stand a chance. Maggie. She was my youngest sister. We'd lived together in this flat—number fifty-two—and he used to visit. He was her first boyfriend. But Maggie had decided it was over. She wanted out. Well, he saw to that! He was such a passive, silent bloke. But he had got the kitchen knife and just kept stabbing at her. I tried to stop him. I was shouting at him, "Stop it! Stop it!" and I tried to get the knife from him. Blood was everywhere. It was in her bedroom—the white duvet had slipped onto the floor and was covered with bright red. Poor Maggie just lay there. A neighbour heard the cries and called the police and ambulance. But it was too late." Tina gave a long sigh.

41

"I only went back to the flat once to pick up our stuff' she continued. "It's hard to sleep sometimes, even though it's five years now. I don't tell people—well, they don't like to hear that sort of thing, you know—to hear that my sister was murdered in our flat. These things don't happen." She gave another long sigh and her breath caught in a small sob. My heart was banging in the silence of the room. My hands, clutching the armrest, were white and cold. I wondered if I was going to be able to bear witness to the violence and fear of her story.

Over the next weeks I started to know Tina. She had gone to night school and college and now worked as a manager with responsibility for a small team; was buying her own flat and was a spirited and determined young woman. She had a stable relationship with a man called Dave.

Despite a childhood of desperate poverty and the terrorising temper of a bullying father, she, her two sisters Daphne and Maggie and elder brother Steven had survived. Huddled together as the beatings were delivered to a cowed and terrified mother, the four children took care of each other.

"We used to run upstairs and hide by the bed and put our fingers in our ears," she told me, and glanced down at her hands. "You know, when I was trying to grab the knife from him, he had his hands on each side of it, and my hand was in the middle, on the blade, and he was pulling and tugging. And later, much later, I found I had this tiny cut, here on this finger. That's all. It's the only wound I got."

Two months after we met this letter arrived at my office.

Dear Sandra,
Unfortunately I will not be able to attend my session with you tomorrow at 9am. My mother died suddenly—after she seemed to have recovered from a minor operation—and I am still in a great state of shock. However, I intend to come to my session next week on Thursday.
Yours sincerely,
Tina.

On Thursday when she came back she looked drawn and pale.

"She was better. The doctors said the operation was successful," she said. "They said she'd recovered and then there was some 'internal bleeding', or something. It's odd, I was going in to see her that evening but as fate would have it, I had to stand in for a member of staff and so I was about ten minutes late getting to the hospital—and when I got there a nurse took me into her office and there was my Dad and Steven. 'I'm sorry,' she said. 'Your mother died ten minutes ago'.

We always managed to miss each other, my mother and me; we spent my whole life not meeting. I think she wanted out, what with my dad's temper all her life; and then Maggie's death. You know she never cried—except once—in the police station the night Maggie died. Her face was completely blank, just like it used to be when Dad would lay into her. But as she looked at me this curtain of tears tore down her face—and then stopped. And the blankness came back."

"But what about you?" I asked.

"I don't feel anything much. I should have been there, something else happened, and she'd gone. You never know what's going to happen, do you? It was just an ordinary day. But I should know by now—the worst *can* happen. So, now there's just Steven, Daphne and me. And Dad. I wonder how he'll cope without Mum to shout at? Dave, my boyfriend's been good, but I don't love him. Not really. He's just a good friend. I need to finish with him. And Steven's ill. He's become very manic again."

Our hours together turned into a year. Tina's forgotten childhood would reappear in the concerns, relationships, fears and dreams of everyday life; in my room; in the relationship between us, as we wove back and fore from then to now. In time, her concerns for her brother grew. He had had several manic episodes between desperate states of depression. He had three children by a first partner but now was in a very erratic relationship with another woman. They broke up and he became agitated, disappeared for weeks; turned up angrily at their father's home, floridly disturbed, threatening him. He had been hospitalised before, was supposed to be on medication. Tina would try to calm him. "*He* was the one that got the worst of it when we were kids" she explained. "My Dad would beat him so hard he'd have to stop for breath. No wonder he's like this now."

Steven eventually was admitted to hospital and Tina would visit him and tell him she loved him.

"I feel so helpless" she told me. "I can feel his pain and all that shame. All my Dad's self-loathing beaten into my brother. One day

Steven disappeared from hospital. No one knew where he was. Eventually he telephoned me from a call box. He was chaotic. I tried to persuade him to return: I'd help him; I loved him; we missed him, were worried about him. I implored him to return. Three weeks before Christmas, he leaped from the platform of a London station in front of the 3.52 train and was killed.

On the day of Steven's death, my boyfriend later remembered that as we were returning from visiting friends by train, the driver had made an announcement: "Owing to a fatality further down the line, this train is being diverted.

"It's weird" she explained. "I always seem to be present, when bad things happen. First Maggie's murder; then being on the same line on the same day that Steven killed himself. It's as if everything's connected, as though we're all involved with each other. I feel like I'm a player in a drama that's unfolding around me, affecting me, but I've got no choice in the script."

Then two weeks later her boyfriend Dave met his football mates as usual for a drink. One of the men had brought along a friend— in fact the very train driver involved. He said to them, "Cheer him up lads. He's been signed off by Rail Track. Some young bloke jumped in front of the train he was driving on Tuesday. Not good for drivers, someone leaping in front of their train. Can do their head in." Like Tina, *I* started to wonder who was writing this script.

Steven's funeral took place at the local church and Tina's grief finally erupted in rage at her father's elaborate display of mourning. "Grieving?! Feeling guilty more like! *He* did this; no wonder Steven killed himself. All he ever got was violence. The only time my father ever told me he loved me was once, after he'd whacked me and later he said he'd hit me *because* he loved me. I don't know what love is; it always seems linked with loss. I think I felt love for Steven, and Maggie of course. And the stray cat that comes around my flat. I stroke her and she purrs and lays on her back and shows me her belly. She's that trusting. Love was a stranger to her.

Months passed, and Tina finally decided to separate from Dave. I was glad that she was beginning to emerge from this symbiotic and largely unsatisfying relationship, yet I felt my own anxiety, along with hers, as yet another separation was looming. How would she cope as she relinquished this support? During the months of the break up, Tina worked through much ambivalence and real sadness.

She and Dave had a genuine affection for each other, but Tina's intellect and passionate nature were never matched by his. I was concerned how he would react to the split. The spectre of a brutal killing, when a young woman had told her boyfriend it was over, hovered. Dave, however, took it 'like a man' and was engaged to be married within months of the break up.

Slowly the gregarious, spirited side of Tina began to strengthen. As time passed she entered the dating scene: through friends, the internet and lonely hearts columns, she began to meet young men. She very much wanted a loving, lasting relationship. This was a real challenge, but she managed to weather the hopes and disappointments of blind dating. Then one day, she came into her session agitated and breathless. "I went to a club on Saturday with my friend Helen. We were all on the dance floor, having a laugh. Then I saw this bloke nearby and I said to Helen, 'He looks quite tasty'. The next thing, she's gone over to him and says 'Why don't you ask my friend to dance?' I was embarrassed, but he came over and then, we were dancing together. He was good fun, and I was leaping about, enjoying myself. I liked the look of him."

This is the first time Tina has shown the slightest interest in any of her dates. "So, at the end of the evening, we're having a bit of a flirtation and he suggested we all go on to another place. Helen decided she wanted to go home, but I was keen to go on. His mates were coming, too. His name was Chris and I liked the way I felt with him, safe. And I wasn't about to do anything risky."

I began to feel excitement. Could this be the start of something good for Tina?

"So we got to the next club and we danced and we had a bit of a snog—well, it's ages since I've had a man's arms around me who doesn't exactly resemble the Elephant Man—who's polite and sparky, a good dancer and wants to know me. We sat down and started to talk. 'Where are you from?' he asks. 'East London', I say. 'What about you?' 'I'm from Liverpool', he told me, but he'd been here for about eight years now. 'Where do you live?' I ask him. And he says he lives in Dalston, where I used to live. 'What road?' And he says Sumatra Road. And I say, 'I used to live there!' He says, 'Yes, Conway Court'. It's a huge old place, with about a hundred flats. It's a bit Art Deco, quite a nice building." Tina speaks breathlessly. "And I tell him, 'but I used to live in Conway Court in

Sumatra Road with my sister. What number flat do you live in?' And he says, 'Number fifty-two. It's got two bedrooms. I rented it first, then I bought it three years ago. It's got a real nice feel to it. People say it's got good karma.'"

In my work I've come across many different stories from people with different experiences and backgrounds, and together we use psychotherapy to make sense of the past, where it belongs, with the hope for greater choices in the future. Although our theories and clinical knowledge may go some way to make sense of Tina's experiences, none of them, to me, explain this extraordinary chain of events and synchronicities. What comes across, in Tina's own words, is how closely our lives may be entwined, "Like we're all connected somehow".

As psychotherapists, in some situations perhaps all we can do is bear witness. We are the ones who are there, alongside, whatever happens.

Synchronicity and Serendipity

Paul Thompson

I am an only child and grew up in a rather remote rural village in an English countryside that had been barely touched by the twentieth century. I was therefore not too good at making new friends or striking up acquaintances. But Ann, who came to work in our office one day as a clerical assistant from a casual work agency, was friendly and open. She was a young black woman from a South Africa that in those days was still very much in the grip of the apartheid regime. I knew little about apartheid but remember being struck by her quality of innocent openness, almost emphasized by an ungainly way of moving about the office, sometimes dropping things carelessly, or sloppily and cheerfully misfiling documents. Ann made an impact of difference-ness upon me, and when she just did not turn up at the office one day I very much noticed the gap, but I just assumed that her agency had moved her elsewhere.

One decade on from that time my own life had changed completely. I had become a social worker and a trainee psychotherapist in a large psychiatric hospital, one of the largest in the country, that has long since closed its doors to patients and been converted into a luxury private estate. One day, walking along a corridor, then the longest corridor in Europe, I was stopped in my tracks by a voice echoing behind me.

"Paul! Paul!"

I recognized the voice and turning, was amazed to see Ann rushing up to greet me, seeming to find rushing difficult with her ungainly gait that seemed to have become more awkward since the last we met. She greeted me effusively and I was warmly pleased to see her. She said that she was a patient, and I told her that I was a social worker and, curiously enough, attached to the ward where she was placed. Thus I became her psychiatric social worker for a time.

As I grew to know Ann in this different capacity I discovered another curious coincidence. She had been living in the same road as me, just a few doors away, very shortly after we had got to know each other in the office ten years before. At that time, according to her records, her family had been followed and stalked by the South African police; not simply a psychiatric delusion, this had been confirmed by documentary evidence. Not only that, but when I had been living at that address, I had on one occasion been woken in the night by ringing on my door bell. On answering the door I had found nobody there. Had that been the South African police, I now wondered, looking for Ann? I did not mention this in my supervision sessions, not wanting to spoil my chances of qualifying by appearing to be a *folie à deux* with a patient.

In my capacity as a psychiatric social worker, I learnt that Ann had a sister, who also suffered from mental illness, and a mother who was unwell from time to time. Ann seemed to be the more integrated of the three. I understood that her sister, to whom I shall refer as Sara, had a particularly severe manifestation of schizo-phrenia. Over time I helped Ann to recover from her illness, supported her in the transition back to independent life outside the hospital and helped her find better accommodation. Once she was settled I withdrew support and, as it is said in the professional vernacular, 'closed her file'.

A further twenty years passed. I had by now qualified in psychotherapy, but retained my position as a psychiatric social worker. I sought to integrate the skills from each of my professional backgrounds in improving my contribution to each. In particular, I developed the notion that psychotherapy skills, if applied to social work, provided access to psychotherapy for patients who might not otherwise afford it. Freud had spoken about a 'new Salvation Army' of social workers qualified in psychoanalytic therapy and the idea that this might be viewed as patronizing had not occurred to me.

My commitment and ideas were to become tested to the extreme by an all-out strike by my social work colleagues that threatened to cease all mental health social work services (formerly referred to as 'psychiatric social work') across the borough. This strike had been called in response to restructuring proposals and what some perceived as low pay. From my perspective of working daily in mental health, what worried me was the life-threatening nature of psychiatric illness—for the patient, possibly for their family or friends, and possibly for the community. I was not sure that my colleagues understood the depths of distress experienced by people with severe mental illness or the damage that the withdrawal of their services could cause. Hence I volunteered to strike break and not only continued to work but to actively provide a crisis assessment service for urgent referrals.

I am not sure I knew what I was taking on or what was driving me. It could have been my unresolved omnipotence; I suspect in part it was. Equally it could have been a commitment to mental health. Whatever it was, I had by then forgotten about Ann and her family, and indeed it was three decades since I had first met her in the office. It was therefore a considerable surprise that the first referral that should come my way was for Sara, her sister, although I did not know at first that it was she.

The referral came from the housing office: the patient, whom it was believed had had her child removed by the child protection team, was apparently hiding in her flat. Nobody could be completely sure of her whereabouts or her child's because of the strike. Mother had meanwhile barred all access to her flat, although neighbours had seen smoke seeping from under the door. It was only when I was told her name that I properly appreciated the possible full extent of Sara's mental health needs. This assessment needed the full mobilizing of all the emergency services—police, fire and ambulance crew. Normally, to force access to a person's flat, a magistrate's court warrant is needed. However this referral was so urgent the fire crew could lawfully force access in order to put out the fire.

Doctors and myself, supported by police and fire crew, entered the flat, which was indeed so full of smoke that fire could have broken out at any moment. We found Sara sitting in an abject, crumpled heap of misery in a chair. She was mute and desolate. Her child was not in the flat but I was able to discover that he was safe in care. Sara was taken to psychiatric hospital under a section of the Mental Health Act. The fire crew made the flat safe.

This was the third decade of my contact with Ann and her family through a series of otherwise unconnected events. It cannot be clear if there was meaning to these coincidences or whether they were random incidents in a haphazard universe. Suffice it to say that, psychotherapeutic awareness combined with my knowledge of the severity of Sara's illness through contact with Ann meant that, by being in the right place at the right time, appropriate intervention was able to occur where otherwise her life could have been lost.

Four decades on and I now visit psychiatric hospitals in an official capacity to monitor the welfare of detained patients. Sara is intermittently detained in a hospital in my patch and I see her from time to time. I am reminded of the old copperplate admission ledgers in the hospital where I had met Ann for the second time. One entry, dating from the nineteenth century, refers to the admission of a woman experiencing '*melancholy following the loss of child*'. The ledgers have gone, along with the hospital. Prisons and the streets are awash with people with profound mental health problems. Psychic pain remains. Perhaps, when a synchronic moment occurs, we are riding the waves of a history that never change but subtly and endlessly repeats itself, in constantly changing forms.

Homecoming

Jan Waterson

Getting into therapy, when I did and where I did, was an accident—or so I thought at the time. As I write, it is years later and I am preparing to finish therapy. Now, I am not so sure. In one sense it certainly was an accident, for I hadn't planned it. I had no preconceived ideas of what I wanted, or what sort of person I wanted to work with, or where. Looking back I now realise that if I had known these things in the beginning I would probably have never started. As was, it just seemed to happen. Or did it?

The world is a very small place, you know. How often had I heard that saying? I had experienced it at times. There was the sea ferry journey when I had unexpectedly met some longstanding, close friends. Normally we would have sent each other postcards when on holiday, but on this occasion I knew very well that I had not sent the customary card and was already feeling guilty, hoping that they would never know I had been away. Suddenly, coming face to face on deck, I was found out. Needless to say, their postcard to me arrived a few days later. Then there was the time when it was easier to arrange to see close friends who lived near me in the UK when we were both thousands of miles away in South Africa. In the course of conversation over dinner with my cousins there, we discovered that many years before my aunt had been employed by my friend's grandmother in a town nearby. Both were now dead, but we had unearthed a precursor of our current relationship that had occurred in previous generations, between people living thousands of miles away, and again, my world seemed small.

Later on, pondering the saying, I saw that it usually involved un-expected personal encounters, either in time or place, and sometimes in both. I knew about the known small worlds. Friends in training as psychotherapists had often complained that the world—the therapy world—was indeed too small a place. They couldn't have their training-therapy with A, because she was supervising B—their training consultant. They couldn't go to C's training session, because he was in therapy with D, and so on, round and round in endless circles. For them, negotiating the myriad and seemingly incestuous, interconnected relationships of the therapy community, avoiding any inappropriate encounters, seemed to require a massively conscious, considered and careful touch.

When I got into therapy I wasn't at all conscious, considered or careful. In fact I had no intentions of starting. I had been involved in some counselling a while before. I'd learned what feelings were and, to my surprise, I seemed to have them. I had had some theoretical interest in group dynamics and humanistic approaches, which could be used for personal growth, but that was where it stopped. No, I started therapy by accident. An important relationship had finished a couple of years before. We had been living together in the provinces for a few years and had intended to return to London. I'd even applied for a new job there but when we split up I withdrew from the interview. Subsequently, I'd had difficulties with my boss and had decided to take some time out from my career. It was time for pastures new and to spread my wings. I decided to attend a weekend training workshop on group and therapeutic dynamics. It was well run—and was definitely a training not a therapy weekend—but in the course of it some things were said to me that had me thinking that perhaps there was a little gap between my self-image and the persona that I projected.

It was only at the close of the workshop that my conscious assurance was really shaken. Suddenly my unconscious took the law into its own hands and delivered a sledgehammer blow. It was a small thing, noticed only by me, but big enough to change my life. As is often the way with such weekend happenings somebody suggested that we list our names and addresses. As this was going on, I was listening to the conversations going on around me—I was practised at this and quite able to multi-task at the same time. When the list came to me I started writing my first name as usual. Then, naturally, I started on my surname. I wrote the first two letters as usual but I inserted one that didn't belong there at all. In a horrifying flash I realised that the five letters together would now spell something questionable, derogatory and disturbing. I quickly scrubbed what I had written out, rewrote my second name correctly and passed on the piece of paper like a hot potato, abruptly leaving the workshop with this new, troubling name ringing in my ears. The ringing didn't lessen even when I did manage to get some sleep that night. It just came along too. I woke the following morning with the new and appalling epithet repeating itself over and over in my mind. It hadn't gone away as I'd hoped. I was really shaken.

Later that same day I decided something had to be done. I telephoned the person who had run the workshop asking to see her individually. She said that was fine in principle but that there was no space until later that year in a group. We specified the sort of help I might seek and what sort of person might be able to provide it. Gender was important, as was level of experience and intelligence. I came away from the conversation with a suggested name, a telephone number and a promise of further suggestions if that did not work out.

I wasn't at all sure about all of this. Things seemed to be out of control. But still reeling from my self-inflicted body blow, and heeding what by now had begun to feel like an injunction, I took the advice and telephoned for an appointment. Two assessment sessions later, I very tentatively began therapy. At first there was no possibility of a regular appointment time for me, which was probably just as well. Such regularity of commitment would probably have scared me rigid and if there had been any mention of several appointments each week at that stage I would have disappeared in a cloud of dust.

It was only some considerable time later, when I had come to recognise that my unconscious imperative could not be ignored, and that I was committed to the process for as long as it took—and given my childhood history, was likely to be longer rather than shorter— that I even thought at all about my therapeutic encounter in terms of place. Certainly, an unexpected turn of events had produced an unforeseen encounter with the past; I knew I was exploring my childhood. Obviously I realised that I was living back in the city in which I had grown up. But more strangely, and apparently by chance, my therapist not only lived in the same suburb where I had grown up, but just round the corner from my childhood home. Moreover it was the very next block. In my disturbed state I had hardly noticed this proximity. It certainly would not have been of my choosing. Only very slowly did the full significance of this dawn on me and, once it did, I knew I would have preferred to be journeying to therapy anywhere than to the neighbourhood of my childhood. I longed for my world not to be so small.

When talking of that house, which my mother had left due to illness, I had often described it as the place where everything happened. Now, completely unintentionally, twenty years after she had moved away, I was re-experiencing those early years both in mind as well as geography. I was being exposed to the unavoidable reminders of a neighbourhood which had barely altered. I knew it from a child's eye view. I had always walked to school and knew every twist in the streets, the names of all the roads, almost every tree and kerbstone. These were tangible and visible reminders of times past. Now, simply travelling to therapy evoked all sorts of memories—some just a fleeting sense, hardly a memory at all but an echo of some far distant and inexpressible sensation. I even saw the very house if I drove that way after a session. It seemed there was no escape from what I had consciously been avoiding. I began to think it was no accident: I was encountering an unpredicted and unwanted small world.

I would avoid going past the house, preferring to turn one way rather than the other to get to a main road which would take me out of the area. But eventually, turning that way lost its horrors. Today I can drive comfortably past the house where I once lived. Its terrors, although still potentially powerful, no longer imprison me. The bricks and tiles may be unchanged, but it is no longer the same house; it is simply where I once lived when I was a child. Other people unknown to me live there now. Whilst I still, and always will, carry the child I once was within me, I have grown up, but only by coming home.

In my case, home was my heart. It had been on hold in a psychic time warp from a very early age, smothered by the protective webs I had knitted. The task of therapy was to understand and disentangle the ravelled pile of wool and then to cast on fresh stitches, only this time to harmonise the design and construction between my internal and eternal worlds.

When I started therapy I described myself as hollow in the middle. Therapy has helped me to create a weight-bearing cover for that hole, without erasing away the substance of those early years. Indeed, covering that space has meant I have had to take account of its dimensions. I have returned home in a way that I could not have imagined—let alone engineered—and I realise that the world is in indeed a small place. Now I understand why T.S. Eliot wrote:

> *'And the end of all our exploring*
> *Will be to arrive where we started.'*
>   (From *Little Gidding Lines, Four Quartets*.)

HEALING

The Honeysuckle Man

Marika Henriques

I looked at the man in front of me. He was tall, thin, slightly stooped, with deep-set eyes and masses of black hair. I thought he had a lonely face, like a desolate and ravaged landscape. He sat with his arms crossed over his chest, his hands resting lightly on his shoulders as if shielding himself from an imaginary blow. He often sits like this, I thought.

I remembered that years ago, when I first saw Adam, he reminded me of a terrible story I had read in the papers at the time. The article described an experiment—to what purpose I could no longer recall and could not ever even imagine. They put a dog in a cage and locked the door. The dog walked to the right. It was given an electric shock. It ran to the left. It was again given an electric shock. This treatment was repeated several times. Eventually the dog lay down in the middle and stayed there. It did not bark, it did not move, it did not protest. It just lay there. It did not leave the cage even when the door was opened. It had simply given up.

I had a disquieting sense that Adam was like this dog. And that the only way he might inch out of his particular cage and begin to trust his environment again was if I joined him there. If I could endure the anguish and despair which was smouldering below, if I could bear with him the unsurvivable, he might then move on and out. I have to admit that I definitely did not look forward to this painstaking and tortuous adventure. I braced myself and listened to his story.

Adam was born in a romantic part of the West Country well remembered and much loved by him. His father was a diplomat however, and the family had to move every three years. Adam carried on stoically throughout the burden of losses which these

59

moves forced him to suffer, but the pattern imprinted itself in his being and in later life he continued to move frequently. Things did not last. He described his father either as absent or as looming large with a terrifying presence. His father had thrown him into the sea to teach him to swim; Adam nearly drowned once. He dangled his little son over the balustrades to teach him courage but Adam only learnt to fear heights. In a tight rageful voice father issued commands which often were incomprehensible to the little boy. His mother on the other hand was always there, inconsistently, tantalisingly there. She was a small, deeply fearful woman who loaded her anxiety onto her child to carry, and made him her "little man" in her husband's absence. Adam was swallowed up by his mother like Jonah by the whale. "She is like delicious honey laced with heroin", was Adam's colourful description of her.

He had learnt early in life that love does not allow one any space. None at all. He felt emotionally bound to his loving and devouring mother, hand and foot. As a matter of fact, when he was two years old and his sister was born, he was regularly tied to his bed at night for some inexplicable reason. He was terrified. On occasions, when he failed to be mother's compliant little companion he was given a brown liquid to drink—goodness knows what it contained—to calm him down. He completely identified with his mother which I believe was his only protection against being constantly overwhelmed by her. When sometimes I commented on some trait or achievement of his, or some episode in his life, he would say "oh, that's mother" in a way that was as confusing as it was frustrating. He came to therapy, as he so succinctly put it, because, "Only the other exists. I don't".

He was, he felt, a football, bouncing between his terrifying father and overbearing mother. As time passed, I realised that Adam had quite simply, like the dog in the cage, given up on himself. He had found a way of being in the world that worked. It was simple. He fitted himself like Zelig in the Woody Allen film, chameleon-like, to the needs, wishes and opinions of others. A friend said, leave your job, and he left it. Sell your house, it's too big for you, said another, and he did. This was his "official" self, Adam explained as we got to know each other better. This official self was often literally robbed. It happened the first time at school when he was eleven. He allowed an older boy regularly to go through his pockets to help himself to the sweets and coins or whatever precious things he held there. Before he came to therapy, he was massively defrauded by a man, who then humiliatingly succeeded to defend himself in court. Then there was the Iranian predator, who coaxed hundreds of pounds out of him for some probably non-existent charitable cause. Similarly, a psychotic and desperate drug user regularly borrowed substantial sums from Adam never of course repaying any of it. But why, I asked in exasperation, are these thefts allowed to continue? Adam explained patiently as if to an obtuse child, "Well, because they need it and deserve it, and I don't".

Well qualified and with masses of experience, he worked for a pittance well below the average salary for his type of work in a small company in Central London as a senior administrator. For many years he worked seven days a week, and never, of course, took a holiday. We often talked about how being swallowed up by this firm bore such a resemblance to his relationship with his mother. It existed now, and he did not. He understood that when a child is small, mother is his whole world. We thought it was remarkable and unbelievably apt that he found employment in a company that was omnipotently called 'Wide World', and how it was that his job now became his whole world.

Adam agreed, but carried on wearing himself out. It seemed that he grew even thinner by the minute. He fell ill, but still did not take even a day off work. He fell from his bike in front of a car. He dreamt he lay down on the road in front of a truck. He dreamt of the cathedral in Barcelona, half in ruin, half complete. He wore the same khaki trousers and checkered shirt—summer and winter, and on rainy days he carried the thinnest anorak I had ever seen.

Over the years I heard in the minutest details about his workplace. Of files and computer programmes, work schedules, minutes, deadlines, the position of desks, meetings and canteen lunches as well as the private lives and intrigues of his colleagues. I suspected that, like a bird pretending to have a broken wing to lead one away from its nest of young, Adam was leading me—and himself—away from his lost and injured self. Nevertheless I began to hate 'Wide World'. In sessions I was often sleepy and imagined that Adam had left himself outside the consulting room. Occasionally I attempted to converse with the person on the other side of that door. Sometimes I was heard, and often not. In the early days when I said too much,

Adam was overwhelmed and withdrew with knitted brows. But if I said too little he felt abandoned. I too felt like the unfortunate dog in the cage, nowhere safe to go. I felt helpless, frustrated and wholly ineffective, but I was not going to give up.

Very gradually and tentatively Adam's "unofficial" self' began to emerge and reveal to both of us a reservoir of furious feelings—as tumultuous and raw as stuff gets when held in the dark. Rage—"you will go to hell, all of you"—grief and despair, underground resistance against all authority, myself included, but especially envy and resentment. These were mingled with good humour, a satirical turn of mind, practicality, tenacity also, and kindness and endurance. Adam himself was astounded by the rich emotions of this inner self. Slowly, as these feelings were aired—and this time there was to be no mysterious brown liquid—Adam became more enlivened. There was now more room for both of us in which to be ourselves. We found quite a few reference points and began to enjoy each other's company. We had animated conversations about all sorts of things: culture, politics, the nature of man. 'Wide World' was not mentioned in these hours—thank goodness. I no longer felt sleepy and, rather than dreading our meetings, I looked forward to the twice-weekly hour.

It was during this period that Adam told me about the honeysuckle. He delighted in and revered nature, through which he expressed—I felt—his need to love and be loved. Mother Earth did not overwhelm or abandon him; she was not unpredictable like people, and to some extent could be controlled. He had a quiet passion for the honeysuckle, a regard which I only fully understood later. When he was little the family house had a walled garden in which Adam felt safe, like nowhere else before or after. And there, on the old stone wall, grew the first honeysuckle he could remember. Since then, for the last two decades, he carefully nurtured one plant—the kind, he said, which went from "white to gorgeous cream". He took cuttings from it and planted it again and again, whenever and wherever he moved. And he moved often. This plant went through horrible adventures and hardships that it was not meant to survive but somehow did. Initially, he told me, the plant climbed from a beautiful antique terracotta pot with delicate decorations. But the pot was stolen and the honeysuckle trampled on. Adam saved as much of it as he could and planted it out in his small garden, where it thrived wonderfully but threatened to overtake other plants. So he took some of it, and planted it out on the common, behind his house. He stole out to water it at night, when no one was there to see him. After a while however, what the wind did not take, people vandalised. A little of it survived though, and when he moved again he replanted it once more. It now blooms near the patio he has built. I began to think of Adam as the 'Honeysuckle Man'. The resemblance was obvious. Both plant and man were tenacious, enduring hardships, intent on survival. The honeysuckle was not entirely milk and honey though. It had a whiff of Mother's dangerous sticky sweetness about it. Entwined with ruthlessness, it nearly took over Adam's small garden after all. But it was a hardy species, and I noted with satisfaction that Adam never gave up on the life of his plant. He hung on to it with stubborn determination. There grows hope, I mused to myself.

Adam came in as he always does. He carefully double-checked the front door to make sure that it was securely closed, scanned my face for my mood, checking that all was well and that it was safe for him to enter. I greeted him with a smile, as I always did and, reassured, he smiled back and sat down in his usual fashion. This has been our ritual for the past few years. He began with a particularly savage attack on a colleague he envied for his many absences and frequent leaves. I had heard these tirades often by now, and my attention drifted. Then suddenly, somewhere from my own long-forgotten past there surfaced unaccountably, and in my own language (which I have not spoken for many decades), a poem I used to love. It was by the Hungarian poet, Dezso Kosztolanyi. It had no title but the first line reads "I shall commit suicide . . ." It describes the lamentations of a little boy who is very sorry for himself. He imagines that if he killed himself then everybody—all who wronged or dismissed him—would be very sad and sorry indeed. He will leave, he says, and no one will see him, not ever again. Only his little coat will wonder in the morning where he had gone. But he would have by then left a world which so disappointed him, and he would lie with blue-veiled face amongst scented roses. There is a barely observable but powerful feeling of revenge hidden in his self-pity. But at the end of the poem there is a shift in mood and self-pity turns into genuine compassion—for himself and for others. When I told Adam of the poem there was a sudden intake of breath and then a shocked and stammered response, "But that is me—absolutely.

This poem contains my essence. This is why I am in this room. This is why I came".

When he calmed down he told me that when he was four years old he fantasized that he would be run over by a Bentley—he loved cars—and then just like in the poem he thought that everybody would be very sorry and remorseful. He also told me of his suicide attempts, of which there was more than one. He thought of the idea of suicide as his 'secret weapon', always there: available, reliable, ready at hand if life became intolerable. This made me think of his ever-present mother. Something which was in his control when nothing else was, something to depend on when all else has failed and betrayed him. But he was ashamed of his feelings and had never disclosed them before.

This was a moving and intimate hour in which a genuine exchange had taken place between us. The Irish poet Seamus Heaney once described a poem as "an echo coming back to us". Through this poem a bit of the past—mine as well as Adam's—returned in the present, in this particular room, at this particular moment. It came unbidden, and was stunningly apt. And something of my essence was touched as well. The connection was experienced powerfully by both of us. Something shifted inside Adam in this hour. If depression is about loss, despair is about something hopelessly missing. The poem had restored that missing something, which had to do with abandonment. It became also a bridge, a link between his "official" and "unofficial" self. Because his deeply hidden feelings had been experienced by a poet from another time and from a different land, he did not feel alone with them anymore. And he was no longer ashamed. As he said, he was in distinguished company.

Did I have a copy of the poem, Adam inquired? Could he borrow it? I only have a few books in my native Hungarian and luckily I actually found the poem in an anthology. Adam did not want a translation. What already he knew of the poem was sufficient. He meticulously copied the original and asked me to help him with the strange accents. He copied it again, this time on beautiful vellum. He then framed it (he made the frame himself) and triumphantly hung it in his living room. He relished the fact that his secret was now displayed openly, for all to see. Yet, visible as it had become, it also remained hidden and his own. "I could not tell it to anybody, therefore I told it to everybody" as another poet had said. Adam did not bring the framed poem for me to see, and I was glad of this. Though the poem was shared between us it remained in some respect mine and he too made it his own. It was neither wholly mine nor his, but existed between us. He could now retain something precious for himself without regard to the other. Slowly he began to matter to himself and he no longer thought of himself as inconsequential. The poem after all describes the thoughts of a lonely little boy who was leaving the world, unseen but for his little coat. Together with our evolving relationship, it had a transformative effect on Adam. The coat did not remain empty much longer; it had a person in it. A person, who was seen and heard by another and was no longer abandoned or overwhelmed. Adam realised that if something had to die, it was not him, but the belief he had held so strongly for decades, that suicide was the only authentic act which he was capable of. In time and with much courage he dropped his 'secret weapon', calling it a "childish thing".

A few months after this session Adam decided to leave the job which had sapped his vitality and deprived him of any life outside it for so many years. This was a momentous decision. It meant not only leaving 'Wide World' but in a sense it was also a separation from his mother—the 'mother world' that had constrained and had held him captive for so long. He made several drawings of himself as Atlas with the world on his shoulders as punishment by the gods. The picture changed with each drawing and eventually the figure became a man in a pub leaning against the bar to get his drink, while the globe dropped from his shoulders and rolled away like a discarded object.

A week before he left his job he came to the session saying he had thought of a ritual with which to ease and mark his departure. I was delighted to hear of his plan. On his last day at work he was going to plant a honeysuckle in the courtyard of the building. "The honeysuckle", he said, "is not easily killed and it has such a wonderful scent". We nodded and smiled at each other. There was no poison infused with the sweet honey any more. We both knew that the plant will now grow without perilous adventures, as plants ordinarily do.

In time Adam got a better-paid job, reclaimed his weekends and booked his first holiday in years to revisit his old home with the walled garden in his beloved West Country. Unlike the tortured dog, he could move out into the world. He was right. He was not easily killed, physically or emotionally. The fates might have woven into his early life some dark threads but he had taken destiny into his own hands and, with a newly found attitude and a zest for life, inserted his own brighter colours into the given pattern. Despite its ambiguities, despite deprivations and hardships, the tenacious honeysuckle had triumphed over the deadly secret weapon.

What about God?

Helen Alexander

Sitting opposite the Bishop in his study, I swallowed and was aware of the moisture on my palms. I did not know him well, having been a priest in his diocese for less than a couple of years, but he had the reputation for being a humane man, and receptive. Nevertheless what I had to say was difficult. It had taken me some months to ask for the appointment. I took a breath, and looked him in the eye. "I think I need to leave the priesthood." As I spoke, I glanced away. There was silence, and when I met his gaze again I thought I saw a faint look of surprise on his face. "Please tell me why." Now for the difficult bit, I thought. "I don't think I believe in God any more."

There was more silence. Senior clerics of the Church of England are not noted for being demonstrative. His eyes were looking at me steadily and I suddenly thought how intelligent they were. "You do not think that you believe in God any more", he repeated. "That rather implies that once you did believe."

Now it was my turn to be surprised. Didn't this man assume belief in God when he ordained priests?

"Well yes", I replied. "During my theological studies God seemed to me to be a sort of given. I never thought a great deal about atheism. But lately I have, and I think I agree with people who say there is no God. I suppose you could say that I've lost my faith, though I'm not quite sure exactly what I ever had." I swallowed again, and was aware of my heart beating.

"I find it very difficult trying to relate to people in the church, thinking the way I do. I feel I'm a fraud. It can be hard knowing what to say. It was *awful* trying to prepare the sermon for Easter. I don't think I can go on much longer." The Bishop was looking at me very intently, saying nothing. I was remembering the devastating panic I had felt on Holy Saturday as I had sat at my computer all day and half the night trying to write something about the resurrection of Jesus that would fulfill the expectations of the people, while remaining true to my integrity. There was more silence.

"I've tried praying very hard," I went on, "but it makes no difference. I have absolutely no sense of anyone or anything there, hearing me." I became aware of the intensity in my voice. I knew the Bishop was looking at me, but I couldn't meet his eyes. He'll start speaking in a minute, I thought. He'll give me a gentle lecture on the limitations of human understanding and the spiritual benefit of doubt. He might even say that this is a test from God and mention the Dark Night of the Soul. He might recommend a few books, or he will say that it is a relief to have a conversation with a woman priest who hasn't come to complain about misogyny in the church. He will suggest I have a holiday and come back to see him in six months, then he will usher me out. I had gone over this stage of the consultation in my head a hundred times. Suddenly, I felt acutely aware of my loneliness. The Bishop sat back in his chair. "What does the word God mean to you?" he asked. His question came as a jolt. I hadn't thought in quite these terms before. "A guarantee of some kind of continued existence after death." I was surprised at the speed of my reply. "That death isn't just nothing." I struggled to find the right word. "That it isn't . . . annihilation." I was aware of the emotion in my voice, and of the silence after I had spoken. And then another thought: "And that love and not impersonal chemistry is at the centre of the universe, right at its core. I think that is what Christianity proclaims, but I can't believe it." I looked defiantly at the Bishop and then I felt my heart fill. I was about to cry. I had not realized how deeply I felt about this. I did not want him to judge me as a woman who couldn't contain herself and I struggled to regain my composure.

He looked out of the window for what seemed a long time. Then he reached for some paper and wrote briefly. "This is serious", he said. "I don't think it is simply an intellectual problem. I have written down the name of a psychotherapist. She is trained in the psychoanalytic tradition and I think you should seek some consultations with her before you finally make up your mind what to do about the priesthood."

And that is how I began my journey in psychoanalytical psycho-therapy, a process so intimate, so important, so strange, that it is difficult to convey the experience in words.

I can't actually remember much of what I said during the initial consultation with the psychotherapist who was to become so central in my life. I told her a recent dream in which the living room in my house had been flooded and in which I had crouched, frightened and cold in one tiny dry corner as the water threatened to spread ever nearer. I must have told her about my vocational doubts because I certainly told her that the Bishop had sent me. I know that she asked me about my family, although I remember little of what I said. I probably told her that I had a difficult relationship with my mother. I hadn't thought much about that, but I was to reflect upon it much more in the years to come. I don't think I asked her many questions in that first session when we sat face to face. It didn't occur to me to ask her if she believed in God. Looking back I think I just presumed that she did not, since Freud had been so categorical on the subject. I knew at the time that Freud's view was that God was an illusion to help people cope with their helplessness: a big make-believe Daddy in the sky. With a hollow feeling in the pit of my stomach, I agreed with that view really. But oh, how I longed for it to be otherwise!

The main memories I have of that first consultation are of impressions rather than words. As I arrived, I noticed her ordinary, somewhat untidy garden in an ordinary sort of street. That surprised me. I had expected her to work from a consulting room, not from her own house. The greatest impression of all was of the kindness of her face, and her openness. Not that she told me anything about herself or was all over me in an effusive sort of way—not at all. I just sensed her goodness. I trusted her. At the end of that session, I didn't agree to come back because I knew the Bishop thought it would be a good thing. I went back because without quite knowing why, I knew it would be a good thing.

I went to her house for four fifty-minute sessions each week for six years. From the beginning, I tried to keep to the one prescription she had given me: to tell her whatever came into my mind, even if it seemed irrelevant or embarrassing, or impolite. What I found strange was that almost right away I rarely thought about religion when I was with her, and so I didn't speak about it much except, for example, if I had felt put on the spot by a parishioner and the incident was fresh in my mind. But even then, if I let my mind wander, I would often begin to think of one of my parents or a teacher or someone I had known when I was young, which would set me off recalling memories that appeared to have no connection with my day-to-day life. Anyway, quite early in the process I contacted the Bishop to say that I wanted to be relieved of my duties. I was finding the management of my atheism in the context of ministry too stressful. I had been a history teacher earlier in my career, and quite easily found new employment. After that, I spoke about God even less.

What I did experience in these early sessions was an increasing awareness of anxiety and stress. I became as overwrought in teaching as I had been in the priesthood, though not, of course, because I had to say anything about God in my new working life. I began to see how much I struggled to relate to people well, whether they were pupils or other members of the staff. The psychotherapy sessions were filled with anxious ruminations about my personal failings as I saw them. Day by day, week by week, I would arrive at her house at the appointed time and ring the doorbell. She would answer—mostly quite quickly, occasionally after what would seem a frustratingly long time. We exchanged no preliminary pleasantries. I would go straight to the room she used and onto the vacant couch, while she sat on an armchair behind, invisible and quiet, but palpably present. Usually when I came in I knew exactly what I wanted to tell her, mostly about the problems of the day, or what I had dreamt the night before. Sometimes as I arrived, I was struck by something about her, or by some new thought. If I wasn't too stressed, I would start with that.

Then came the first major break after about nine months: her summer holiday. She took four weeks. I thought I would cope, but very quickly I felt bereft—bereft and terribly, terribly anxious. I counted first the weeks and then the days until her return. It was during that break that I thought about God again. I desperately needed to know if God existed. It was the old problem, but no longer did it arise principally as a vocational issue. It was my personal problem. If I could be convinced of God, I thought, I could face anything. No problem could be too difficult or overpowering if God was there, helping and directing. I tried to pray. There was nothing in response: no word, no sign. It felt less like facing a wall of silence, and more like being poised on the brink of a void; a bottomless darkness that I might tip into with no hope of return; a black hole, where I would be twisted and mangled until the life was drained from me forever. I felt gripped by fear like a vice. One weekend it almost overpowered me. I lay in my bed tight with it. I felt I could just manage if I stayed safe in that bed, in that familiar bedroom; but the idea that I might leave it was impossible to contemplate. Somehow later that week I was able to go to work, to get through the day. I'm not sure how I did. But the memory of that experience stayed with me for a long time, together with the knowledge that God had not answered me in my distress. I had remembered the scriptures, especially the psalms: "I waited patiently for the Lord". I could relate to these words, but then inevitably came the rest: "He took me from a fearful pit, and from the miry clay . . . and set my feet upon a rock . . ." Well, He hadn't done that for me.

Then she came back from holiday. I was ringing her doorbell, seeing her face, entering her familiar room, lying on her couch, and telling her all about it: the suffering, the fear, the longing, the anxiety, and yes, the praying. It had felt like dying, like impending annihilation. As I talked, I suddenly remembered that had been the word I had used to describe my fear of death to the Bishop. During her holiday I had felt as if I was falling into nothing: not a comforting nothing where I wouldn't feel anything—like having an anaesthetic—but a terrifying, persecutory, pain-filled nothingness which felt like the death I dreaded. It had been as if I had inhabited Dante's *Inferno*.

There were more periods like this, sometimes over weekends, often when she was on holiday. Gradually they became less frequent. But if I had thought that by plumbing these awful depths the trouble was over, I was wrong. For the next months—years actually—I felt as if I was swimming painfully and laboriously in a great grey sea of despair; with no sight of land, no comforting ships, no life-belt, nothing and no-one, except her quiet invisible presence four times a week for short—oh-so-short sessions—during which I lay on her couch trying to put into words the depth of my hopelessness. There was no pleasure, no goodness in me. I could survive. I was no longer so anxious, but I had no sense of aliveness, no expectation, no faith that life could offer me anything other than a rather barren path to a death I no longer feared but which would simply be the closing of a life half-lived. Session after session was filled with descriptions of this state, or else with silence, when I felt myself spiral away from her, adrift in the universe of her room, attached to her just by the thinnest of threads which threatened to break at any moment.

Once, memorably, I was convinced that the thread had broken. I had been angry with her, and had said so. The reason doesn't matter now. It was the expression of that anger, that hate, that fury that was so important, but that felt so terrifying at the time. I was convinced that I had severed the thread. Now there was really nothing. Now I was back in the void. But then she spoke. I cannot now remember what she said. But she was still there. She had not retaliated. I had not succeeded in breaking the bond. And as I lay on the couch that day becoming aware of this, and the enormity of what it meant to me, I remembered the biblical phrase "Underneath are the everlasting arms". I was experiencing what it meant to be held.

My struggles in psychotherapy did not stop at that point. I still felt despair for periods. I still knew the longing for her presence, her voice; sometimes in the night, or at work, or anywhere. I still wrestled with difficulties in relating to some people. I still experienced frustration with members of my family. I still went to work and appeared to operate reasonably competently while underneath I felt like a frightened lonely child. But actually I was undergoing a change. Friends seemed to notice it before I did. Slowly and imperceptibly I was becoming stronger. Sometimes I felt hopeful, pleased, even excited. I felt I was re-engaging with life, perhaps really beginning to engage with it for the first time.

Tomorrow I have an appointment with the Bishop. I am going to tell him that he was right that my problem about God's existence was not just an intellectual one. It was bound up with my childhood, and in particular with the failures in that childhood experience. I had not felt sufficiently held, emotionally. I no longer blame anyone; that is simply how it was. I do believe that 'God' fulfilled a containing function for me early on—that is until my belief cracked. Perhaps I went into the priesthood unconsciously to try to paste the cracks. In my psychotherapist, I found a human, rather than a divine container. She was a living, breathing person. She had failings and wasn't perfect, but she was demonstrably and patiently good enough to enable me to stay safe even when I felt that my very being was cracking. I know that through the process of psychotherapy, I have experienced a human acceptance and receptivity that is worthy of the word love. Whether that love is a reflection of a Love that is God, I don't know. I do know that I do not want human love to be diminished somehow by God-talk.

I am going to tell the Bishop that after this psychotherapeutic experience I no longer worry and fuss over the problem of God, though I think there is a mystery at the heart of life that defies neat prescriptive definition. Those who come after us, especially some scientists, may stretch nearer this mystery as they seek to understand the laws of nature, but I wonder if it will ever be grasped. I am fascinated to think, read, talk about this question, but I am uneasy about using the word God, perhaps because it is so overlaid with meanings I can no longer relate to.

Nevertheless, I am going to tell the Bishop that I believe that the stories of the Bible can be entered into imaginatively even in our post-Enlightenment age. I will say that I still like going to church when the service is conducted intelligently and expansively, especially in a lovely building, where music and ritual along with periods of silence provide a sense of continuity and a contemplative and restorative space in a busy week. I can inhabit that kind of space gratefully without trying to dissect its meaning too much. I will tell him that for me religious practice at its best has value as a creative art form. But I am also going to say that unless kindness and compassion shine from the heart of the Christian rite, I am sceptical about its worth, no matter how well it is done. Somehow I think that he will understand me.

I am going to tell the Bishop that I have begun training to become a psychotherapist myself. I will tell him that I have a vision of a centre attached to a church in which people can be offered good quality psychotherapeutic help. I will say that I think this would be a valid 21st Century expression of the ancient ministry of healing, and I will ask him if he would support this and help to bring it about.

But most of all, I am going to thank him for listening to me so carefully during that first difficult interview, and for opening a door which is very possibly the most important I will ever pass through.

Author's Note

While this account is rooted in an actual experience of psychoanalytical psychotherapy, an element of creative license in the construction of the story was introduced by the author.

Angela's Search for Her Identity

Annie McMillan

This is a story about human courage. A story of childhood traumas, which were so horrific that the only way to survive was to cut off from any feelings linked to these experiences, and to bury memories deeply within the unconscious.

Angela was forty-two years old when she first came to consult me. She was married, with four adult sons, and she wanted to find out more about her birth mother. Little did we know that she would remain in therapy for eleven years—two, three and four times a week. By the end of the therapy, she still had not actively sought contact with her birth mother. The reader might understand why as her story unfolds.

In those early days, she talked about knowing that her birth mother had given her up for adoption when she was twelve weeks old. She was not told until she was five, when her parents adopted a second daughter. Angela had always felt herself to be unlovable. Relentless abuse repeatedly underlined and reinforced this belief.

At one session she expressed anger and resentment towards a work colleague who had sexually assaulted her. I asked why she had let him abuse her and this question triggered the beginning of her conscious memories of shocking sexual and emotional torment, involving both parents. Therapy was a slow and painful process. How could this woman, once a little girl who had no experience of trust, allow herself to get in touch with feelings of terror, shame and despair? But she found a way through bringing me her dreams and her poems.

For a long time, she felt as though these were unconnected to her. Together, we built up a sense of trust and safety, which enabled her to begin to make links. Her beautifully written poems often revealed a suppressed awareness of her suffering and an insight into the internal chaos, which had been impossible for her to manage as a child. Her father had sexually abused her from a very early age— perhaps when she was one or two years old. She tearfully told me of how, after bathing her, he would wrap her in a towel before sitting her on his lap. He got her to touch his penis and eventually entered her anus, with threats that if she did not agree to this he would find another little girl to whom he could read stories. She did not know if the painful "thing" inside her belonged to herself or her father, or was something separate. She wondered where he put it afterwards. Angela had loved her father and was full of confusion. The first poem she showed me describes her confusion; her longings and her awareness of her need to bury feelings.

> The cries of terror on the beach
> Echo round the dunes and over the sea
> But help is always out of reach
> And no one sees what is happening to me
>
> If only he would hold me close,
> Without the lies, the dirt and pain
> And I would lie quietly in his arms,
> Then slowly come to life again
>
> The sand is soft beneath my feet
> The sea laps softly as if to say—
> Keep on waiting, keep on hoping,
> Help is sure to come one day.
>
> Then fear and terror will be gone,
> The pain and darkness disappear,
> So bury it now, deep in the sand
> Until that help is really here
>
> Then gentle hands will soothe the hurt,
> And arms will hold you quietly still.
> Then never again will love and trust,
> Be taken away against your will.

At the same time, her fanatically religious mother talked of the devil as if he was God, and was always condemning Angela's behaviour. "If you were my real daughter, you would not do that," she said. Her mother later told her that Angela would not allow her to care for her as a child but preferred her father. To add another layer of confusion, Angela had memories of her mother insisting that she accompany her to the bathroom, where she was asked to tell her mother how lovely she was, as she watched her mother wash and use the toilet. Although her mother did not physically hurt her, Angela wondered whether she had a "bit of magic up her sleeve" like her father. After about three years of therapy, we came to understand this more deeply: on a visit to her mother, now in her sixties, she asked Angela to accompany her when she went to the lavatory. Angela refused but, when her mother came out of the toilet, she grabbed her wrist and held her fast, pleading with her to tell her how much she loved her. Angela again refused and was full of horror as her mother stroked her breasts and kissed her. After this episode, Angela struggled with the denied fears and sense of dread, which had always been present on visits to her mother. Eventually, she was able to insist on firm boundaries with her and to relinquish some of the child's helplessness, which she had carried around for so much of her life in response to others' abuse.

It was an exploration of Angela's fear of moths, which took time to emerge, as if out of a chrysalis, that increased my understanding of how she used words to keep feelings buried and unknown. She had often spoken of this terror and described how she would run out of a room when one appeared. One day she brought a dream of an eight or nine year old girl who was in the bath and who was being watched by various people, though she could not actually see them. She was terrified when a very large moth flew into the room. It landed on her and had huge yellow wings. She tried to hit it so that it would leave her shoulder. It would not move and no one would help her. In the end, the wings stayed stuck to her shoulder and the body fell into the bath—eventually going inside her. It was "disgusting".

As sometimes happened in our sessions, I was struck by the sensation that the dream represented an actual experience. There had been a past reference to the possible link between her adult fear of moths and their presence when she was abused in candlelit surroundings. I referred to the "tickling" of the wings—perhaps another "gameword" used by her father when he masturbated her?

"Candles", I suggested, "are like penises . . ."

"Moths", she said, "are more like penises than candles. I remember being given a book as a child. On one page was a picture of a huge moth with yellow wings. Alongside it was a chrysalis—hard and big. The caterpillar was soft, then hard, then soft again when it became a moth." She talked about her confusion about the sequence of this process. She linked this confusion to her father's penis and to his garden shed, where moths often appeared, and where he often abused her with his chrysalis penis.

These memories put her in touch with her efforts to try to work out frightening experiences by referring to books, particularly the moth book. The chrysalis had a line down the centre and so did her father's penis. These thoughts led to the "disgusting" moth exploding inside her. She spoke about the bookcase at home which was full of natural history books. She had spent hours searching their pages, trying to make sense of confused feelings, and to some extent the information alleviated her turmoil and distress. This confusion around reality and fantasy, and Angela's preoccupation with actual understanding in order to manage feelings, had damaged her capacity for ordinary, child-like imaginary play, which is an essential ingredient in every human being's development.

At times she would lie on the couch, a shivering, frightened child, awakened by a dream's unconscious meaning. Sometimes she did not tell me about a dream until nearly the end of a session in an effort to keep her feelings under wraps. It was the same with her poems, as if the act of writing them formed a barrier which protected her from linking thoughts and feelings. She brought the following poem to me on a screwed up piece of paper. She was too frightened of the feelings that might be evoked if she read this poem herself. As I read it to her, she slowly allowed her hands to drop away from her face.

> She had no one to see the tears in her eye,
> No one to hold her and help her to cry,
> No one to share all her fear and her pain
> No one to stop her from going insane.
>
> So without any fuss she quietly died,
> Unable to live with such darkness inside.

They cut out her heart for Satan to keep.
Then she lay very still as if asleep.

They buried her body in a hole deep and black.
She had no white shroud but a rough piece of sack.
The black wings of evil hovering there
Filled all the others with terror and fear.

"Where are the angels with wings shining white
To take away all these terrors of night?"
"Angels guard good girls who do no wrong.
So not for you, child, the angel's sweet song."

No cross to mark the place where she lay.
No flowers to show where she used to play.
No memory held dear in anyone's mind.
No one can see her, for everyone's blind.

Again and again I marvelled at Angela's capacity to survive such abuse. One of the ways she had stopped herself from going insane was to develop different child selves, which we discovered when she talked about becoming different people to handle different situations. They all had names. At first, we thought Holly, who was very "prickly", was the youngest, but we were wrong. The smallest child, Holly Berry, was quiet for a long time inside Holly. After several years of therapy, she screamed so loudly that Angela found she could not move. The headache she suffered was intense and would not respond to painkillers. This pain lessened as Angela remained silent in the warm womb-therapy room. (Silences were difficult for her. She had said on one occasion, "If I have nothing to say, I don't exist.") It seemed that Holly Berry had at last been heard instead of left to die.

As each child was recognised, listened to, accepted and enjoyed within the therapy, Angela's trust was strengthened. At times, I felt humbled by her courage in the face of such a lack of childhood love and care. She wrote,

I want to trust you with all that is me,
There is no reason not to, that I see,
But how do I know what tomorrow will bring?
To frighten or crush this butterfly wing.

As each new tomorrow comes, then departs,
The trust that I have for you grows in my heart.
You are real, you are honest—I hope you can see—
That the doubts and the fears belong just to me.

I think that this poem is about her developing trust in me.

At first Angela had talked of loving her father, and, because she was adopted, was convinced that they should have married and lived happily ever after. This understandable distortion of reality slowly and painfully shifted as she faced the horrors and details of the sexual abuse she had suffered until around the age of thirteen. She had been distraught when the abuse had stopped at this time. She remembered feeling suicidal when she experienced this as her father's sudden and shocking withdrawal of his love for her. She had had no mother to turn to. In therapy she began to feel her painful longing for motherly care. Later, she wrote,

I used to believe in angels
There just had to be someone out there,
But why did they let me suffer so much
Were they blind or couldn't they hear?

Now I believe in an angel
Whose safety is human, though rare.
There is still so much that I don't understand.
But you see me, you hear me—you're here!

For many years, Angela expressed suicidal thoughts. She was convinced that I would abandon her, and suffered from many anxieties about her relationship with me. All of this was very difficult for her to handle, let alone speak about with me, since the fears were rooted in her childhood experiences of severe parental control and abuse. It was something to celebrate when she risked getting angry with me about taking a break, or when she wrote to me saying that she was not going to attend the next session. Needless to say, the safer and the more trusting she felt with me, the more she could relate to me as a separate human being, instead of feeling as she had as a child—an extension of both parents who was there to meet their needs. She began to entrust me with fantasies about her growing relationship with me. These could be explored and understood but remain safely as fantasies, rather than become frightening and unsafe realities. Little girls often dream of taking their father away from their mother but their experience is that this does not happen. They are free to grow up and to find their own partner.

External events contributed to changes and to Angela's developing capacity to become confident about the woman she was, and would become. She adopted a feminine style of dress and became more comfortable with the womanly aspects of her personality. She knew that her more masculine response and dress had been partly a protection to ward off sexual abuse and partly because, at some level, she had felt an extension of her father's masculinity. Then she celebrated the birth of her first grandchild, a girl. She had wanted a grandson because she felt she would know how to relate to a boy. She was glad that she had had sons herself and was convinced that she would not be able to relate properly to a little girl, since she had had no experience of this being offered to her. She (and I) experienced enormous joy as she responded with so much love and delight to her granddaughter. Angela was free to play, to laugh and to become a well-loved and loving grandmother.

Around the ninth year of therapy, Angela's mother died. This stirred up many difficult feelings for her around loss. She had a deep understanding of her mother's mental ill-health, which had ruined any chances of Angela being able to expect or receive a necessary level of care. One of her first observations in therapy was that she liked the fact that my house was near a pub in one direction and a church in the other. This was to do with the way she had had to switch between child selves. Cynthia (linked to "sin") was the naughty one and Mary (Magdalene) was the good girl who behaved well in church every week to keep her mother happy.

In the past, Angela had studied to be a lay preacher, and one of the friendships in her life, which had meant a lot to her, had been with a woman minister. Angela's successful career had always involved caring for others and, just before her mother's death, she had begun to pursue the possibility of retraining as a minister. We acknowledged a deep-rooted desire to transform her mother's distorted beliefs into a genuine expression of Angela's belief in God. There were many doubts and questions in her mind about whether she was right to undertake the training. It felt important that she was able to find a way of continuing to restore a good relationship with a 'father'. We talked about the male dominated ethos of the church, and the inevitability of confronting and developing the more assertive, confident aspects of her personality.

We ended the therapy shortly before she took up her trainee minister's post in a different part of England. At that time, she was still thinking about if or when she would seek contact with her birth mother. This is an excerpt from one of her poems. It speaks of her desire to fulfill a potential.

Oh moon in the sky I love your appearance,
I understand why you shine down on me,
You lend me your brightness to guide my long journey
In your light is my safety, my joy and my dreams.

Oh Annie of the small room I love your appearance,
But I don't understand what you do to me.
Are you lending me brightness to guide my long journey
Or is this a mirage, one more shattered dream?

Oh moon keep on shining and Annie keep on shining,
'Til one day I shine back for the whole world to see.

It seemed that she was well on the way to achieving this when she wrote to tell me that the Training Committee had said that she was "an exceptional minister", and that their vote that she should be ordained was unanimous. Subsequently, when she wrote to me after her ordination, Angela commented that she had begun to believe that she might have found a way of "shining on her own".

Author's Note

Angela has given permission for this story to be published. Both she and the author have changed their names to preserve confidentiality.

Waking in the Blue*

William Bedford

I was in my fifties when clinical depression returned to my life for the second time. My wife had been ill with cancer, but once her recovery seemed secure, I began to have trouble sleeping, lost my appetite and was soon spiralling down into a familiar misery. The trouble was, because of my past history, I could not seek help.

I had attempted suicide in 1968. In the four years that followed, I plunged into a frightening underworld, suffering the side effects of Largactil and Tofranil, being sectioned, having ECT, losing touch with my daughter, and seeing two relationships wrecked. Thirty years later, the dread of entering the same whirlpool prevented me from seeking help.

But I was ill. I was a university teacher and a writer. I had published novels, children's novels, short stories and poetry. My academic work was well-known. Yet I could scarcely leave my room. The anxiety attacks were so bad that I thought I was in danger of having a heart attack. I spent hours in my study, the curtains drawn, staring at the bookshelves.

Fortunately, the Macmillan nurse caring for our family intervened. Our GP wanted to put me on Paroxetine, but I refused, so she arranged for me to see a psychologist at the nearby hospital. He was a senior consultant, close to retirement, and used to dealing with university staff. That seemed important, the security of the familiar, though I think it was the Macmillan nurse who recognised this rather than me.

We met in Andries's book-lined study. There were two large windows, so there was always light whenever I visited. Beech trees grew just outside the building. Andries relaxed in one chair, his long legs sprawled out, looking me directly in the face. In the three years we were meeting, he never varied this position. He went quickly through my details, an obvious formality because he must already have read them.

In the coming weeks, we seemed to talk about nothing significant. He had been a university teacher himself, so we talked about the university, and my work, the books I had published. I thought this was odd, but I was reluctant to say anything about how I felt. We seemed to be going nowhere. Finally, I asked him how this was supposed to work, simply talking about a life already lived. We talked briefly about determinism, whether we could escape the experience of a lifetime. We had both studied philosophy, and he told me his favourite philosopher was Spinoza. If there was freedom, we would find it in knowledge, in consciousness, Andries suggested. This session was more like a philosophy seminar than a psycho-therapy session.

I returned the following week, wondering whether to abandon the meetings. Quite casually, Andries asked me why I had been reluctant to seek help. It seemed a shocking question, this sudden intrusion into the turmoil. From everything I had heard, direct questions were supposed to be deemed inappropriate. But Andries was far too experienced a psychotherapist to make errors of judgement. He knew exactly what he was doing. I started to explain my reluctance. I told him about the overdose I had taken in 1968, on the day Robert Kennedy was assassinated. The overdose was clearly influenced by the hysteria of the times—the cultural and political upheavals—but in my own life I was struggling to leave a disastrous marriage, unable to stay, unable to leave my three-year old daughter.

In the following months, I was put on heavy doses of Largactil and Tofranil. Largactil was thorazine, the wonder drug of the 1950s, rendering violent patients peaceful, inducing lethargy, mental vacancy—the 'zombie' effect, and spasms. Whenever I visited the hospital, I would see groups of patients waiting in the corridors, their legs kicking up involuntarily. Largactil soon became popularly known as the 'liquid cosh'. In my case, Largactil also rendered me impotent, wrecking a second relationship. I spent hours sitting in a corner, seeing hallucinations of my daughter playing with gifts I had not bought her. I ended up being sectioned to a grim Victorian hospital, where I was put on the 'terminal ward', a ward for patients unlikely to recover. I took this as a sort of punishment, as I did the ECT, a treatment which terrified me and gave me nightmares for years afterwards. I was sectioned twice in four years, and then miraculously the depression lifted, energising me for a period of intense creative work. For thirty years I experienced little more than the 'blues' common to most of us.

Andries listened quietly to this sudden outpouring. I must have talked for almost the whole session. As I prepared to leave, he told me that on the night of Kennedy's assassination, he had been in Democratic Headquarters in New York. He spoke simply, matter-of-factly, adding what a shock the terrible crime had been. I suppose some patients might have been frightened off by this apparent irrelevance. It had the opposite effect on me. Quite irrationally, I felt he was there on the day I attempted suicide. He understood in a way that had nothing to do with words. In the coming months and years, there were further examples of this historical synchronicity. They were always reassuring, never intrusive. They established trust as we embarked on our journey together.

This session was clearly the turning point, and in the coming weeks I talked in great distress about the years after 1968. Andries rarely commented. He simply listened, in the same relaxed, un-flinching posture, apparently enduring the story I had to tell. I have very little recollection of any order to these sessions. I know I cried often. There was no anger.

Over these months, the feeling which emerged most powerfully was guilt over abandoning my daughter. I felt hardly anything for my first wife. In one session, we talked about guilt, and what guilt means for Catholics. I learned that Andries had been a priest, working in Latin America before leaving the Church in 1968. After training in Harvard and at the Tavistock, he married an Anglo-Saxon don from Cambridge, travelling to work between London and Cambridge.

I had studied Anglo-Saxon myself, and knowing that the god-parent of Andries's son was Dorothy Whitelock, the eminent Anglo-Saxon scholar, simply served to bring us closer together, in the straightforward sense of mutual understanding. There was also the shared experience of Catholicism. Catholics, even lapsed Catholics, always recognise each other: a way of thinking. We never spoke about guilt again. I began to realise that in psychotherapy, there were only the memories, the psychic dramas, no judgments.

The trust went on deepening and one afternoon, Andries finally asked me the question I knew I was avoiding. I had talked of abandoning my wife and child, but they were not the only figures in the story. What about my parents? They had actually been there at the time of my overdose, or at least a couple of days afterwards. What did I feel about them? I was immediately back in 1968. Having made myself violently sick by taking too many aspirin, I managed to call for help. My wife and family were all away. They returned two days later when I was recovering. My father seemed furious, glaring down at me as I lay on a settee. A friend was there, trying to tell them what had happened. My father hardly bothered to listen. When my friend had finished he angrily said that I hadn't taken anything, that I was drunk. Then he walked out of the house. I didn't see him again for almost five years.

My father was a policeman who suffered from periods of debilitating depression, alternating with frantic activity. He would hold down two or even three part-time jobs after finishing his shifts. When he wasn't working, he spent all his free time playing football, cricket, tennis, or looking after his garden. He rented an enormous allotment to grow vegetables. My abiding memory of childhood is of waiting for my father to appear. He was rarely in the house. He had 'walked out' emotionally long before my illness.

My mother spent most of her time with us, taking command of our daughter, running our lives. When my wife was breast-feeding, she sent my father to watch, 'to make sure she was doing it right'. She was a dominating, frightening woman, a delusional psychotic subject to moments of uncontrolled rage. These would alternate with intrusive displays of physical affection, always associated with food, and knowing no boundaries. She would hug me until I could scarcely breathe.

In one of her rages, when I was seven, she stripped me naked and beat me with the heel of a shoe, my father standing by unable to intervene. The day afterwards, she took me out and bought me an expensive gift. On another occasion, a year or so earlier, she invited a coal delivery man into the house with his black sack to 'take me away'. I hid under the bed, listening to her jeers about 'little cowards'. When he left the house, she smothered me with kisses and watched while I ate half a large chocolate cake.

Throughout her life, she claimed that her father was a friend of the Duke of Devonshire, her sister an opera singer, her elder brother the designer of the Brabazon aeroplane. She came from a large, dysfunctional family, growing up in the east end of Sheffield despite her claims of a grand house near a park with servants and a chauffeur. Even in her nineties, she insisted that her father had been a 'great artist' and profiled in *Tatler*.

In the heat of 1968, she sat downstairs all night telling my young wife that she should throw me out of the house. The following morning I left, with the clothes I was wearing and my portable typewriter. Now, talking to Andries, I suddenly knew that I had left my daughter with the two people I detested most in the world. I broke down at this point, and nothing more was done in this session.

This prolonged outburst shook me very badly. The memories were vivid and highly detailed, and yet seemed to come to me in slow-motion. I felt intense anger as I tried to talk, leaning forward and crying. Afterwards, my ribs ached as if I had been physically attacked. I had to get a taxi home. And yet that moment seemed to change things yet again. I felt relieved, began to enjoy food again, listen to music, to walk in the countryside. I also began to think about my father, what hidden pain made him incapable of facing the truth of my suicide attempt. Things that I had always known slowly emerged. His mother had died in a mental asylum after years of serious mental illness. Her elder sister had hanged herself after the death of her fiancé in the Great War. Her younger sister died of a possible brain tumour which was never really explained. In 1974, six years after my own overdose, my father's sister herself took an overdose and died. That explains nothing about my own experience, but a great deal about my father's family, farming people from the Fens with a history of clinical depression.

In a session soon after, I described an incident when I was eighteen. I had published poetry in various magazines, and wrote to Faber & Faber wondering whether I might be able to have a job with them. Peter du Sautoy wrote back, and invited me to London for an interview, paying my train fare and hotel expenses. The interview was on a Saturday morning, and the position was merely clerical, but I was offered the job. To work with the greatest poetry publishing house in the world, when T.S. Eliot was still alive, seemed an amazing opportunity. When I returned home, my mother was hysterical. Ferocious pressure was put on me: I was too stupid to look after myself; I had made a mistake and they hadn't offered me the job at all; I was a 'bloody twisted queer', wanting to write poetry.

In the end I gave up. I was exhausted, and it took another year for me to finally leave home.

This session left me drained and weeping. Calmly, Andries told me that he had a family relation who had once worked for Faber. She was Brigid O'Donovan, the Oxford graduate who was Eliot's secretary during the years when he was leaving his wife Vivienne. This information had an immediate, healing effect upon me. For decades, I had buried the pain of declining Faber's offer, and of turning down their kindness. Suddenly it was back, in all its raw misery. But this time I had somebody with me. My psychotherapist shared my regret, actually genuinely understood it. In both an actual and symbolic sense, 'he was there'.

I tried to understand my mother's behaviour. Her own family were violent, disturbed people with a history of drink and mental illness. Searching medical records, I learned that her paternal grandfather had died in the South Yorkshire Asylum, suffering from manic depression and syphillis. Her mother, my grandmother, had a glass eye which she used to remove and pretend to eat when she wanted to frighten me. According to an uncle, she lost the eye when she was thirteen, serving beer in a pub when there was a violent brawl. According to my mother, she lost the eye one winter afternoon when snowballing in a park.

As my therapy came towards its end, I became obsessed with making a family tree. Andries suggested I was still worried about determinism, whether I could escape the relentless hold of the past. It did seem a daunting inheritance, the manic depression and asylums, the awful suicides. Knowing that my grandmother had been terrified of ECT did nothing to alleviate my own memories of the treatment. Understanding my father's horror of suicide did little to forgive his rejection of my own despair.

But psychotherapy is not about forgiveness, unless it is to help you forgive yourself. In my sessions with Andries, what happened in the past simply happened. Contained in that room, in that generous containing environment, the anguish of the years was carried out into the open and laid to rest. I never think about it now, except that as a writer I think about it all the time. But that is different, that is simply giving form to experience.

Ironically, as I emerged from therapy, the work I turned to was writing for children. In a sense, I was inventing a childhood, both fantasy and phantasy, as Freud suggested and Andries reminded me. In a novel called *The Stowaway*, I told the story of a young boy whose mother had died. In their shared grief, father and son 'find each other,' and even I could see how I was trying to resurrect a relationship with my own father which I had never had. In a few years, I wrote a dozen books for young children, and finally a picture book for five-year-olds called *The Glowworm Who Lost Her Glow*, which has sold around the world, most amazingly in China, where the glow-worm has particular cultural significance. The glow of the female glow-worm is of course the radiance of love.

Andries was not surprised by any of this, and it brought a new atmosphere into my family life. Like many people involved in the arts, I soon became interested in Winnicott, starting with *Playing and Reality* and eventually reading everything he had written. I recognised Winnicott's famous 'holding environment' in the years I had spent with Andries. I even had the pleasure of seeing my daughter from my third marriage go on to Oxford to read Experimental Psychology, where she delighted in talking to me about the adaptive nature of genes. This brought back echoes of my conversations with Andries about Spinoza and the freedom we might find in consciousness. My daughter's cheerful optimism as to the extent to which we might escape our gene inheritance seemed part of a new mental life. Though I have no clinical proof, I know this new life began for me in my experience of psychotherapy.

How can I describe this experience, this doctor of the soul who sat down with me for three years, looked me unflinchingly in the face, and listened to the infantile griefs and furies that had so damaged my life? Critics of psychotherapy argue that it all depends on the luck of finding the right therapist, and obviously Andries was the perfect therapist for me. But I do not believe the concept of the happy accident explains everything. Andries was too successful for too long for the success to depend upon a few historical synchronicities. He knew perfectly well what he was doing, and his knowledge was both wisdom and professional expertise.

'Psychoanalysis is in essence a cure through love' Freud wrote to Jung, and in the Christian sense of *agape*, an informed and genuine concern for the true welfare of others, I have to say that is how it felt.

* Robert Lowell, "Waking in the Blue," *Life Studies* (Faber, 1959).

Desert Rose

Diane Helliker

It was on my birthday, 1 December 2004, that I received a call from Dr Pas. It wasn't unusual that he would remember this occasion, as his father and I shared the same birth date. After the death of his father, Dr Pas always remembered. I somehow became intertwined with his personal life, through someone close to him that I didn't know. I was rambling on about the perils of moving to a foreign place, when I noticed something was not right in his voice. "Do you have a cold?" I asked. "No," he replied, "It is much worse. I have cancer. I am dying. I have six months." Neither of us spoke for at least a minute. I was struck not only by the weight of the words, but by the sharp, concise way that he chose to tell me. Dr Pas taught me that when you repeat things that are painful, enough times, the words lose their power. He relayed the news of his impending death as though he had rehearsed the lines over and over, until he attained sufficient distance from them. "I have had to close my practice," he went on. "I wanted you to know that I admire your courage, your tenacity and strength. I remember you with fondness always. I wish you well."

Several months before I had moved away, I wanted to end our sessions. I wanted to know if I could manage without therapy, without Dr Pas. He saw this move as asserting my independence from him. He was disappointed that I was leaving before our work was complete. There was more to do, to make me into a fully-functioning individual, rather than a semi-functioning one. Now Dr Pas was leaving me, for good. I knew that I could always call if I needed to. I never did. Perhaps, he wanted to see how I would react to the news; if he was worthy of my falling apart.

I have not spoken to Dr Pas since. I have no way of knowing if he outlived the six month prognosis. There have been no obituaries to be found. I search every day for this. I ponder this unique relationship between the psychiatrist and the patient: the deep, dark secrets that no one else is privy to. This is a professional relationship, yet based entirely on the intimate details of one's life. For seventeen years—two, sometimes three days a week—we met for sessions. I am not family, I am not even a friend. I was the patient and he was the doctor who more than once saved my life.

Some of the old thought patterns are re-emerging, feeling responsible for events out of my control. I awaken with nightmares that if I had stayed in therapy and hadn't moved away, he may have avoided getting the cancer. I read that pancreatic cancer often appears after a lengthy depression. In states of semi-consciousness, I talk to him as though he were here. "I let you down by becoming well, by becoming strong enough to fly, to leave the safe nest of therapy. If I remained unwell, I could keep coming to see you, but then you wouldn't be a very good psychiatrist, would you? I was, as you often said, your "project", a broken, psychotic young woman, who was heading for the back ward of an institution. You were the first psychiatrist that believed in my ability to become well."

We met while I was in the acute care unit of a psychiatric facility where Dr Pas was a resident clinician. This wasn't my first hospitalization, there had been many before in my twenty-five years. When he made his rounds and came into my room to ask how I was, I believed that he really wanted to know, not merely to write something on the chart, but because he genuinely cared about his patients. When I left hospital, Dr Pas made arrangements for me to meet with a psychiatrist. This was the first time that I left hospital with any follow-up. I met with Dr B for a few years. He was frustrated by my slow recovery and my reluctance to follow his solid, good advice.

I returned to hospital again, the same ward where Dr Pas was a resident seven years before. My marriage was over. My daughter, now nine years old, was living with her father. I was living in a rooming house—attempting something grand. I had completed the pre-university course necessary for admission to the University of Toronto. I had begun my first course that would lead to a degree in drama and history. The stress was overwhelming, the auditory hallucinations returned, drowning out all that Professor A. L. was lecturing on Medieval theatre. After three months I was discharged, without follow-up. I looked for Dr Pas' number in the directory, and called his office. He answered the phone. "I don't know if you remember me," I inquired nervously. "I was in hospital when you were a resident. My name is Diane D."

"I think I do," he replied, "you are the model."

"I'm not modelling anymore," I said, "I'm calling back to ask if it would be possible to make an appointment."

It was six weeks later when I met with Dr Pas. He was encouraged by my enrollment at the university, my valiant attempt to earn a degree against incredible odds. I had lost the credit for the course on Medieval and Renaissance theatre. Dr Pas and I discussed the best strategy to return again for the following term. I would choose one course and spend the next three months doing some preparation such as acquiring the reading list and course outline. I chose another theatre history course, on the Greek and Roman theatre. I was able to finish the course with a B+. For the first time Dr Pas made me realize that my inability to do well in school as a child—the dyslexia, the failing grades, the streamlining into what I called the Dummy School—was not my fault. I was not the stupid, lazy child that I believed I was. I was hampered by a lack of self-worth, not believing that I could do anything worthwhile, reinforced by family and certain educators. Dr Pas and I dissected every thread of my life. It was excruciatingly painful to relive the past, yet I realized that this was necessary if I was ever going to become well, and Dr Pas created a safe place for this. We unravelled the events leading to my first attempted suicide. "When did you first become aware of suicide?" Dr Pas would ask. He would pull the lever on the side of his lazy-boy, adjust his body and nod his head once, which meant whenever you're ready. I began.

"I was ten years old, when a neighbour of my grandparent's shot himself in his barn. This was the first time that I became aware that if things weren't working out the way you thought they should, you wouldn't need to wait around for your regular death date. At sixteen, I would give it a try by slitting my wrist, hoping to bleed to death. The school guidance counsellor sent me to see a psychiatrist, without my mother's consent. My mother didn't believe in psychiatry, and tried to convince the school that there were no problems at home, and that I had created these scenarios for attention. I only saw the psychiatrist once. When my mother found out, she threatened to sue the school board."

"Go on,"directed the voice from the chair.

"I was ashamed that I couldn't 'snap out of it' or 'pull up my socks'. I thought of death. I made Novenas to the Virgin Mother, asking if she could please consider taking me now. I seriously doubted that I could ever be of any real use in the world, although I longed to be—how I longed for this."

Dr Pas was interested in how I defined "useful" in terms of the life journey. He pointed out examples of how I had proven to be just this. He recounted my stories of being with children as a child and adolescent. How a deaf family's children taught me sign language in exchange for babysitting, and that I taught my little brother to read and write by playing school. More recently Dr Pas was surprised to find me in the waiting room holding my infant niece. She slept in my arms for the entire session, and on this day, Dr Pas didn't pull the lever on the side of his chair to recline. He sat perfectly straight taking in what he considered a defining moment in his continuing assessment of me.

It was around this time that Dr Pas wrote a letter of recommendation for the University of Toronto's Sesquicentennial Award. It was given annually to two part-time students, for outstanding achievement, who were attending University despite insurmountable challenges. On November 24 1989 I was one of the students to receive this award and the first to receive it for mental health issues. It was an incredible boost for my academic studies. The award dinner was splendid and for the first time I believed that I could achieve the unachievable. My family couldn't quite understand why I got the award. My father, half-jokingly, said, "What did you get that for, finding your way around campus?" Neither of my parents understood what a remarkable achievement this was for me. "What matters," Dr Pas said, "is not what anyone else thinks of your achievement, but that you believe in it yourself."

In 1990, I married for the second time, at Hart House Chapel at the University. It was a small ceremony. My niece was now seventeen months old and was my flower baby. Douglas, my new husband, was supportive and loving. Dr Pas gave me a gift for my wedding. It was a bone china cup and saucer, with the name "Persian Rose."

He explained, "I bought this for you, because you are like that rose in the desert, you continue to bloom against the odds."

I'm afraid to say, the rose would have to weather more desert storms. It seemed that the closer I was getting to the end of my degree, the more ill I became. It wasn't the end of lengthy hospitalizations. Dr Pas greeted me one day for what I thought was a regular session. I arrived with Vanessa, a doll that I had been bringing to sessions for several weeks. "I have cancelled my 3:00 appointment. I'm taking you to hospital. I've called, and they're waiting for us."

"No!" I screamed, clutching Vanessa. "I won't go, you can't make me," I pleaded. "Would you rather go with the police?" Dr Pas asked. "I would rather not go with anyone," I wimpered. "Please don't lock me up again."

Dr Pas tried to defend his professionally sound decision, "You aren't safe, you are wandering the streets with a doll that you believe is a real baby. You aren't aware of where you are, how you got there and all along you are plotting ways to drown yourself and the doll." I sat on the shaggy carpet cross-legged rocking Vanessa to and fro. Dr Pas sat on the floor beside me. "What I want," he said in his usual calm voice, "is for you to be well. You need to be in a safe place where you can be cared for." He tried to reassure me that after I was stabilized and released we could resume our sessions. I reluctantly climbed into the back seat of the car. My husband Douglas sat in the front with Dr Pas. I clutched Vanessa tightly. "Vanessa," I whispered, "I'm afraid this time we'll never get out." I kept a journal of my stay after I left the acute care unit. I was angry with Dr Pas. After a month I wrote to him from my hospital room.

Dear Dr Pas,

If I were to be honest, I would say, I felt betrayed of late, because of your decision to commit me to hospital. In retrospect, this is an unfair conclusion on my part and I owe you an apology. You did everything humanly possible to prevent a hospitalization. The truth is, I did some things I know were against my best interest to regain a healthier state of mind.

I feel saddened and confined. Your card gives me hope that I shall soon again return to my classes at the university. I look forward to resuming our sessions if this is favorable with you. Thank you for your caring attitude towards me.

D.

It wasn't until the end of summer that Dr Pas and I resumed sessions. He did call me once in a while to ask how I was, and consulted regularly with the doctors at the hospital. I returned to classes in September with two courses and fingers crossed. I thrived at University and was always the first to arrive. I needed twenty credits for my degree and I now had seven.

By the next term I was taking three courses, the following term three more. I thought I was on an unbroken track to my degree. Alas, there were other breakdowns, more hospitalizations. Dr Pas warned that as I neared the end of my university studies, the negative self-talk would resurface. I had just received another award for high academic achievement. The fear of success brought out the demons and the incessant ramblings. "Remember, you went to the Dummy School, you aren't and never will be university material," those were the words of Mr. G your Grade 8 teacher. Remember the sandbox? You printed your letters backwards, your mother beating you with a wooden spoon couldn't turn them around . . ."

The more I wanted my degree, the more I believed that I didn't deserve it. There was someone who was quite willing to support my undeserving side. It was Helen, my other personality. As a small child, I conjured up Peggy. She helped me to survive a violent and disruptive home. I came to believe that all families had an alcoholic father and an abusive mother. I believed that this dysfunction was somehow my fault.

"It was Peggy," I told Dr Pas, "who knew this was not a normal family and that I was not to blame." Dr Pas said that if Peggy knew this, then on some level, I understood this too because after all Peggy was part of me. He had difficulty convincing me that Helen was also a part of me. I don't recall the day she decided to tag along. Unlike Peggy, Helen was a malevolent force, not willingly evoked as a companion. Helen had one goal only and that was to destroy me. I began to pick up signals when she was around, my head would feel hollow and echoey. She would natter at me with repetitive statements such as "you must die and I can help you with this. What makes you think you can go to a university? What makes you think you can do anything at all." Dr Pas prescribed heavy anti-psychotic drugs in the hope that Helen would go away. He would talk to her often, as she would frequently take over our sessons. He befriended her with the sole purpose of eventually convincing her that she didn't need to hang around with me anymore; that she could take on a life of her own, without having to share a personality with me. Of course neither Helen or I thought we were sharing a personality with anyone. Helen was interfering more and more with my academic journey. Exams were approaching and my ability to concentrate was seriously marred by auditory hallucinations.

The problem became exasperated when I began to believe Helen. I began to take seriously her directions to end my life. Helen planned that I should die by drowning, and pushed me closer to the lake. Helen and I, not surprisingly, landed in hospital again. Helen disappeared by the time I was discharged, but I had lost three credits and would have to repeat these again.

The next summer my daughter offered me her apartment in another city, if I wanted to apply for a transfer credit to her university. Dr Pas was reluctant, but after several sessions weighing the pros and cons, he agreed that we could have sessions on the phone. I studied 19th Century Europe. It was a liberating experience for me and Dr Pas was surprised and pleased at how well I coped. I would return home at the end of summer, with only three credits left to complete my degree. Helen reappeared. Dr Pas expected that she would. In the last year I worked with an occupational therapist at the University. I wrote my exams in a special room, with other students with various disabilities. I couldn't write a political science exam because Helen wouldn't stop badgering me. I crawled under the desk holding my ears. I stayed there for the entire hour. It meant losing my honor average, as the professor was not willing to allow a re-write. Basically, he believed, if I was that screwed-up, I shouldn't be at University. I am so grateful he was an exception.

My final exam was written with the occupational therapist in her office. Helen would bother me, and the OT and I would take a break, and do some deep breathing exercises. "This is your last exam for your degree," she said, "You can do it. I know you can." And I did. On June 16th 1997, I graduated with my B.A. It took twelve years to complete! What made the day extra special was that my daughter was graduating at around the same time, at another University. Her friends who were graduating with me, asked her what she was doing there and she proudly stated, "This is my mom and she is graduating today."

My niece, who I held in my arms in Dr Pas' office eight years before, was wearing my sesquicentennial medal. My husband, my father-in-law and mother-in-law were there to offer their congratulations and to share in the celebration. I asked my mother if she wanted to attend. Her response was, "I can't very well go to yours and not my granddaughter's." My father's agoraphobia meant he wouldn't be able to attend. I doubt he would have come regardless. It didn't escape me for one moment on that day that it would not have been possible without the unfaltering belief Dr Pas had in me.

It has been two years since I have been in therapy, since I moved away. Whenever I feel discouraged I replay Dr Pas' voice in my head. "You are a good, decent person. You deserve to be happy." I always believed that, no matter where I was, Dr Pas would be there, a phone call away. It is difficult to accept that he won't be here anymore for those of us he dedicated his life's work to. I have fleeting thoughts, that maybe I should die now too, because I can't possibly go on without him in the world. I know he wouldn't want this. He spent seventeen years of his life trying to persuade me that I can wait for my regular death date.

The Picture

Bernardine Bishop

Anita was moving her consulting room. She was also moving house, but her patients did not have to know that. For all they knew, her daily journey to the old consulting room had always been from the new house. There was no secret about the old consulting room being rented. That was obvious from the type of building it was in. Now she was going to work in what she hoped was a nice room in her own house. For the first time, and it coincided with retirement from her NHS position, she was going to work at home. Not that it felt like home yet. She hoped it one day would.

She prepared her patients for the move. Some went to have a look at the new address. They may have thought she was there at the time, looking out of a window. But it was only in her imagination that she saw them drawing up briefly in their cars outside it. For it was not until the August that she moved.

People sympathised with her for not having a holiday. Close friends did not, and she herself saw it as a bonus that she was spared the trouble and misery of the fortnight in Andalucia which threatened that year. When it came down to it, she enjoyed August much more than usual, and wondered briefly if that should send her back into analysis.

Close friends and friends interested in houses helped with the move in different ways, and Anita's daughter promised a carpet. Anita did not like transition, or have strong tastes, so she got things done quickly, and for her there were none of those enduring cardboard boxes or uncertainties about colour that she met with in other people. She left the consulting room to the last, wanting to get it immutable and right, and as the end of August arrived, she found herself quite pleased. Her daughter's carpet had fitted nicely, some of the furniture from the old consulting room reappeared comfortingly in the new setting , and the familiar ornaments were in place on the mantelpiece. On the last day of the break she bought an extra picture from the Oxfam shop. The right size and shape for the gap in question; sea, a bit of windblown shore, a broken fence, a distant lighthouse. Neutral and timeless, but offering a mythic perspective if required, thought Anita, who was soon to spot a Matisse print that would have gone better with the blue in the carpet, but by then the patients were back and it was too late.

Enid was not a patient to go and reconnoitre the new house in July. She was much too afraid of getting a glimpse of Anita off duty. It would be unbearable to see Anita happy, and unbearable to see her unhappy. The danger of either, or even the thought of either, made Enid's intense and gnawing curiosity about Anita a bed of nails. If Anita was to be seen relaxed and smiling in a front garden pruning roses (did people prune roses in July? Enid did not know. Picking roses then—worse) with a handsome and adoring husband, Enid's anguish would be intense. And if, on the other hand, Anita was involuntarily on show on the pavement, staring, unkempt, lonely, perhaps looking vainly in a bag for keys, Enid's anguish would be irrecoverable. She arrived exactly on time for her first session in September. Anita came to the front door to let her in.

"The couch feels different," said Enid after a short silence. "It must be a new one, properly yours. The old one must have gone with the room. I thought the big plant was yours, but perhaps it belonged with the room. It isn't here, anyway." She looked round, insofar as a person on the couch can look round.

"Or perhaps it died in the break and you tidied it away, she added" Anita began to make an obvious interpretation, but Enid, now in tears, interrupted with "It's lovely to hear your voice again— although you're saying something so predictable. What was really extraordinary was you answering the door. I tried to foresee things about this session—I tried to foresee everything—but I never foresaw that. You coming to the door and letting me in just as if I was arriving at a friend's. I can't have seen you standing up since I started. Two years. I need a minute to get over it." Anita gave her a good minute, and then said, "You may have felt I was wanting to tidy away some of the new and difficult feelings before you had properly talked about them." She was aware that she had not, indeed, thoroughly thought about what her unprecedented appearance at a front door might mean to Enid.

Now Enid's glance fell on the new picture. "That's new," she said. "The pictures in the old room were obviously theirs, whoever they were. But this one must be your own." She contemplated it in silence for a minute. "Perhaps you paint. It may be by you. Or perhaps it's by someone you know. Someone you love. Or perhaps it's a scene that comes from your childhood." Enid fell silent. It was impossible to understand or express how painful she found it to think about her therapist's life. 'Real' life, she had once called it to Anita, and Anita had taken up as a painful illusion that by implication Enid believed their life together was not real.

"Perhaps your father is a little-known painter, and he painted that on a holiday in your childhood. So it has sentimental value for you. And you want to see it while you're working to keep you going."

"Do I need keeping going?" said Anita. She had heard a warning in the term 'little-known' and she was bracing herself for Enid's familiar scathing eloquence. "It's not very good. It's blurry, but it's not impressionistic, there's no atmosphere—it's just unskillful. And what's that in the front—that brown thing?"

Before the break Enid had been in diatribes over a recent clinical paper by Anita, lest the disguised clinical material was about herself, or worse, not be about herself. Now it was the picture. The picture ran and ran. Enid was sure the lighthouse was not really there, but had been romantically imposed on the scene by the brush of Anita or of a lover. The lighthouse was despicable. It did not look like a lighthouse. The light from it was incredibly badly executed, as was the sea. Sea is difficult to paint and this hapless dabbler should have left it alone. Was that brown thing a gate or a tree-stump? It drew pointless attention to itself only by making you wonder what on earth it was. As Anita knew what the picture did to Enid, how could she leave it smugly on the wall, session after session, undermining thereby Enid's expensive analysis? Why did Anita intrude what should be her private life into her patients'? Was she so insecure that she needed to tantalise? Why were her patients invited to a peepshow? It was an exercise of power. It was a deception. She who pretended to value honesty. A deception, because patients were supposed to think it was just a picture. They might even, poor things, make their own story out of it, while Anita gloated. But actually it hung there to offer Anita a treacherous means to preoccupy herself with her own exciting life while pretending to pay attention to her patients.

Anita had some hope for the lighthouse at first. She said that its real existence was being denied, put out of the picture, rendered fraudulent—and that therefore the light it might otherwise shed on things was erased. She said that Enid was putting herself in the dark. She said this darkness imposed by Enid was not necessary.

Anita liked Enid. She respected Enid's struggle. Enid's distress caused Anita pain. But Anita was pretty sure the distress was Enid's own and not, as Enid supposed, inflicted on her by her therapist. So Anita endured. She said that, as Enid alleged that patients made their own stories out of the picture, what of the story Enid had made, and continued to elaborate? Was that not just as much Enid's own story? But Enid always believed that whatever she surmised was fact—as Anita well knew. Yet it seemed worth saying anyway, as did quite a lot of other things that Anita continued fairly imperturbably to offer. But the only one that seemed to strike Enid was when, weeks later, Anita said, almost to herself, "I keep being pushed out of the way."

"What do you mean?" There was a tense silence. Anita kept quiet, though she was longing to follow up what suddenly seemed a toehold. "Do you mean it is my version of you that gets in the way, and you—you yourself, your own self, are trying to, well, get in between, save me from it?"

"Yes." Anita spoke firmly. It was a new thought, and one that Enid was ready for. Later that week Enid said, "Actually, I've realised I don't know your version of the picture." There was a tone of wonder, of relief, of achievement in her voice, as well there might be; in the next session there was a dream of a beached dolphin being freed into the sea.

The idea that a picture so personal had been allowed by Anita to find its way into the consulting room changed gradually for Enid, though the certainty that the picture was so personal did not. It became possible that its presence was not a taunting and sadistic act of self-display, or the concealed entrance to a voluptuous secret world, but an open-hearted sharing of good things. Inch by inch, Enid began to quite like the picture. One day she benignly recognised the brown structure in the foreground as a broken fence. Time passed, and she saw the picture in all its available different lights, as the days shortened or lengthened, as the sun came into the room or failed to, as electric lights were reflected in the glass. Spring was returning, and for Enid, who all her life had assumed she would always be alone, there came stirrings of new and different possibilities.

Anita had become seventy, and thought she was beginning to look it. Retirement from the NHS job had been harder than she had expected. It was lonely. She missed the team, the unsought contacts, the coteries, the shared stress. Between sessions nowadays she would find herself going downstairs to her kitchen, not for a coffee, though of course she had one, but, she thought, in search of the staff-room. Had her new house become a home? How could she tell? Certainly she was more anxious away from it than there. She was never actually happy, and according to an article she had unwisely read, this meant she would probably soon get cancer. Not having grand-children, she was inclined to be stoical about global warming and terrorism, and her daughter showed every sign of being able to look after herself. Thus Anita was spared many worries, but she was no stranger to dread, and she bore it uncomplainingly. She thought and talked a lot about retirement, and made the decision to take on no more new patients. If money got tight, she could get a lodger; two, if she no longer needed the consulting room. The idea of not working frightened her, but she had seen too many colleagues go on too long to want to take their path.

The loss of Enid's four sessions a week was soon to bring retirement closer, though not to ease the prospect of it. Enid was moving to Scotland.

The time came for their last session. "I've brought you a plant," said Enid. "It's a very nice one and I hope you like it. I imagine it on the shelf under the picture. I chose it not to be too tall for there, and not to get too tall for there, either. But you might put it somewhere quite different. I'm going to be so sad saying goodbye, but it's also masked by the move. I've got my cheque here, and I'm putting it on the couch beside me now, because I don't want any truck with it while we say goodbye. Is that OK? I know it is, now— you don't have to answer. I remember there was a long time when if you didn't answer, I thought you hated me. I must have changed so much." She was silent for a minute and then said "I'm saying goodbye to the picture. Poor picture, it has been through so much from me, and it meant no harm. Goodbye fence, goodbye beach, goodbye sea, goodbye lighthouse." The tears were coming now, and not only for Enid. Enid went on "Now I can be curious about you and the picture, and it's all right—all right for me to be curious, and all right—well, almost—for you to have your life. I don't have to own you because I love you."

After a pause, Anita said "That's about trusting, isn't it?" She was having a moment she recognised, with the difficulty of long estrangement, as happiness. Enid said "I wonder what you will look like when I leave. I always look back at you in your chair from the door, and sometimes you are big, sometimes small, sometimes old, sometimes young, sometimes fat, sometimes thin, sometimes pallid, sometimes rubicund. Sometimes you are more male and sometimes more female. I'm a bit worried about what the final one will be."

"You mean in case it proves the definitive one?"

"Yes. But you saying that makes me think it doesn't have to be. They can all be there."

"That sounds right," said Anita.

"I will want to give you a big hug when I go," said Enid, "but that would be cheating, because you couldn't really stop me, this last time. My heart might break if you recoiled, and there would be no you to put it back together, and you wouldn't want that. Giving the plant was cheating a bit, because again you could hardly turn it away today." Enid looked at her watch. "There's the sadness, but there's also the future," said Anita.

"Yes. I have so much still to do when I get home. And tomorrow night I shall be in Motherwell."

After the front door closed behind Enid, Anita picked up the cheque from the couch and straightened the couch cover for the next patient, whose car she could see already nosing into a parking space. She then put Enid's plant carefully on the shelf under the picture, where it flourishes to this day.

A couple of years later Enid was on a coastal path in Scotland on a summer evening. She stood stock still suddenly, which did not surprise her partner, for they were bird-watching. Enid stared out to sea, ignoring the proffered binoculars. There was the angle of the beach, there was the perspective of sea, there was the lighthouse. The lighthouse was not attempting to shine at the moment, for there was still daylight; but there it was. This was the place. There, immediately in front of her, was the broken fence. Unbelievingly, as if a fairy story had come true, she put out her hand to touch it. It felt rough but very solid, as it would, having endured in its brokenness. "Here I am," said Enid, and her partner, who had spotted what might be a cormorant, stood close and let her be.

This was where Anita had stood, familiar with this territory, with this beauty, at home here. Anita's dreams of childhood, of hope, of love, might still sometimes, for all Enid knew, take this place for their setting. And at last, at this moment, Enid could assent lovingly to Anita's separate life with its private intensities, intensities shared by people other than Enid, painful though it was not to be part of them. Anita's having been here, Enid was realising, did not have to bludgeon Enid's own experience now into one of wistfulness, exclusion, hankering, or guilty voyeurism. Neither Anita nor Enid owned this sea, and Anita had not tried to requisition it for herself. Enid too could have unique experiences, and Anita wanted her to. The experiences were different from Anita's, but they neither supplanted nor were belittled by them.

It was at this moment that for the first time the idea entered Enid's mind that this place might not be of importance to Anita. It was possible, she now realised, that Anita had never set foot here. Was the picture, to Anita, possibly just a picture? Had Anita not been, as Enid had believed she was, uneasy at Enid's having penetrated and exposed the secret of the picture, but, rather, perplexed by Enid's clamourous version of it? Enid staggered, and put her hand on her partner's arm. She saw now that the picture itself had been her way of taming and framing Anita's otherness. She stared now at the moving and uncontrollable sea, as different from the picture's rendering of it as Anita was from the scribbles and daubs, whether shining or murky, that Enid had produced.

"Look," Enid's partner was saying. "Watch. They are putting the light in the lighthouse on."

Life Drawing

Alice Bree

I've heard it said if you take a large group of people who have
never met before, and ask them to pair off randomly, they will
unconsciously choose partners with whom they have something
significant in common.

Several weeks after my mother's funeral my employer suggested
I should see the counsellor. Mother and I had lived together happily
for twenty years after father died, but after her death I fell into
depression. People were kind, but I retreated into myself. Life was
meaningless; I found it hard to get out of bed and get myself to
work. But it was with a sense of shame I agreed to see the resident
counsellor, because I never imagined I would ever need something
like that. I am not used to talking about feelings but the pain of this
loss took me back to the day my father died. I was an only child, and
it had taken several years to come to terms with that bereavement.
In the back of my mind I knew I would lose mother one day, but I
put the thought aside and concentrated on looking after her.

After I had attended the standard six sessions the counsellor said
she wanted to refer me for long-term work. I was alarmed. Did I
have a serious mental problem? The counsellor said depression
needs more time for exploration than she was able to give. I was
reluctant to start with someone else as I had just got used to her, but
I decided to take the plunge after she had given me the name and
phone number of a psychotherapist.

When I met Helen, I wasn't sure what to make of her. I trusted
her, but she didn't say much. I wondered how psychotherapy
differed from counselling, but she didn't answer questions and I
think I accepted I would find out by doing it. A significant difference
now was having to pay a fee, and it was quite a lot. It made me feel

sometimes she was just earning her living and didn't really care about me, but intuition told me she did care and also that I was embarking on something important. It was interesting that paying made it feel safe to be with her, as I realised without a fee I would have felt threatened by the intimacy of our unique relationship.

She suggested if I had dreams I might like to bring them to sessions, and she also encouraged me to lie on a couch. I was reluctant, but one day I decided to give it a try. It was odd talking to someone without looking at them, but I got used to it, and soon I agreed to go three times a week. Things began to change after that. I had not foreseen the dynamic effect this was to have on me. I had to tolerate some painful episodes, looking with her at past disappointments in which I cried like a child, or sometimes I became unreasonably angry and felt humiliated. But there were other times in which I felt listened to for the first time. Not that people don't listen, but maybe the right word is heard—heard in the sense of being really understood.

We had been working together for some months when suddenly one day my senses woke up. I experienced a startling moment of heightened awareness. I remember it was one morning as I was making toast. I became acutely conscious of its warm, comforting aroma, and revelled in the melting butter, which I allowed to run down my chin. I savoured to the full some thickly spread, chunky, bittersweet marmalade and found myself searching for other sensual experiences, feeling needy, but vaguely worried if now, living alone, I was turning into a hedonist. My life till then, as you may guess, had been heavily overlaid with moral rectitude.

I was a thirty-seven year old civil servant. Life with mother had had well worn routines with which I had been content until I became depressed: work Monday to Friday, shopping Saturday, and maybe a film. Sunday brought mass at eight thirty, a walk, cakes for tea, dinner at seven, and bed by ten. But recently I had lost my appetite, was omitting meals and certainly not baking cakes. The highlight of my week had been an embroidery group on Wednesday, and I did manage to keep it as a focus. We designed abstract collages, stitched reverse appliqué, couched gold thread, and quilted swirling patterns. We were an avant-garde of the sewing world, commissioned by churches to make tapestries and vestments. Sometimes we worked on a big tapestry, seated either side of a vertical frame, passing needles full of coloured thread to each other; occasionally we would agree to work at the weekend on a big commission. I had found this group activity fulfilling to the exclusion of everything else till depression hit me. We had been together for six years; loosely knit, harmonious, with commissions to keep us going into the foreseeable future; we put no pressure on each other for friendship outside this mutually creative activity. My role was practical only. Others designed, agonized over colours, and mapped out patterns. I was a meticulous co-worker, valued for my attention to detail, and unquestioning acceptance of decisions made by others. I began to feel a need for friendship but lacked confidence to do anything about it, and in fact insisted I was "fine" when some of them offered help. But it was the one activity that held me together at this time.

Sunday morning, after the 'awakening' experience, when the alarm assaulted my ear at seven o'clock, I extended my arm from the warmth of the duvet, switched it off, and drew it back again. I stretched, aware of the sensation of arching my back and extending my legs, and a thought dropped into my mind. I didn't want to go to Mass. It had never occurred to me to question why I went. It was part of a mindless Sunday routine, so I started to think about faith. After the funeral I had arranged for a Mass to be said for mother but was embarrassed when people wanted to know if I was all right. Again I had said I was fine and changed the subject. I knew my faith was integral to me but something was missing. Surely I could find a place that felt ... spiritual? I'd never allowed myself to explore like this before, so I stayed where I was to cogitate. The following week it was easier not to go again, and soon I had to admit I had stopped going. I decided to leave the answer phone on and not return calls in case someone would try to persuade me to come back. One day maybe, but after I had dissented. I was a thirty-seven year old rebel! When the priest inevitably called I'm ashamed to say I lurked behind the unopened door with a racing pulse. I explored guilty feelings with Helen, and she listened but said nothing, so I was not sure what she thought and I imagined she disapproved, but she told me I didn't know what she thought, which of course was maddening but true. But I was also thinking how shocked mother would have been.

The next phase of my metamorphosis was an impulse to dispose of things from the house. I wanted to transform mother's home into my home. Out went all the things in various shades of brown: some of the furniture, ornaments, carpets, curtains, and even paintings. I took them to charity shops and an auction house and spent a manic week on leave, painting the walls white and buying replacements, but only things my eyes liked. I gave away mother's clothes, keeping only one thing—a silk scarf my father had given her. I had begun to feel optimistic as I worked on this project.

I bought Scandinavian furniture, cheerful curtains, towels, sheets and duvet covers in jewel colours, and modern light fittings with spots; I focused on new ceramic sculptures and translucent coloured glass. I took my small embroideries to be framed and bought watercolours and prints. I had the floors sanded to a blond sheen, the spicy smell of shaved wood lingering deliciously that day. I laid modern rugs and kelims, one of which was too precious to walk on and had to go on a wall. As I placed each new thing in my transformed home, I gave a sigh of pleasure. Had I been blind before? A quotation from the Hebrew Scriptures came to mind, "They have eyes but they see not". I knew it referred to idols and for an instant feared I could make an idol of my home, but I was also aware I had discovered part of me that had been lifeless, like stone. Making my home reminded me of Vanessa Bell and Virginia Woolf, when they swept away the heavy Victorian décor of their upbringing in Kensington, to replace it with a light airiness in their house in Gordon Square where they were 'at home' to the intelligentsia of the Bloomsbury Group. They would be my role models, particularly the artist, Vanessa Bell. It was as if I too had swept away a heavy weight. Now if I saw something my eyes didn't like in my environment, the sight of it was painful, an emotion which surprised me by its violence. But I was aware also of some joy, of beginning to find words for positive emotions. I struggled with guilt when I realized I had destroyed my parents' home in a dismissive critical way, even though I was pleased with the result. That's enough for now, I thought nervously. I imagined Helen was pleased for me but she didn't say anything to encourage me. She did however comment on how excited I was and wondered if I had any thoughts about the décor in her home. I said I liked some things but not everything. I had to admit some of my ideas had come from there, though others were my own.

Inside a month I felt further stirrings. I hated my job. I was conscientious, my salary was adequate, there was a pension to look forward to, but it was dull, and the people seemed dull, and I felt dull. Could I leave? As a teenager I'd wanted to go to Art School. Father said a secretarial course was wiser, and I dutifully agreed. Could I become a mature student? I arranged an interview. The only portfolio I had was my embroidery. It was thought to be "innovative". It was clear, they said, that I had potential, and if I went to life drawing they would give me a place on their Foundation Course the following autumn.

Depression was fading and it was no longer possible to tolerate my stultifying career. Life was swiftly passing me by, so I handed in my notice. I had savings and mother had left me a considerable legacy. At my leaving party I asked for a framed print by Matisse, and hung it in the hall. (It's the first thing I see when I come home.) I went to life drawing and found it difficult. I couldn't achieve the lively, flowing line I wanted, but I persevered and the tutor taught me elementary things about drawing. The course tutors were impressed by my ability to "keep at it". That autumn I entered art school, leaving my embroidery group with regret, but promising to return with new skills.

I was the only mature student in a Foundation Year of eighty school-leavers. They looked at me in disbelief. They too were intent on escaping mother figures, but they accepted me after an initial wariness. I looked conventional wearing black trousers and a smock; artist's gear I thought. They had wild, spiked, brightly coloured hair, and squeezed their bottoms into hipster jeans. The girl's flat tummies were enticingly bare, my plump one hidden under the smock. The boys looked as if they had just got out of bed. But I liked how they looked, and their cheery sexual banter, which I listened to with secret delight, hiding myself behind a drawing board propped up on an easel. I had never had a boyfriend or even wanted one. I laughed at the contrast between this uninhibited, creative place, and the office I'd so recently left. I gradually discarded my office persona, had my hair cut into a chic new style and began to dress as it took my fancy, but not before I had had a humiliating experience. The department held a jumble sale to find extra money for materials and I bought a white tee shirt. It had beautiful leaves on the front in two sharp shades of green. After I'd worn it a couple of times a tutor told me quietly they were cannabis leaves. Later I was able to smile at my naivety, and even to save it as a funny story to tell the embroidery group.

I was pleased when the tutor said we would do still life. I pictured flowers and a bowl of fruit, maybe a wine bottle and glasses. I wondered how you would draw something transparent. He asked us to pile all the tables and chairs into a heap in the middle of the studio and draw them. Most of them were stained with paint. Every time I looked at my drawing, and back again at the tangled pile, I'd lost my place. Two hours later I was exhausted, astonished to find a static activity like that was such hard work. But I began to see the spaces between things and the value of the overlooked reality around me.

I took a sketchbook everywhere, and discovered that drawing heightened visual awareness. It was meditation, or prayer even. Was this the spirituality I looked for? Although I experienced only occasional bleak moments now, I was becoming insular and self-absorbed. My tutor saw the difficulty of being with teenagers, and suggested another life drawing class, mainly attended by mature students, with a teacher from Fine Art who taught Zen drawing. "Are you trying to get me to join a cult?" I said. He laughed and said he thought I'd find it helpful.

Before the class began some of the in-students clustered round a guru-like teacher. He was old, round-shouldered, had a long face and never smiled. He rarely commented on our work, or even looked at it. He had paintings in the Tate so I was impressed, but shouldn't he come to see how we were doing? At the end of one class I asked for an opinion. "They're frozen," he said. That was all! I felt a surge of anger. Bloody man, I thought. I wanted you to tell me what to do. But I didn't dare to say that and I thought some of the in-group looked at me disapprovingly. They were mainly women, most of whom were extra-mural. Of the few men, one, who like me was new and about my age, took up a place beside me. He introduced himself as Francis and said he was on the Fine Art degree course specializing in painting.

The group worked standing, two to a table, the model in the middle, and prepared piles of paper, because no pose lasted longer than five minutes. It was impossible! That was the point. You couldn't get it right, and one drawing was followed at speed by the next so there was no time to think. Sometimes he asked us to draw with both hands. I watched a young woman near me who looked as if she was dancing, as if her whole body was making the drawing and I longed to be that free. Sometimes we were asked to start with the paper on the floor and a brush dipped in dilute ink held between our toes, and sometimes to make the first marks holding the end of the brush in our mouths. And we might start lying on the floor, or standing on the table. It was bewildering. Sometimes we worked in twos on the same drawing, takings turns to add marks. Francis and I then shared responsibility for each drawing, but I thought he was better than me and wondered apprehensively what he felt about my contributions. He didn't comment or ever say much to me.

One week the teacher played us a tape of German Lieder. I didn't understand the words, but the song was beautiful and sad. All of us, including the model were to listen with closed eyes and describe the music in the air with our hands. After doing this for a bar or two a wave of emotion, the gush of a melting glacier, opened in me, starting at my belly and ascending through my chest. I knew I was going to weep and searched in panic for a handkerchief, couldn't find one and had to sniff. The music stopped, the model posed, I drew with my eyes full of tears. When we had finished that series the teacher came silently to see my work, and sifting through the pile he pulled out six, lay them on the table and still unsmiling remarked, "They're beautiful". And they were. I found it hard to believe I had done them. Francis gave me a handkerchief, pressing it into one hand and holding the other in a comforting grasp. He said, "I think it's about not allowing your mind to come between your hand and your eye".

"Yes" I said, making full eye contact with him for the first time, astonished to see tears there too.

That was how I met Francis. And after we spent time together we discovered our shared Roman Catholic origins and our sexual continence. We discuss how we feel about that, our faith and our spiritual longings. Like babes in the wood we have set out to explore all we could have experienced long ago. I still go to see Helen but we have cut down the number of sessions and set an end date because I have reached a place where I know I can do without her. Francis has decided to start therapy himself, because he sees how I have discovered myself by doing it, and knows he wants that too. The love I was given by my parents gave me a valuable start in life, but also made it difficult to dare to become an individual in my own right. My Foundation Year has come to an end and I have been accepted on a Fine Art Degree course. After that? I don't know and I don't much care, because my life is transformed and the future full of promise.

Shadow Man

Sandra Primack

I have been a therapist for many years and find my work endlessly fascinating. Sometimes someone has a story to tell that is unusual and David was one of those special people you never forget. For the sake of clarity and brevity I think it would be best to write his story as it unfolded in my counselling room.

David was referred to me by his GP because he had asked the doctor if he knew of a therapist. The only information I had was that he was a man in his early thirties, living alone, with a job as an IT consultant in a university. When he arrived for his first session—an assessment interview—I opened my door to a very ordinary looking man with short dark hair and brown eyes, wearing chinos, a blue shirt and loafers. After the initial introductions, I lead him into my consulting room. As I turned towards him I felt the room darken slightly, which was out of the ordinary and somewhat unsettling. Offering him a seat opposite me I waited for him to sit down. He looked around at my minimal furnishings and two Monet posters then sat on the edge of his seat, hands clasped in front of him. His face was covered in a shiny film of perspiration, which I took as a sign of nervousness. He looked at me expectantly. "I've never done anything like this before," he began.

"Perhaps you would like to tell me what has brought you here?" He looked around again seemingly trying to decide what to say. "It's hard to know how to start." he said.

"Take your time."

"How long do we have?"

"For this assessment session we have an hour and a half. If you decide you would like to come for therapy then it would be fifty minute sessions. Everything you tell me is in confidence. Perhaps you would like to tell me about yourself" I said, thinking he needed a little help to get started.

Obediently he gave me his history which in itself was fairly straightforward. He grew up in north London with his parents Elizabeth and Martin, who were still together, and a younger sister, Susan, who was married and had recently had a baby boy. He got on well with his parents, who he said were very loving but perhaps a little over protective. Otherwise he had had a very happy child-hood. After school he went to university and then found a job in IT. He now managed a department and his job, though not incredibly stimulating, suited him. He lived alone in a one bedroom flat and had recently met a woman with whom he had fallen in love. It was at this point that he stopped and looked at his hands. "This is where it gets difficult" he said. I waited. "The trouble is . . ." he faltered again. "I know this is going to sound completely mad but," he paused and then took a big intake of breath before he blurted out "I have a shadow." He looked at me expectantly, probably to see what my reaction would be. I nodded reassuringly, which seemed to encour-age him to go on while I wondered about the feeling I'd had when he arrived and the room had darkened.

"It's always been there ever since I can remember. When I was very little it was like my imaginary friend though it has no name, only Shadow. My family accepted Shadow and so I thought everyone had one. When I went to nursery school and met other children I realised that no one else had a 'companion' like me. I quickly learnt not to talk to it—or him—when anyone else was around. Because Shadow has always been there, most of the time I don't think about it. But lately, since I met Chloe, always having its presence with me has begun to bother me. I have used Shadow as a friend and con-fidant. I have been able to vent my frustrations, cry, or be happy, but now I have a real person to talk to and confide in I think I would like Shadow to go away."

"And that is why you have come to see me?"

"Yes. I want you to help me to . . ." he faltered trying to find the right word, "Let it go. I don't want to be dependent on it any more."

I noticed he didn't say "my shadow" but called it "Shadow" like it wasn't really part of him at all. I felt he didn't want to say get rid of it in case he hurt its feelings. I was curious as to how it came into existence in the first place. Time was running out but he certainly had me intrigued and a little puzzled. We arranged to meet again the following week and, though I held out no promises, hoped we could uncover the mystery together and help him manage without this other being.

During the week I thought about this young man. I read Christopher Bollas' book *Shadow of The Object* again, hoping it would give me some idea of what David's shadow might represent. Bollas talks about the early experience of 'the shadow of the object' as it falls on the ego, leaving some trace of its existence in the adult. The object can cast its shadow without a child being able to process this experience through mental representations or language. He goes on to say that the therapist will partly be preoccupied with the emergence of early memories of being and relating into thought. So was there a parent or someone very close to David, who used him to bear something of their own that was unmanageable? Only time would tell.

The following week I felt the same slight darkening of the room as he came in and sat down. "I felt relieved when I left here last week," he began, "that I was able to say something about Shadow as I wasn't sure I would. This week has been very difficult because I feel so guilty that I don't want it any more."

"Can you say more about the guilt?"

David went on to say that it felt as if he would be discarding someone who had been very important to him his whole life and now that he wasn't wanted what would happen to him? I asked him if he would tell me more about it. "He's more than a friend but not a parent." He said.

"Like a brother."

"Yes exactly, like a brother."

"Did you ever have a brother?"

"Not that I know of."

"You said your family accepted Shadow. Do you think it is possible there was ever a brother?"

"I don't know." He paused, thinking for a while. "Maybe I need to ask my mother but I would have thought my parents would have mentioned it if there had been a brother." It seemed that David wanted to go away and find out about this, so the rest of the session he talked about Chloe: how wonderful she was and how happy she made him. He didn't mention Shadow again until the following week.

It was obvious from the moment he came in that he had something urgent to tell me. "I nearly phoned you but thought it best to wait until I saw you in person. My mother was shocked when I brought up the subject of a brother. She didn't know what to say but I could tell from the way she behaved I had hit upon something. She told me I had a twin." David could hardly contain himself. "Can you believe it—a twin, another boy—who was stillborn but who they named Sheldon. I have grown up all these years without knowing I had a twin. Do you think that could explain who Shadow is?"

"Perhaps."

"I think that must be it. Somehow deep down I knew and sort of kept him alive in a way by having Shadow—a shadow of my baby twin brother. How bizarre!"

"You said that your family accepted Shadow. Maybe you were keeping him alive for your family too."

"I hadn't thought of it like that."

"I imagine there was a lot of sadness at the loss of a twin you didn't even know existed but he was always there in an unspoken way."

David sat for a while thinking. "I feel very sad," he said after a while.

"That is understandable. It seems the family hasn't really mourned the loss. No one has ever really let Sheldon go."

"And I have been carrying him around with me, talking to him as if he was real. I think I feel even more guilty now. It means I have to let my brother die when all my life I have been keeping him alive. I don't know if I can do it now. I'm afraid that if I let Shadow die then something inside me will die too.

"I didn't know what to say.

"The trouble is I've only just discovered I had a brother. Is Shadow Sheldon? Do I start saying Sheldon instead of Shadow? It feels really odd."

"I'm sure it must feel odd to give Shadow a real name."

"If I do that then am I making it—him—more real? I feel very muddled. I wanted to get rid of Shadow then discover I have

Sheldon and think maybe they are one and the same but that isn't how it feels."

"Maybe you need time to get used to the idea."

"I haven't told Chloe you know. I tell her most things but don't know how to talk to her about all this."

"Perhaps you are frightened of something if you do tell her?"

"When we met Shadow was a part of me. If I don't have Shadow any more will I be less of the person who she has come to know and love? Do you think I am going mad?"

"Maybe you think you are going mad."

"I thought I must be mad going around with something I call Shadow. It has been a real presence for me."

I knew what he meant. The darkness I felt wasn't exactly sinister but it was disturbing. How must it be to have the presence of a dead twin brother with you all your life?

"Were you identical twins?" I thought it would be even harder if they were identical twins to let go of this other being.

"I didn't ask. Though my mother did tell me there was a twin she didn't go into any detail."

"Perhaps you'd like to know more?" I wasn't sure if he wanted to know more—maybe it was me who was curious. "Yes. Yes I would but I suppose I am frightened of upsetting my mother."

"What about your father?"

"I never thought of talking to him. Maybe it would be easier than going to her."

We talked some more about whether he would talk to his father and also whether he would tell Chloe and his sister. David did talk to his father, who explained more about Sheldon. Apparently, the doctors didn't know there was a second baby because it was smaller than David and lying underneath him. It was another boy but not an identical twin. Because Sheldon wasn't expected it made it easier for his father to accept the fact he was stillborn, but apparently his mother was very upset and became depressed. His father thought it would be best if they didn't talk about Sheldon and so he was never mentioned. It wasn't until his mother seemed to come out of her depression and his father was so relieved that he didn't think it would do any harm for David to keep this imaginary companion. When their daughter came along Shadow was firmly established as part of the family.

"I have kept Sheldon alive all these years for my mother," he told me. "If I let him go now I am afraid my mother will get depressed again."

"Do you still talk about Shadow to your mother?"

"No, not for years."

"So if you did let him go . . ." I didn't get to finish my sentence.

"She wouldn't know I had let him go. Mmm." He sat for a while pondering. "The strange thing is that Shadow helped me so often while I was growing up it is hard to finally not want him in my life any more."

"Maybe now you don't need him and his work is done." I suddenly felt a shiver as if I had been blasphemous and realised that this was how David must be feeling. "It's hard to let go of someone that has been so precious to me." He looked at me and I could sense his relief. "You understand, don't you?" The session finished without any decision. I knew it would take a long time for David to let Sheldon, or Shadow go. It was like killing off a part of himself and it seemed that he had to do a lot of mourning first.

David phoned very near the time of our fourth session to say he couldn't come because he forgot he had a dentist appointment. I wondered if he was feeling ambivalent about my role. Did he see me as an accomplice in the assassination of his lifelong companion?

Subsequent sessions were taken up thinking about the relationship between Shadow and Sheldon. They hadn't merged into the same person; it was as if Shadow belonged to him and Sheldon belonged to his mother. He wondered if he could let go of Shadow and talk to his mother about his lost twin. He wasn't certain if he let one go that the other might not go too. Because all this was so entwined with his mother and her depression he felt he had to talk to her some more about Sheldon.

During our times together David was in turmoil, thrashing around trying to understand how he felt and to find some answers. I wondered who I represented for him. I didn't think it was the depressed mother, but had I accepted Shadow too readily, like his family, when we first met? Was he feeding my curiosity and did I want to keep him alive for me too? David's fantasy seemed to be that for him to survive someone had to die. After much soul searching he decided it would be best for him to talk to his mother even though he was very apprehensive and afraid of upsetting her.

Several weeks passed, and by our twentieth meeting David had been able to talk to his mother and a great weight was lifted from his shoulders. She said that when his sister had been born—and she didn't become depressed—she realised that, although she would never forget Sheldon, she had come to terms with his death. It was a great relief for David to realise that he didn't need to keep his brother alive for her any more. He asked her if she thought Shadow was Sheldon and she said yes, but she hadn't seen any harm and thought he would grow out of it. She didn't know that Shadow was still with him. David felt angry with his mother but realised it wasn't her fault and Shadow had helped him so much he shouldn't be angry with her. What he thought he could do right now was acknowledge that Sheldon, who he had never known, had died and he was able to let him go.

David was also beginning to understand that Shadow was a part of himself and maybe it wasn't so much about killing him off but somehow recognising that it was a part of him he had kept separate or outside of himself. This developing concept seemed to calm him and made it easier for him to accept that perhaps we all have some sort of shadow but not quite in the same way as him. When David left this session I felt he had come to a place where he was more at peace within himself.

Next week the David who came to my door looked much happier. When he walked into my room—for the first time since he had come to see me—the room didn't seem to darken. I didn't need to be told that Shadow had been integrated; David had never needed to eliminate him; he only needed to accept that he was a part of him. He smiled at me and I smiled back. "You know don't you?"

"Yes."

"It feels strange and yet a relief. I will have to get used to not having him with me but it is like I am living independently for the first time in my life. I don't need him anymore. I'd like to come once more just to make sure nothing changes but I think I have got what I came for."

We talked about real shadows and how the negative feelings we have can be called shadows, but this was just an intellectual exercise and it was evident that David was now able to move on with his life. "I am getting married." Were the first words David said to me the next week.

"Congratulations."

"I am so grateful for all your help."

"My pleasure." As I wondered if he had told Chloe about Shadow, he announced, "I told Chloe. I didn't want to have any secrets from her. She was cool and now I don't need Shadow it isn't a threat to either of us."

"I hope you will be very happy."

"Yes I think I will now I am able to live a full life. Before I came to see you I was being only half a self, living in the shadow of a dead twin."

I am sure that was true and he had said it all.

THE PSYCHOTHERAPY RELATIONSHIP

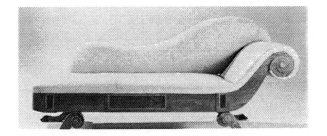

Getting There

John Welch

I have rung the bell and I am waiting to see if this small act will have worked its dependable magic and summoned the presence within, signalled by a confused stirring on the other side of the frosted glass. Actually there are two doors, an outer and inner one, and he has told me I am welcome to open the outer door and wait inside the porch until he comes. But today I prefer to stay out in the street. I find myself half-hoping that I will be released into an absence, which is where I have so often contrived to be. I picture myself upstairs in his room, and I imagine that perhaps, when I do get up there, there will be no one but me, the desk, the books, and below, the garden—that I will have managed to cut myself free and to float.

As I wait I start to invent a character, someone who has been in analysis for a long time. The analyst is horrible, the whole process seems negative, but still he keeps going. Finally, he begins to wonder why. He thinks perhaps he should try and get in touch with some of this analyst's other patients. So he starts to keep watch outside the house or—in another version—he hires a private detective to do so. The watching goes on for a week, the hope of catching sight of him outside that sacred frame, but in all that time no one goes in or comes out of the house other than the analyst himself.

My therapist comes to the door. As I go up the stairs behind him I am smiling a pleased sort of smile and at the beginning of the session, I tell him the story I have made up. "This useless analyst," he says, "might be a reference to me, and to the time you saw me at Kings Cross." He is referring to an occasion when I had cancelled a session, and by chance had seen him near the tube at the time of my session. "When I was playing truant?" I suggest. "When you thought, perhaps, I was looking for you, to punish you for not being here?"

"Or, perhaps, you were looking for me, to see if I was all right."

"Perhaps you are hoping for forgiveness for missing the last session?" he changes tack.

As so often I am silent. But afterwards I thought of the story of the prodigal son. My father was a clergyman and those parables made a powerful impression on me as a small child. Prodigal with absence. That was how I decided to punish my parents, a long time ago.

Sometimes there's that moment at the beginning of a session when I don't know what to say. There's a peculiar noise in my throat and a bereft expression on my face before I get control again. Afterwards I am usually angry, and I wonder if the transference is a kind of spell. The rules of the session—the absolutely fixed time for starting and finishing, the limitations on the analyst's own intervention—are what make the spell. I compared these rules once to a game and he thought I was trivializing things. "It's not a game for me", he said. Above all there is the sense of a container arising from this small set of arbitrary rules. There has to be time, all the time in the world, which seems paradoxical given the strict limitations regarding the beginning and end of the session. Once you create this container something happens. What if I were to break the rules, go back, after the session has ended? What will I find then? There was the occasion when I realised as I was walking down the street away from his house that I no longer had my travel card. It had been in the back pocket of my trousers and must have slipped out in his consulting room. I hurried back and rang the bell. Who exactly was this man who came to the door, in slippers and cardigan, holding an LP, entertaining himself after I had gone?

Soon after I started my therapy I had a dream about arriving for a session. I was going to a house on the edge of a city, a part that was unfamiliar to me. I found the house but it was my house, though at the same time I felt myself to be a stranger there. Diffidently I went in, not sure whether I was supposed to be there at all. Although this house seemed to be empty it was full of a powerful sense of presence. I went through to a sitting room at the back. There was a sense of evening sunlight, the half-drawn curtains swaying in a slight breeze, and the pulsing life of the city somewhere beyond. It had been a complicated journey and I identified the city I had crossed as Lahore in Pakistan, where I had spent a year teaching. Indeed now, going into the therapist's house, I occasionally encounter an Indian woman—I assume she is his wife—whom I only ever see two or three times, and who I imagine keeps herself discreetly out of sight, as if she were in purdah.

When I get home I cut some slices of cod's roe for my lunch. I have time to admire its appearance, the soft pinks, reds and purples, subtle and the near transparency of a slice when you cut it, the way the slice is on the verge of breaking up into thousands of eggs. When you go to the 'Bagel Bakery' where I buy it, it doesn't look as if there is a shop there at all. You push the door open and inside there is a food counter. His house is a bit like this, a secret place you visit, slipping in and out, with nothing on the outside to indicate what it is, this place where you will be fed. Three years into the analysis I once opened his outer door myself and waited inside the porch. On opening the inside door to let me in, he leaned back looking startled. He referred later to my need to make myself visible, and then invisible. Arriving early, arriving late; everything can be interpreted.

The stormiest confrontation I had with him was on an occasion when I got there a good ten or fifteen minutes before the start of the session, rang the bell and waited. I wondered if he was out. I looked back out of the door and down the street to see if he was coming, then rang the bell again. I heard a noise inside, and the door opened. But it wasn't him, it was a woman who stood awkwardly in the doorway, then smiled and pulling the door half shut behind her slipped past me. This had never happened before. I stood there peering in, not sure whether to go in or stay outside. I thought that if I stayed outside he was sure to make something of that. I'd better go in. I manoeuvered myself awkwardly right into the house just as he was getting to the bottom of the stairs. He gestured me into the room where I usually waited. When the session began he was upset. I had, quite involuntarily as it happened, succeeded finally in making him angry. "It's as if you think I don't know my place", I said. "Exactly", he replied.

Looking back I do wonder what happened during the second half of my analysis. We had stalled and there were times when I felt, stretched out on the couch, as if I were lying in a shallow grave. Once, I was early for a session and there was a perfectly ordinary explanation: I had left work promptly to do an errand in the West End, which in fact it took much less time than I thought. I lay there, not telling him this, with a tightness at the top of my spine. More and more he was commenting on my reluctance to express any aggression towards him. The point is that, so long as I withhold, it means I have in my possession knowledge he does not have, and this means I can feel superior.

Much of the time I was acting-out in the sessions in the same way I had behaved all through my later childhood and adolescence. My parents had expectations of me and perhaps my aim was finally to defeat those expectations. Not in any obvious way, such as by being an obvious failure. That would have been, paradoxically, to give them too much. It was by being an apparent success, while feeling inside that I'd not been much of a success at all. So I go as near to being a failure as I dare: passive, watchful, aggressive, camouflaged. You may come and look for me, but you won't ever find me. I'll be lying so still you won't even see me. And, if you do, I'll sit up and give you a nice reasonable smile.

I had been buying books, more books than I can read, and I had started to collect antique coins. I had been dampening my need, blunting its sharpness. Greedily, seeing always through the glass, the reaching out and then the cold touch. Always peering, taking covertly; food there to be thrust in quickly before the need sharpens, and then to feel bloated, the discomfort a punishment. The other, shadow-self is gnawing on hunger, waking and hoping, but snappishly. Envy? Did I believe that a feeling *shown* was a feeling wasted? Feelings that have to be saved up like money and not spent all at once, if at all? Because I wasn't sure whether my parents wanted my feelings?

I never stopped wondering about his domestic arrangements. I wondered about his son. In the room where I wait downstairs there's a photograph of him bending down and showing something to a boy. There's a model warplane made from a kit on the book case, and once there was a war-game laid out on the floor. The door at the top of the stairs is covered with stickers. This must be the boy's bedroom. I have only once seen this boy, a brief glimpse, though I did hear him once as I came in, calling out to his father in a repetitive jokey sort of way. Overall, the layout of the house is still hard to work out. There is my own brief passage through it, which is always the same and absolutely predetermined, leaving no trace. As I come into the house and just before I turn up the stairs I face an inside window with bars across it and, on the other side, a heavy curtain. Various domestic noises come from the other side of this window, a radio maybe, and sometimes there's a smell of toast. There is something about time in this process and the way it passes. Or doesn't. Years later, when he had moved house, I was commenting on his son's apparent absence from the scene and he asked me to work out what age he might be. I had to admit that by this time he would presumably be in his early twenties.

Another session. I lie there, silent. I have been silent for some time. Eventually I say, "You give yourself the license to interpret my silence in a negative way. How come?"

"You're trying to provoke me into doing it again so you can come out and punch me on the nose."

"If this was Wimbledon, I'd say that was a good return of serve."

He grunts, then laughs.

"You sound pleased," I suggest.

"Perhaps we're both pleased"

He talked a lot that session and I said "Thank you" and came home feeling light-hearted.

In another session that felt different, I started to talk in a heartfelt way about how I felt before I started analysis. It started with remembering how I would drink at lunchtime, and then feel wretched. I talked, with absolute sincerity, about how simply unhappy I sometimes was. It was as if I had spoken about it and in doing so recognised it for the first time. When I finished I sensed before me a dense blackness, as if a mirror there had been smashed. I commented on this and he said "You feel that when I am silent, I am not reflecting you back." He hasn't turned the light on, and now the room is bathed in twilight. "The last two sessions you have been much more *here*" he says.

So I had given him a licence to interpret my behaviour, behaviour on his part that in any other circumstance might be seen as unacceptable. There is always the reductive element, as in "You're only saying that because . . ." But I am paying him and that does give me a kind of control. One might think of it as consulting an oracle, the point of which is the question that ritual of consultation obliges you to ask. An oracle is simply there, available. "Take that track up there, then first left and it's just round the corner, you can't miss it." That was what I felt when I decided to make that original phone call. I think, simply, that all I had to do was reach out and pick up the phone.

So here I am now in this room in North London, it is early evening, and just getting dark, and he hasn't put the light on yet. Perhaps he doesn't want to break the atmosphere. There may be noises drifting in from outside; often it is a little boy playing in one of the neighbouring gardens and a sound of birdsong. This is the site of our peculiar encounter, and somewhere just behind me is this shadowy oracle, part absence and part presence, speaking as it were from the place of the dead.

Being expected to take a dream there is what causes you to remember the dream you had, and not simply overlook it in the moment of waking. Lying half-awake in the outer reaches of the dream, surfacing slowly and feeling quite relaxed, such a dream recalls other dreams, briefly remembered like hints of another life, a life of richness and liveliness. As I lie there running the dream through my head, and gradually become more awake, it will assume its quality of otherness. And when I get up, notwithstanding the fact that I have now lost the dream, I feel more relaxed, more in touch with all the time in the world, turning over the pieces in my mind, a process of digestion. The time I have, to move into and to occupy, my own time which is, in the end, coffin-shaped. I have all the time in the world, but one day the world will have no time left for me.

So here I am lying on the couch and feeling I am nowhere; in an odd, dark, semi-fluid vacancy. Somewhere, impossible to locate, is a hard kernel, and all this floating about is as if in dark ectoplasm, not unpleasing exactly, but a blankness. Shallow and brimming over at the same time; safe but vacant.

"I feel transparent", I say. Transparency is absence, is having no borders, no boundaries. Lying here, I believe he knows me inside-out. There is nothing he does not know, there is no space at all between us. "You are very intuitive", he says. "Much too intuitive for your own good. You get inside other people and can't find your way out."

I am talking about the piece of prose I'm trying to write, how I needed to get outside it, in order to be able to work on it. "You need to get outside me", he says, as if I am fused with him. The paradox is that, unable to be separate, I can never get close enough. I say to him "Why should I get angry with them, give them my feelings, when they were unable to give me theirs?" And this became, "why should I get angry with him?" To this he replies, with passion, "Because it would be good for you." Then I describe a fantasy about eyes. There is a thing like a feeler coming out of an eye and waving about, and then a whole bunch of them like intestines breaking out of an eye. I talk about how I had felt about eyes when I had my breakdown all those years ago, a sense of there being nothing there, a sense that there, if nowhere else, there must be the person, but there was only this lump of cold jelly.

Halfway through another session and I am saying nothing. I have drifted off into a doze and this time I actually dream briefly of a female head with strange needle-like teeth. Actually there are two of these; there is a pale one with a flattish face rising up as if from a pillow where it had been lying and floating there, blank-faced and sad, and then another which is part baby and part woman, crying— but still with those same odd teeth. It rises, it sways on its long neck. I tell him about it. Lying there I say, "They seem to be growing out of me."

"Like a tapeworm?" he suggests, and at once I understand that he's getting at this 'mother', who feeds on me in secret, whom I must feed, as if I feel she is not properly separate and leading her own life. All the time I am on the run, and all those bits of me that so nearly existed, so nearly came into full being, call back to me tantalisingly in fragments of memory, sense impressions, odd bodily sensations—as if inch by inch edging towards separateness?

A Headache

A. H. Brafman

It was many years ago that Julius came to see me for psycho-analysis. He was twenty-one years old and coming to the end of his medical training. A brilliant student, he had always achieved considerable academic success and had a large circle of friends. Intelligent and articulate, he could handle most adequately his social life. But the preceding two years of his life had brought much unhappiness: he had fallen in love with a girl whose origin led his parents to oppose their relationship. This produced intense conflicts and Julius came to analysis in the hope this might help him work out some solution to his almost permanent state of anxiety and depression.

Julius was the firstborn son and he had grown up aware of the extent to which parents and grandparents saw him as their dearest child, the one who would represent the family's successful entry to the world of professionals. His father ran a profitable business and the family lived in comfort. They were no strict practitioners of their religion, but this still represented an important element in their sense of identity. Julius was well aware of their feelings and he only brought his girlfriend to the house after months of going out with her. Sadly, his worst forebodings were confirmed; the parents praised the girl's qualities, but could not conceive of her joining the family. Great agonies followed. His girlfriend decided she would adopt the family's religion, even if this entailed complex and protracted steps. But Julius' family still were not satisfied.

We embarked on our therapy and each session was filled with painful accounts of endless episodes where Julius had clashed with one or the other of his parents. He would speak about his medical placements and some encounters with friends and colleagues. He told me of his relationship with his siblings and other family members, but the main *leitmotiv* was the girlfriend and his agonizing conflict of loyalties: he didn't want to hurt his parents, but he loved his girlfriend and didn't want to hurt her either.

After some weeks of therapy, Julius recounted what was his first dream since starting analysis. He dreamt that he was celebrating his marriage to his girlfriend. Friends, colleagues, family, lots of people had come to the ceremony and there was universal joy. After the religious rituals had been performed, the young couple went down the aisle and as they got near the door, Julius felt some uncomfortable itch in his ear and could not resist putting his finger there. To his surprise, he had brought out a little ball of wax, which made him feel quite embarrassed. The dream finished soon after that.

Much in line with the "correct technique" of inviting the patient to free associate to the dream, I asked him what the various events of the dream had meant to him. He voiced his disbelief and pain at the thought that only in a dream could he imagine his longings coming true. He made one or two comments about some people in the dream and then focused on the "ball of wax". He smiled and told me that only the preceding morning he had attended a lesson at the Pathology Department and he remembered looking at a bottle containing a specimen of a brain tumour: its shape and colour reminded him of the "ball of wax" in the dream.

The only comment that I felt justified in making about this dream was much the same as Julius himself had made: that the dream depicted the fulfilment of a desperate wish—which confirmed one of the main assertions Freud had made about dreams. But I was aware that this did not add much to what Julius already knew himself. Our work continued and session after session I found myself wondering in what way was I really helping Julius. From the point of view of the senior analyst who supervised my work, I was doing all I could do to help Julius understand the nuances and implications of his feelings vis-à-vis his parents.

After some six months of therapy, Julius complained of a recurrent headache. I used to see him early in the mornings and he himself attributed the headache to nights where he had slept little and badly. I found some more complex possibilities to link the headache to his emotional pain, but his complaints continued. After some weeks, he decided to consult the medical services attached to his university.

He told me that the physician had considered the headache "psycho-somatic" and encouraged him to continue with his analysis, while resorting to various analgesics. We carried on.

But the headaches did not disappear. They were not continuous, but appeared quite often. After some more weeks, I encouraged Julius to look for a second opinion. In those days, the split between private and NHS facilities was not as dramatic as it has become nowadays, but Julius would never consider using his father's money to gain access to private doctors. He sought the same student services, but this time the consultant who saw him took a different view of the situation: he referred Julius for further tests and for a neurological consultation. Julius informed me of this by telephone; he had to cancel his next session because the neurologist was due to see him the next day. And what followed took place very quickly indeed. X-rays and other tests confirmed the doctors' clinical impression of a brain tumour. An exploratory intervention left Julius virtually comatose and he died a few days later.

When I visited my supervisor, I was very shaken. This was not just "another patient". He was someone I liked as a person and his being a medical student brought in that dreaded dimension of "there, but for the grace of God, go I". For this and many other reasons, I could easily see myself in Julius' position and I was shocked by the way in which his emotional struggles had been brought to an end. I was comforted by my supervisor and he reminded me that it was part of a doctor's life to have a patient dying, whatever the treatment he had been receiving. As we came to discuss the months of therapy, I brought up the contents of Julius' first dream. Could this be seen as evidence of some unconscious awareness of a diseased body? As true believers in the psyche-soma unit, surely we had to consider this possibility?

My supervisor was Michael Balint, an eminent psychoanalyst who pioneered analytic work with groups of General Practitioners. Psychosomatics was very much a speciality of his. But he laughed, a typical open, warm laughter, and said, kindly but firmly, that I should feel free to take the dream as evidence of that "awareness", but sadly, he added, how would it help me if and when I found another case with similar features? Would I really refer my analytic patient for neurological screening?

I was disappointed, but my puzzlement has remained alive to this day. The ironic final touch came with the pathologist's report on Julius' tumour: he had been presented with a history stating that headaches had been present for some weeks, with no other symptoms. But in his report the pathologist said he had found areas of the tumour showing changes that indicated the tumour had been present for many months.

The Doubled Therapist

Valerie Sinason and Melanie Skye

The Story by Valerie Sinason

Ten years ago, Dr Rob Hale and I were conducting research into ritual abuse whilst at the Portman Clinic, an NHS outpatient psychotherapy unit, when a woman named Melanie sought an appointment. She had witnessed a criminal act of violence against a child and wished to report it to the police and the project.

Melanie attended the appointment with two friends. She was a pale woman who seemed to have gone through great pain. She told us that she had troubles with her memory. She had experiences of losing time, she said, and finding herself in places she did not know. Sometimes she found herself waking up in a strange place in clothes that were not her own. However, she could put up with all of that. That was not the reason why she had come to see her. She had come because she wanted to do right for a helpless unknown child.

Once she was sure her account had been heard and accepted and was able to give it to the police her eyes gave a sparkle and some colour came to her face. After ten meetings the research part of the project was over. With further discussion it also became clear that psychotherapy would be an important step for her and we agreed that she would come on her own the following week for her first session.

Although she had been very punctual coming with her friends to speak about this child, her first session alone came and went without a call. I was concerned and, rather unusually, decided to telephone her. "This is Jayme," said a bright voice.

"Sorry," I replied, "I must have the wrong number."

"Who did you want?" asked Jayme. I was silent thinking of confidentiality. "Don't tell me it was Melanie?" asked Jayme.

"You know her?" I asked. "Know her? She has people ringing me all the time for her. Nobody seems to ring me to talk to me." I apologised again and put the phone down, concerned the secretary had taken the wrong number. The next day Melanie rang. "I am sorry I couldn't come. I found myself in a part of London I did not know and I couldn't find where the car was." I wondered aloud whether she had felt nervous at having time for herself. She was silent. I said how hard it must have been to not find her car and said I had the wrong number for her. We checked the number and she said it was the right number. We were both confused. I said someone called Jayme had answered the phone who said she kept getting calls for Melanie. Melanie said she knew no-one called Jayme. I said I looked forward to seeing her the next week and we decided it would be helpful if I rang her just before the session to check she was finding her way alright. This was not a usual thing for me to do but there was something about Melanie's pain at not arriving the week before that had powerfully lodged with me.

The next week I rang before the session but Melanie did not answer and I left a message on the answer-phone. A moment later my phone rang. It was Jayme. "Why have you rung me again?" I checked the number with her and there was no doubt it was the same number. "Are you still hooked on this Melanie," she asked, " or was it me you were wanting to talk to?" A thought started appearing in my mind. Could it be that Melanie and Jayme were connected? I started thinking again about Melanie's experiences of lost time, of finding herself in places she did not recognise, of missing her last appointment. Could it be that I was dealing with DID—Dissociative Identity Disorder, the new term for what was called Multiple Personality Disorder or, as The Diagnostic and Statistical Manual of Mental Disorders says:

The presence of two or more distinct identities or personality states (each with its own relatively enduring pattern of perceiving, relating to, and thinking about the environment and self). At least two of these identities or personality states recurrently take control of the person's behaviour. Inability to recall important personal information that is too extensive to be explained by ordinary forgetfulness and not due to the direct effects of a substance (e.g. blackouts or chaotic behaviour during alcohol intoxication) or a general medical condition (e.g. complex partial seizures).

Although the international psychiatric criteria here describes very clearly what constitutes this condition, British clinicians have on the whole ignored or condemned both the condition and the clinicians who recognize it and offer treatment. Indeed, the British Journal of Psychiatry has published only five papers on DID since 1989, all of which are unanimously critical. Psychiatric and psychotherapy trainings offer little understanding both in the past and now. This leaves British professionals uniquely vulnerable to emotional stress and British child patients particularly vulnerable to misdiagnosis and disbelief.

American and European research links DID to extreme abuse and deprivation in early childhood where fragmentation was the only means of emotional survival. It provides a double trauma for the child for it comes from trauma that the child is too frightened to speak of and leads to symptoms that most professionals cannot recognize. As Melanie and I worked further it became clear that she did have DID and Jayme was the first of several other alters, personalities, self-states or people that I was to meet.

At the start of the new therapeutic relationship I so wanted to protect the new relationship and how it was contained that I did not see how much less flexible and accommodating I was in my manner. I learned later that my voice and even my phrasing changed— becoming full of sentences like "I wonder if it could be that . . .?" Gradually as our work progressed I became aware of the different approach that was needed for Melanie and Co—as I started to think of her and her alter personalities.

I had only recently got myself linked to the internet and had just discovered the pleasures of sending and receiving emails. I had always found addressing envelopes a chore and emails felt so quick and easy as a means of communication! I knew that Melanie had also got her computer linked to the internet and we wondered if this could be an extra-therapeutic means of communication in this very complex set of circumstances. Perhaps it would be a means of helping other personalities to keep in touch and it proved a great success. Some, who never even appeared in a session, were able to stay in touch through email or phone.

In my weekly consultations with psychoanalyst Pearl King, we conceptualised that separation had a different meaning in DID when people could lose their psychic identity at any moment and never know when or if it would return. After several years in therapy, Melanie told me a close friend, who had offered support throughout the Portman Project, had mentioned meeting a new alter personality also called Valerie Sinason (my name!) inside her. This Valerie Sinason was a psychotherapist too. What's more, Melanie's friend recognized this "twin" Valerie when she "came out", as she spoke the same way as I do, and had the same facial expressions and body movements. This was something completely different to consider.

From the moment I heard of the existence of this other Valerie, I was nervously aware that I felt reluctant to meet her. At the same time I was aware of the irony of the situation. Here I was interpreting Melanie's fear at the thought of linking with her other personalities, and here was I not wanting to make contact with someone who had my name and some of my mannerisms.

I was informed that she had a separate email address. It was my name. Sorry, *our* name. As the internet cannot allow identical names she had attached the numbers 123 to "our" name to herald the difference. I entered this address into my "buddy system" so I would be able to see if and when she was on-line and stored the information reluctantly.

One morning, unusually, I was not at my usual supervision time with Pearl King, and going on the internet, I found to my shock that not only was there a Vsinason123 on-line but there was also a PearlKing123 on-line as well. Of course! Melanie knew that her case was supervised by Pearl, and she knew when I went for supervision—so others "inside" had worked this out too. As Melanie commented with great amusement when we next met, just as I went for my supervision at a fixed time each week so did the internal Valerie with her supervisor. Only their supervision (as they were both personalities within the same body) was on-line rather than face to face.

Vsinason123, as I prefer to call her, became a source of amusement between Melanie and myself—until a frightening moment. Another person "inside" was threatening suicide. This was not a genuine personal wish. It was something that happened to this poor internal person to destroy the progress of Melanie and everyone else whenever there was a major step forward. In trying to work with this alter, who we will call Kay, it emerged that Vsinason123 was her therapist.

Melanie said I needed to contact Vsinason123 now as she had no possibility of doing this and the danger was very real. That evening, as I turned on my computer, Vsinason123 was on-line. I sent an email. "Hello Valerie," I mistakenly wrote. A formal reply was returned: "How did you know my first name was Valerie when my email address is Vsinason123. I don't know you." I felt fury. How did I know her name was Valerie? That was obvious wasn't it? It was my name!

I digested my anger and apologised for my familiarity. When else would I have sent an informal email to a stranger, using their first name before checking how they liked to be addressed? In my working with learning-disabled clients it has been a huge issue to check how people like to be addressed—let alone in all my other work.

I sent an apology saying I found it unusual seeing someone else with the same surname as me as not many people had that surname, and as her first name began with V, I wondered if the coincidence went further. I added I had heard from a joint colleague that she was a therapist and that had added to my interest.

It was clear that finding someone else with the same name was not of interest to this Valerie at all. But that seemed to be the main point of difference. As our conversations progressed I was witnessing a difficult look at my earlier therapeutic identity. "It seems that . . .", "I wonder if . . .?", "Could it be . . .?" were phrases that her language was peppered with. I found, to my further discomfort, that I disliked myself as heard through this new twin. I disliked her language, her lack of self-disclosure, her formality. Even deeper, I disliked what I experienced as a rigidity and stubbornness behind her use of language.

Melanie found this very amusing. She chortlingly informed me that my language used to be like that all the time. She reminded me of my lack of self-disclosure in which she was supposed to say everything and I nothing. More significantly, she spoke of ways in which my training mirrored her's, that I looked and sounded like a robot therapist. When I broached the issue of suicide in our shared client, Vsinason123 courteously informed me that it was a matter of confidentiality and she could not reveal the name or confirm that she was seeing such a client; she was concerned by my breach of ethics in possibly seeing a client who was already in therapy with her. I informed her that the client, Jay, had given me permission to contact her and that Jay had been in therapy with me first. We therefore needed to think together about the very complex needs of a client who was seeing two therapists; moreover two with the same name. Vsinason123 could not take in this new information and did not try. She kept to the ethical code she had been trained in and mirrored back to me the very things that I had most wanted to move beyond in my own work.

Despite all the ongoing traumas in her life, Melanie was overcome with amusement at watching my difficulty at dealing with the double Valerie Sinason. But I also tried to broach the matter in a more collegial way in discussing therapeutic attitudes to technique when working with a suicidal patient. Vsinason123 was very clear: the job was to provide a contained space in which the client could express her fears and wishes and be enabled to make a decision. She could not breathe for a client once they left the therapy room. It was their own responsibility. If a client of hers was determined to commit suicide then they would. It was not her job to dissuade them. Her supervisor (the alternative) PearlKing123 was in agreement with this. Kay was going to die on a particular day and Vsinason123, through her formal analytic manner, was going to follow a path of neutrality.

But I, Valerie Sinason, the one writing this, was faced with a terrible sight. The unknown abusers inside and outside Melanie had perfected their own ingenious attack on their victim, who was slowly leaving them. Their new weapon was a robot therapist.

Pushed to a point of desperate authenticity, I spoke passionately to Kay about all we had gone through, about the triggers the abusers had planted, the mind control games to cause death and destruction. I was not the Valerie Sinason Melanie and her alter-personalities had first encountered. On behalf of them all, on behalf of the life that had been crushed and stolen from them, I was pleading. It was two large tears that came out of my eyes and slowly rolled down my face that allowed Kay to finally alter the programming that had been set off.

The robot had become human.

The Story by Melanie Skye

The singleton (what I call someone from the general population who is not DID) Valerie Sinason (my therapist) had a lot of trouble writing to our inside personality called Valerie Sinason. It was quite amusing at times like holidays, when she wrote to all the personalities she was in contact with to tell them, hearing that she had emailed all the personalities but Valerie Sinason.

The inside Valerie sounds and reacts just like singleton Valerie did years ago. A robot, who through her training shows no emotions and who gave nothing about herself.

In that way she was just like us and just as our programming taught us: don't cry, don't get angry and don't tell. It reinforced our idea that this was how everyone behaves; emotions do not exist.

We have been in and out of treatment with different robot therapists for thirty years. The usual standard treatment can work for many but for us with programmed DID we need to be shown how to talk and relate to a human not a robot. We had been brought up around robots. To be asked for years "How do you feel?" yet not knowing what a feeling was. Then being faced opposite a therapist robot who also didn't seem to know or that their training taught them not to show. The training though is alright for some but (as I have said) our needs are different.

I feel singleton Valerie had a real taste of hearing a mirror image and knowing the difficulty of trying to communicate with a person who is frozen in time, and has our old beliefs and feelings.

To actually be faced with a self that is stuck with the old thoughts and feelings with no room to move forward at a speed that was needed for us to relate to, can be painful, embarrassing, frustrating and at times dangerous. Having DID and being told about the other alters can be like this. We have to try to face, help, accept and communicate with others that highlight our old feelings and behaviour that we would rather ignore.

The breakthrough in our treatment came when singleton Valerie changed, showed some emotion, showed she cared and taught us what a feeling was and how to identify it. This difficult experience for singleton Valerie with her double insider (something her training or reading could not have helped her with) has made the rocky road of therapy lighter and real. We are side by side on this journey and that is thanks to both Valeries, especially singleton Valerie for her patience, commitment and willingness to change. Inside Valerie is trying hard to undo this work through email therapy with other alters but now singleton Valerie has seen her old self and training and experienced change, which helped many of us move forward, I am confident she will get through to inside Valerie as inside Valerie did her.

Unfinished Business

Carole Smith

The selection procedure involved two interviews, one to be with a registered psychiatrist. Laura couldn't really remember much about that one, except that it was a rather dry affair. Being screened for any signs that might indicate unsuitability for psychoanalytic training was not unlike being body-searched before boarding an aircraft; it was best to avoid making manic jokes, and offer oneself with the correct degree of decorum. A depressed psychiatrist and a suitably detached candidate shouldn't produce anything untoward to report to the training college.

She anticipated that the second interview, this time with a psychotherapist, would be a more personal encounter. She arrived for the appointment punctually at the Victorian house in Primrose Hill, and was asked by a voice on the entry phone to come in and wait in the hall. Sitting there alone, she could hear the sound of running water coming from somewhere near the landing on the stairs above her, and then a door opened and shut and a man with wild hair and a beard, his shirt unbuttoned almost to the waist, descended jauntily and, giving her a rather studied look with his blue eyes said, "You wouldn't be Laura Mansfield, would you?"

Rising to her feet, Laura smiled and offered her hand. The interview which followed lurched wildly from one lane to another: "You don't want to do this—why would a woman like you want to be a psychotherapist?" And then, "Well, I think you should do the training. You'd be good. Film-making's far too manic for you, anyway." This was followed by, "If you've been making films, you'd find psychotherapy too passive. Why don't you go on making films?"

The truth was that she had been fascinated by psychoanalysis since her early teens, when she had discovered, quite by chance, a book of case studies. Her children were the centres of her life, and her interest in them had diminished an earlier drive to create celluloid images. But now she found herself unwilling to talk about such private feelings to this man, who chose to submit her to this some- what reckless style of interview. Might not such an approach owe something to a defensive need to show that being a psychotherapist was no tame job for a man? This wouldn't be the first time that Laura had known men to react resentfully when they heard she was a film- maker. Uncomfortable with the man's manner, disoriented by his tactics, she felt car-sick and wondered if she should have filled in that application form after all. Perhaps it would have been better just to have gone on reading Freud.

Following the initial interviews, candidates were instructed by letter to attend a meeting as a group. It was not clear whether their selection had been provisional and whether there would be further assessment based on performance in the group. A tense atmosphere prevailed as people arrived at the spacious redbrick house in Hampstead and mounted the staircase to the first floor. There they followed a sign saying "Group Meeting" outside a large room in which they were to assemble.

Attempting to appear neither nervous nor relaxed, since the situation seemed so tenuous, Laura entered to find some twenty straight-backed wooden chairs arranged in a circle. People arrived and as they seated themselves, seemed very swiftly to lose any inclination to acknowledge each other. This may have been due to the imposing presence of a short elderly lady of European appearance sitting on a chair at one end of the circle, with her back to the windows. Her short hair was sparse and tinted a dark reddish colour. There was a handbag sitting in the middle of her lap, and her short legs were noticeably swollen. Both the imperious angle at which she held her head, and her rather pugnacious features, gave her an air of remarkable indifference to the people in the room. Laura assumed she was the Clinical Director, Dr Stekel.

When most of the chairs were taken, and Laura had managed to look around the room a little, she saw there were five men and some fifteen women. Eight of the women were wearing pearl necklaces. The silence continued for many minutes, inexplicable to Laura who had never attended such a group before, and where the apparent virtue was that of withholding speech. All of a sudden, a man, who must have been the Assistant Clinical Director, came in, sat next to Dr Stekel—who completely ignored his arrival—and said, "Well, we can begin."

Any hope that help might have coincided with the man's arrival soon vanished. Many minutes seemed to pass with the tension swelling. Could this be all it is, this final test, Laura wondered? Is it a matter of holding out without speaking? Another age of minutes passed in silence. When at last a young man found the temerity to speak, it was alarming to hear a voice. It now occurred to Laura that all along the session might be devised as a test of courage to see who could speak first. Perhaps it was all a question of showing initiative.

"It's difficult to know what we are supposed to do," said the young man who was wearing a fair isle-patterned jumper. Dr Stekel turned her face in his direction. In a heavy Austrian accent, she spoke with slow deliberation, "Why? Is there something which you must do here?" Everyone now swung to look at him. It was of great importance to hear his answer. He muttered defensively, in what would in normal circumstances, outside this hellish room, have seemed like sanity, "Well we didn't come here for nothing, did we?" This inspired a ripple of terror amongst the group who all then turned on hearing the Doctor speak. "You think we should be giving something to you?" In the silence that followed, Laura mournfully concluded that Fairisle's future would not be as a psychoanalyst— at least not with this organisation.

A very English, refined—looking woman was sitting next to Laura, and she could actually feel her shaking. When the woman spoke, her face was flushed, and her voice trembled with indignation, "I must say, it would be a basic courtesy to be greeted when we arrive." The Doctor was impervious to the charge of discourtesy in this wildly delivered assault. "What you think it is, this place?" Laura felt she must speak, if only to support her neighbour. "It's rather like a cocktail party without the drinks." At this Dr Stekel smiled—not so much a smile as a betrayal of some inner satisfaction. Laura felt a little dizzy, as if she had displaced a human force-field.

When the phone rang three days later, it was the guttural voice of the Clinical Director. It appeared she had been accepted. "I want that you commence your training analysis. I have been thinking *very* carefully about whom you should see. I know *exactly* the man." She deliberated over "exactly" as if to accentuate her prowess at casting. The unctuousness in her tone, after the calculated misanthropy of the group meeting made Laura shrink but she obediently wrote down the name and telephone number of her appointed analyst.

Years later, she understood that analysands, trainee analysands in particular, had some say in their choice of analyst, but it didn't occur to her now to query this magisterial command. It was in this rather enthralled state of mind that she rang to make an appointment with he who would be the keeper of her soul. She wondered what it was about her, or about him, that had coupled the two of them in Dr Stekel's mind. She felt as if the Laura who had been identified by Dr Stekel might not really exist, and that she had perhaps been viewed with refracted vision. Marked out as more hardy than she actually was, she was now launched on a clinical training course that required the tincture of bravado.

Uncharacteristically for a training analyst, Dr Westmore was also a psychiatrist in a large London hospital. He had only recently been invited to join Dr Stekel's training programmes, the latter being keen to recruit the power of psychiatry to strengthen the cause of psychoanalysis. When Laura rang the bell of the mews house, which was his home, a shortish man in his fifties, wearing a navy blue blazer with brass buttons, answered the door. He had small intense brown eyes, which looked at her swiftly with a sense of anxious arousal, and then looked immediately away. Beneath his deep-set eyes, his jutting nose gave him an avian quality. His dark hair clung closely to his skull, which was set on a short neck in keeping with his rather thickset build. Laura's instant reaction was to turn her back and run for her life. He said "Hello, come in," adding as he turned away, "we're upstairs." He gestured for her to go first.

As she walked up the small staircase, Laura could feel the uncomfortable intimacy of this complete stranger following silently behind her, and when she reached the landing, she hesitated. He directed her silently, his rather bullet-shaped head lowered, towards a room on the right. Venturing towards it, she passed a room on the left, and through the half open door, glimpsed a large screen hiding the rest of the room from view. The screen was covered with swirling, naked, renaissance-style cherubs, set against an azure background.

The consulting room was immaculate and furnished almost entirely in leather. The couch awaiting her was brown leather, the analyst's chair black leather, and the chair facing the couch, white leather. On the wall to the left of the couch, hung a painting of a bowl containing what she thought were nuts. She sat on the couch, facing the Doctor, aware that at some point she would be expected to lie down. It was then, while he defined the terms—the fees and the times of the twice-weekly sessions—that the strangeness of the situation struck her: that she should reveal her most intimate thoughts to this man, whom she did not know nor with whom she felt safe—at least for the present. He told her it would be best for her to use the couch.

His voice, which was to become the embodiment of his presence, was soft and insinuating. He avoided her glance when she looked at him, and it seemed to her that if she chose not to lie down it would be seen as an act of resistance. She felt also it would contribute to his unease if she didn't comply with his wish. Perhaps he didn't like being looked at. She lay down and wondered, self-consciously, if the feel of the soft leather was supposed to elicit tactile memories of skin, but wasn't emboldened to say so. He instructed her to say what was on her mind, but this she was unable to do, being so acutely aware of an atmosphere which she couldn't help feeling might arise from mutual revulsion. In an effort to cleanse them both of this feeling, she launched into an anodyne history of her life, all the while fixing her gaze on the white leather chair.

The initial term of lectures for the training course was given by a youngish man with a conceited air and a clear dislike of being challenged. This intractable manner unified some of the more spirited women trainees through their shared dislike of him, and although this was probably a regressive move to schooldays, it was no less diverting for that. Laura found a great deal to admire in some of her companions, amongst whom were a very bright woman who wrote novels, and the refined woman, a philosophy graduate, who had shown her indignation in the group meeting. This lady often grew irritated with what she felt was the tutor's specious logic. If she intervened to question him, he would pause, frowning, his eyes fixed to the floor. Laura also irritated him when she asked him on more than one occasion whether he shouldn't make it clearer that his theoretical assumptions had a Jungian bias.

The trainees were organised into two large therapy groups, Laura being assigned to that of Dr Stekel, which was to be held at the group leader's home once weekly for two hours in the evening. Attendance here was to prove the most arduous feature of the training course, causing much conflict amongst its members. The group appeared to be forming a highly destructive culture, against which the exposure of vulnerability or the sharing of tragic events in a life history seemed contra-indicated. The trainees hoped vaguely that there would be some evolution from a primitive group into something enlightened, but it was not encouraging to find on arrival one night that Dr Stekel was involved in an altercation with another resident of the street, the owner of a black taxi cab, who she was berating for leaving his cab parked outside her house, in what she was describing as a "residential area."

Under such pressures, there was a tendency for the trainees to mould their personal analytic space into a refuge, in which trust was transferred onto the analyst in an attempt to find protection from the vicissitudes of the group. She spent a lot of her time entertaining her analyst with observations about the group, a procedure which he appeared to enjoy. As the months passed, however, Laura found herself, in her analytic hour, moving back in time and uncovering layers of forgotten memories. Analysis was progressing well enough and prompted by Dr Westmore's gently spoken affirmations, she was able to start deconstructing the world of her earliest childhood. She had been the youngest member of a family whose outward adaptation to life was made at the expense of inner personal location. Laura felt that part of her had been mummified as an adjunct of her mother, whose own emotional survival had been so attenuated. Praised for her practical capabilities, her common sense and maturity, she had nevertheless lived in a very private inner world.

Out of the miscarriages of the past, transformed infantile beginnings indicated the resurgence of long repressed feelings to her father. Dr Westmore, having negotiated the maternal role, sensed in his feline way, the shift in the transference. Laura dressed more carefully and one day, as she lay down, she felt alarmed by the Doctor's furtive glance at her breasts, and then realised that this was what she had unconsciously designed. When her hour was over, she felt a surge of sexual shame. Arriving, however, for the following session, she found, pinned to the door, a small handwritten note saying "Gone to the chemist for prescription. Go upstairs and wait."

She pushed open the door, went upstairs and hesitated outside the room where she had often glimpsed the erotic screen. Deciding to steal a quick look behind it she saw that there were two single beds pushed together and realised with a shock that it had never occurred to her that her analyst was either married, or had ever been married. She wished she hadn't looked. Entering the consulting room, she lay down, but lying there alone she felt absurd, and the situation suggested an inappropriate act, as if that of a woman waiting for a lover.

She heard the door downstairs open and someone came bounding up the stairs. Turning her head as Dr Westmore entered the room, she saw that he looked excited. Trying to calm herself as he sat down behind her, and feeling it was necessary to start speaking quickly, she heard herself saying that she felt rather like a child who had been sent upstairs to bed. She was startled to hear his voice, purring, "Du bist mein bub." She recognised the line from *Der Rosenkavalier*, although she was neither very knowledgeable about operas, nor particularly fond of them. She tried, though, to register his meaning, but remembering the cross-dressing in the plot, wondered whether he was addressing her as a girl, or as a girl dressed as a boy—or even a boy dressed as a girl. When she went home that night she looked up the scenario. There it was, "Du bist mein Bub, Du bist mein Schatz."—"You are my boy, You are my darling."

This incident was to mark the onset of what she was to remember as the 'erotic reverie'. Although at the time, she felt the couch to be a raft floating in a warm sea, and her analyst's comments to be caressing, she was always aware of being at a distinct remove from reality, that she was somehow being coaxed into playing out a part. But it was not within her power to play this part at the same time as questioning her analyst's judgement about whether they were floating in the right direction.

One day, she heard him ask, "I'm wondering if you regret having given up your film-making." She answered, "Not really", but she also knew that her answer came partly out of a wish to reassure him that the work he did, the work of the psychoanalyst, was of value. Dr Westmore seemed to answer her unexpressed thoughts, and contributed information which she had not sought, "I went into medicine for all the wrong reasons."

"Oh", said Laura. She felt the constraints of her position, and that to offer consolation would require significant reorientation of roles, so she remained silent. She also felt that he might be implying that she was unsuitable material for training. Or was he trying to tell her that he wouldn't wish the job on anyone? When he announced, "I used to be very interested in photography", she became distinctly embarrassed. "Still or moving?" she managed to ask. "Still", the Doctor answered.

In the weeks following the incident of the note and the *Der Rosenkavalier* quote, Laura felt that she was playing a part that had been allocated to her but that the next lines of the script were not forthcoming. This phase, probably narcissistic, seemed so split off from the person she felt she was that she could not enjoy it. To have so much arousal of sexual energy, and not even to like or want to look at the person conducting made her feel trapped. The energy which should have been channeled into her work, or at least into the recovery of past experiences, had been somehow deflected and become stuck to the person who sat behind her, as if she were iron filings adhering to a magnet. She understood enough about the analytic encounter to know that something needed to be done, but she didn't know what. Unable to talk to him about sexual feelings of the present, she felt compelled to regress to childhood experiences. One day she ventured to tell him that as a child, she had often blushed since she was teased so much in her family, but that she had managed to teach herself not to. "And without biofeedback!" he said.

This joke was the response of a behaviourist-influenced psychiatrist—at least, so it seemed to Laura at the time, taken aback by the pleasure he took in its delivery. Years later, she knew he could have asked her then if there was something she wanted to tell him that made her blush. He might have known, or felt, that if a child is forced to suppress its blushes, then there is a good chance that she has had to suppress a great deal more. At this moment, however, his remark seemed like a blow, elegantly delivered, but hurtful. And it cut off another effort to escape from the erotic claustrophobia. There seemed neither sufficient oxygen to survive, nor any way of emerging from this elemental state, and as she lay there she wondered how she would be able to negotiate the act of getting up and going down out into the street without severance from internal reality or complete loss of dignity.

The next night she had a dream about sexual intercourse with her father. She understood how important this dream was and summoned the courage to tell Dr Westmore, but when she began, "I had a dream about my father last night" he answered her immediately with an amused tone, "Was he fishing?" She thought he must be making a reference to himself as the object of the transference, but the effect of his wit was increasingly double-edged. It disarmed her since she felt obliged to enter into his humour, while at the same time colluding with what might have been his discomfort at being the recipient of difficult intimacies. Once more he had silenced her, and at a critical moment at which the whole analysis might founder or progress.

The same night she woke up very sharply, with the clear recall of a dream. In this dream she was arriving with her father in a taxi at a pine house. In front of the house there was a grassy hill. She and her father drove into the house and got out, but when they did, her father was no longer apparent, although she knew he was somewhere. Dr Westmore now appeared, welcoming them in a routine friendly manner. There was a girl or, perhaps two girls, in the background, one of whom was watchful and unwelcoming. Dr Westmore gave Laura a polite kiss, but there was something in his mouth—it might have been a pencil. Laura said, "My father's gone around the corner." They were in a long front room looking out or down onto the grass. "Around the corner" indicated the unseen side of a veranda. Laura spoke again to the Doctor. "He's gone around there. But he's quite deaf. You'll have to shout."

Laura planned to tell it to Dr Westmore, but she found it difficult to find the right moment. Perhaps she was looking for some natural way of embarking on what seemed a risky enterprise, but when, on arrival, she saw Dr Westmore he didn't seem to resemble either the doctor in the dream or her father. He must have caught something dissimulating in her manner. He broke the silence with a question: "Who are you today?" At this Laura, disorientated, wondered if he was implying that she was playing a part—perhaps imagining herself to be an operatic star. She couldn't imagine what else he could mean. She didn't tell him her dream. Later she understood very well the pining (pine) for her father, the guilt towards her mother (the house), the erotic past of her feelings for her father (the grassy knoll—the veranda), the effort to transfer to the professional doctor with the taboo on incest (the pencil), the split depicted by the two girls, the premonition of her father's death, the appeal to the analyst to be trustworthy as a replacement father figure.

At the end of the session she was further surprised when he told her he was sorry but he wouldn't be able to keep the following appointment as he had booked for the opera.

"Falstaff", he said with an apologetic little laugh. He seemed not to understand what an effort she was making to hold everything together. She couldn't tell him that she was doing her best to contain this weird erotic transference, one that she believed he had gone out of his way to encourage. If she appeared to be acting, it was her only defence. On leaving, she felt unspoken resentment. As the opera was being broadcast live that night, she watched it, wanting to be connected in real time through the shared experience. The tragic-comic character of Falstaff served only to remind Laura of men at their crudest, and she felt no sympathy or interest in the old fool.

The summer approached. With the long break imminent, Dr Westmore told her he would be going away for five weeks. Attempting to hide her desolation, she heard herself asking, "Are you going to China?" She had no idea where the thought came from. She heard an intake of breath from him. "Hong Kong", he said. "Oh", said Laura, as if no great importance attached to it. "You'll eat well, then."

"Oh, yes", he said with feeling, "The food is wonderful," adding—as if making a privileged concession, "I'm going to see my daughter." If this was meant to somehow console her for his impending absence, it had the opposite effect. "I'm afraid time's up." The Doctor stood up, and as she glanced at him she thought he now looked defended against these personal revelations. He said crisply, "Well. You'll have your gardening and the piano to keep you busy in my absence."

Five weeks in analytic terms could feel like five years. Her early childhood had been marked by long separations from her father, and the effect of his parting words was that of the paradoxical injunction: gardening and piano playing were imbued with a feeling of disconsolation.

On the date which marked Dr Westmore's return, Laura set out nervously to keep the appointment, feeling no relief at the prospect of seeing him again. She parked in a nearby street and walked to the cobbled mews, arriving there with her usual punctuality. As she turned the corner, she saw, with a sick lurch in her heart, that Dr Westmore and a tall bespectacled man with light hair, were inspecting a shiny new Italian sports car, its hood down. It was parked across the front of the house, so that she would have to walk around it to reach the door. Dr Westmore heard her steps, and turned, speaking a few quick words to his companion, who went quickly into the house.

Feeling upset by this unsought intrusion into his private life, Laura made an effort to disguise her feelings as they went up the stairs silently together. Would she be expected to talk about this glimpse into his real world? What bearing should it have on her analysis? And yet, how could it not affect her, especially today, after such a long absence which had come at such a difficult time for her. The incident, moreover, seemed to have been carefully staged. Was he trying to give her a message? What was his relationship with this man? The analysis suddenly felt a complete sham. Was he trying to place a barrier between them to protect himself from her feelings? Were those feelings so repellent to him that he must resort to such dramatics? And why today, why straight after the break? As the session began his manner was controlled and there was a coolness about him which confirmed her feelings of rejection—and of sexual rejection in particular. The session was something she just had to get through. Any trust she had sustained in the wait for him to return had evaporated.

From then on she began to feel less like attending to the academic work of the course—work which she had previously enjoyed. She had no way of speaking of her feelings of abandonment. She knew that it was possible for trainees to discuss problems with their tutors, but she felt that to do this would somehow be far too intimate, for she was full of shame. In the sessions she could have cried out to him, like a baby, asking him if was he teasing her, but she felt he would never admit to such tactics, and it would be impossibly humiliating. It was better to pretend that none of what she had felt had ever happened.

Deprived of meaning and losing direction, Laura began to drive past the corner of his street at night, looking to see if the Italian sports car was parked outside. One night, when her son was refusing to do his homework, she lost her temper and shook him. The next day, in tears, she asked him to forgive her. Memories of her childhood beatings came flooding back.

Feeling unable to make any progress, and having lost interest in herself, she became even more sensitised to her analyst's manner and his moods. This seemed to irritate him, but she had to do something, lying there, and her own story seemed to have come to a close. She really didn't know what was expected of her any more. She withheld her dreams from him. In one, she jumped from the top floor of a large water tower into a cushioned paddling pool. There was something ridiculous about this dream—something that reminded her of a McGill post card from the British seaside.

When Dr Westmore gruffly said—as if in disapproval at her performance—that she was not dealing with her feelings about her father, she surprised herself with the retaliation, "Sometimes I feel you have not altogether dealt with your own feelings about your mother," a little taken aback at her own daring. "What do you know about my mother?" he asked, with a hint of amusement. "I imagine she was rather formidable, and you got on better with your father." This did not mark a breakthrough in the analysis so much as a stalemate. If the exchange had occurred earlier, perhaps it would have served some useful purpose, but by now Laura had also lost a great deal of her interest in the training course, and was finding it a struggle to attend the lectures. In her youth, she had angered her father by winning a place at university, thus incurring his enormous resentment at his daughter for having gained for herself the opportunity for the education which he himself had earlier been denied. Consequently, Laura had felt guilty for her privilege, and her attendance at university lectures became less frequent, until eventually she had avoided the day lectures altogether, attending only the evening ones which were repeated for those who had been obliged to work in the day.

One day, she heard Dr Westmore ask, quite out of the blue, "Why do you persist with this course—with these courses you are on?" She was stunned. He continued, "No-one", he paused, "Would be happier than I, if you were to give them up—sooner rather than later."

Laura could not begin to ask him what he meant. He seemed to be saying something in a secret code. It was the language of a father who was unable to speak to his daughter for years at a time, who resorted to strangled euphemisms to communicate. Which courses exactly did he mean? He said, as he got up from his black leather chair at the end of the session, "Well, you have had all sorts of messages tonight."

Laura was so numbed and confused by these remarks that she couldn't form clear thoughts. Was he saying she just wasn't up to the standard required of a psychoanalyst? Was this the only way he could break this news to her? This was not usually a decision to be made by the personal analyst without consultation with the course leaders. Perhaps he just couldn't stand her, and wanted her to disappear? Perhaps he found her sexuality disturbing in some way? She was completely confused and unhappy. To avoid further humiliation, she made a decision. That night she wrote a letter to her course tutor giving regretful notices that she would, for personal reasons, be unable to continue with the course. She received generous and consoling remarks from most of her fellow trainees, and from her tutors with the exception of the lecturer to whom she had been, along with her friends, a bit of a handful. His note read: "Laura, I think you have made the right decision. My opinion is that you would be better suited to less demanding work, perhaps marriage counselling."

When Laura reported this in the next session, affecting light-hearted amusement, she hoped secretly that he might say something supportive—that he might defend her ability against the pomposity of the lecturer. Perhaps he would come out and say that he, the Doctor, was pleased that he and she were no longer shackled together in a professional trap. She felt the unresolved conflicts of desire and repulsion, need and evasion, and a secret terror that she had once more cast herself out—been forced into the wilderness. He said nothing to mitigate her fear. Nor did he, to her dismay, express any concern about her having resigned from the course.

A week later, she received a call from thousands of miles away. The moment she heard her mother's voice, she knew what she was about to tell her. Her father had died. She took herself that day to the session and told the Doctor that her father had died. "What? No tears? No grieving?" he said. She was unable to feel anything at all except for distress for her mother, but felt his reproving tone was both inappropriate and misjudged. "I suppose we ought to decide when I should terminate coming here, since I have no reason for training analysis any more," she said. For the first time since his return she detected a note of warmth in his voice, "Yes," he said in a generous tone, "But don't rush it. Give it a couple of weeks. After all, you've just lost your father."

When Laura arrived home after the final session, she more or less collapsed. The nameless horror of annihilation she felt didn't prevent her from being clearly aware that she was bound on an inexorable process of unravelling, as if some efficient machinery, having been set in motion, would pursue its course until it exhausted itself. She had attempted to act correctly—as if in accordance with the doctor's unspoken wishes, as if to please him—in some repetition of past events which were too amorphous in her memory to help her to save herself from an inevitable disintegration.

It was less clear to her whether he had any real cognisance of what she had done in giving up her course of studies. She suspected that he had not really grasped the meaning of her actions at all; indeed it was probable that he had been relieved of what had become an intractable problem for him.

She managed to cope for a year, and then another few months. She managed to perform outwardly the things necessary in her life, but the imprint in her psyche left by the anniversaries of long-passed experiences found her one spring day returning to Dr Westmore's house. She had been unable to use the telephone and as she drove to the familiar corner, she half remembered the feelings she had when she was forced to knock on her father's study door obliged for some reason to ask him to sign something for school. Throughout all those years of high school, he did not to speak to her. He had wanted her to attend the school known as "Domestic Home Science", which awaited girls who were consigned to the bottom of the intellectual ladder, and he had been extremely indignant when her teachers had told him that she would be sent to the high school in keeping with her ability, viewing their decision as deliberately undermining of his patriarchal authority.

When Laura arrived at his house for this unscheduled meeting, the Doctor answered the door and looked at her as if she was an escaped criminal. "I'm sorry," she said, "but could I speak to you?" Looking alarmed, he glanced at his watch, and said that he had ten minutes before the next patient. She apologised again, thanked him, and climbed up the familiar stairs, and sat down facing him on the couch. Then she asked him whether he thought they had terminated her analysis prematurely. He looked straight at her and said: "I'm not clever enough to do analysis with psychotic people." Laura was too shocked to speak and left.

In the time following her attempt to reclaim the self that she had surrendered, her days and nights were occupied by the duties of looking after the children. Then one day, driving home down a narrow street near the children's school, she found herself confronted by a very large red truck which drove hard up against her car, and halted. The driver stopped, put his elbows on the steering wheel, and grinned. She got out of the car, closed the door and walked away, leaving it parked in front of him. After she had sat down on a seat in the nearby park, she returned to find the car still there, the truck gone.

She began to look at car number-plates, scrutinising the letters—and sometimes the numbers as if they bore some message. They became persecuting objects and the number of cars in the street seemed to have increased beyond all explanation. Indeed the streets seemed to be lined with so many hundreds of coloured metal vehicles that one day she actually asked someone if they had noticed what an extraordinary number of cars there suddenly seemed to be. She tried to make sense of the world around her, but found it increasingly jumbled. She knew that she was unable to continue in this state.

One day she again made the accursed trip to Dr Westmore's house. She had forced herself to keep away for what seemed years. She knew her visit would not now, or ever, be welcomed or even accepted, and that she could only be seen as something dreaded. As she rang the bell, she heard the sounds of Wagner coming from the living room. The door opened. Standing there was the tall man with light hair. When she saw him, she asked for Dr Westmore. He said he wasn't there. She could stand her situation no longer. Ignoring him, she rushed past, through the downstairs hall, into the forbidden small living room, hesitating briefly to satisfy her curiosity about its arrangement. Then, seeing the record player in the corner with *Tannhauser* or *Parsifal*—she couldn't tell which—blaring out of the speakers, she seized the needle, removed it from the record, and flung it down. In the poky kitchen annex which led off from the living room, she saw a bottle of cooking oil. She opened the refrigerator and took out a bottle of milk. The tall man was standing helplessly, bleating something at her. She ignored him contemptuously, took the bottle of cooking oil in one hand, the milk bottle in the other, and poured the entire mixed contents all over the pale living room carpet. She then walked back to the car and drove home.

The next day, a nervous looking young man arrived at the door, holding a sheaf of paper. This was a legal document, which he said he had been ordered to serve on Laura Mansfield. Laura went out into the hall and told him to go away. The articled clerk said he was bound to deliver the document and must wait until she accepted it. Realising that one of the children was due home, she took it, and the boy shambled gratefully away.

Arriving at the legal hearing the following week, Laura was asked to wait in the annex, where Dr Westmore was already sitting with his friend. She had taken her knitting and took it out—a somewhat subversive gesture—but also because knitting had provided a sort of defence against her own unravelling in these long months.

Sitting a few yards apart, they waited for the court to become free. When it was time to go in, the tall friend got up to accompany Dr Westmore into the court, and she was pleased to hear a court attendant tell him that it would be better if he waited outside. Once they were inside the courtroom, the judge entered and everyone was asked to stand. Laura refused to do so, remaining seated, and was surprised to find that no one forced her to her feet. She heard Dr Westmore telling the judge that she had assaulted his property, and that on account of the danger she posed to his safety, a restraining order should be imposed on her. The judge, a pleasant-looking man, looked up from his papers with a slight smile and asked Laura if she had anything to say.

"Yes," said Laura. "I would like to say that psychotherapy can be a very dangerous thing if the therapist treats his patients as if they were characters in an opera."

The judge then asked in an equable tone if the Doctor had anything to add. Dr Westmore said that he had been advised by his solicitor to request an injunction forbidding Mrs Mansfield from coming within a prescribed area around his home. There was then some conferring between the legal team about the precise geographical area which would constitute this injunction. Laura asked if she would be able to use the nearby tube station, which was fifty yards from the

Doctor's house. The judge smiled and said she could. The order was then passed.

One day, not long after this, as she was driving past a skip parked in a street near the Doctor's house, Laura saw that it contained an abandoned washbasin. She got out of the car, calmly picked up the basin and, although it was heavy, she carried it to his mews house and threw it through the living-room window. Feeling a calm satisfaction in this deed, she returned to the car and drove to the shops to buy something for dinner. As she did so she heard a police siren. In front of onlookers in the street, two policemen seized her, one twisting her arms behind her and the other forcing her to the ground. She was then dragged into the back of the police van and driven to the nearby police station. During the trip, sitting opposite a policeman, she recalled that her father had said when she told him she was going to university, that he had washed his hands of her education.

She was asked some questions by a man who she decided must be a police psychiatrist. Certified, she knew not exactly as what, she looked at her watch and saw it was time to go to pick up the children from school. She couldn't register at first that she would not be allowed to do this. When they ignored her now tearful pleas, the real horror of her situation dawned on her. She insisted that they allow her to collect the children, but they refused. She made a bid to escape, but was brought back by the policeman. She then insisted that they allow her to ring her kind neighbour to ask her to pick up the children. Then she was driven to a psychiatric hospital in North London which she had known as being the worst-administrated psychiatric establishment in London.

On arrival, Laura was forcibly injected with some mind-altering substance, and her brain juddered into a state which felt like chemical decomposition. She realised early on that there was only one way to get out of this Gothic horror which housed so many tragic figures, most of them drugged and shuffling up and down the endless corridors carrying plastic bags which contained various articles reminding them of a previous existence. The trick of getting out of this uncaring place was to pretend to be what the doctors considered to be well. If that meant saying that you had become overwrought and behaved strangely but that now you had—and showed—

'insight', this might be the key to freedom. Luckily for Laura, a senior social worker at the hospital took an interest in her, and didn't think she should be there.

Since there was no effort on the part of the psychiatrist in charge to grasp her inner world, the weekly interviews being a group meeting of fourteen or fifteen people confronting the patient in a circle, the intervention of the social worker was an act of considerable independence of mind, if not courage, in view of hospital protocol. Possessing only the notes by the police about an act of disorderly conduct, this woman made a point of speaking to Laura from time to time. One day she said to Laura, "I don't buy this psychotic thing. Can I come and visit you at home with your children?"

Laura was allowed to go home for the day. The social worker came and behaved as if she was an ordinary visitor. The visit went well. Laura cooked lunch for her and the children were relaxed and friendly in her company. When she returned to the hospital the next day, she was told by one of the nursing staff that she was to be discharged, but that if she ever attempted to contact the Doctor again she might even have to go to prison.

Her recovery was more a process of rebuilding and the salvaging of things that mattered. Understanding what happens in a mind under siege gave her the ability to recognise how fear of disintegration expresses itself and transmits fear and closure in others. Fear of madness, being largely the fear of madness in oneself, encourages a process of defensive action which seeks to put distance between the controller and the controlled, and to pathologise symptoms which, seemingly inchoate and meaningless, can offer keys to the illumination of events which have been too threatening for admission to conscious life. Her interest in such matters grew rather than diminished in the years following her own traumatic abandonment. Eventually she was able to contemplate the resumption of psycho-analytic training. She thought she was beginning to understand what the job was really about. It helped her greatly to discover that there were analysts who believed that plummeting to the depths of one's own mind was, albeit perilous, an invaluable source of under-standing about the minds of others. When, later, she began to see patients, her own experience of erosion of the self served in her efforts to enter and contain their terrors without undue fear or pretence.

She did her best not to underestimate the powerful influence that an analyst could assert.

One day, five or six years later, a friend with whom she had done her analytical training asked Laura if she wanted to go to a talk at the Institute of Psychoanalysis—one of a series in which psychoanalysis was attempting to forge closer links with the world of the arts. The Institute had invited two distinguished speakers—one a psychoanalyst, the other a musicologist—to speak before an audience on the subject of "The Incest Theme in Rigoletto as Depicted in Musical Notation".

As they made their way down to the auditorium, in the basement, Laura saw Dr Westmore standing at the bottom of the stairs. He was intent on putting a tape into a rather cumbersome portable tape recorder. As she reached the bottom of the stairs where he was standing, he looked up and saw her. Their eyes met before he quickly looked away. Laura couldn't help noting that he was wearing a navy blazer with brass buttons, and wondered fleetingly if it could possibly be the same one she had seen him wear at their first meeting. It was difficult not to register the contextual irony of the occasion—not only opera but incest. Her earliest impression that there was something shifty about her former analyst was confirmed as she saw him in this common meeting place. Their mutual failure to acknowledge each other was as banal as it was tragic.

She and her friend walked into the lecture hall and sat near the stage where the musicologist was earnestly conferring with a technician about the setting up of the sound system which was emitting rather high-pitched squeals. With the technical requirements set up, and the introductions effected, the two speakers began a rather fractured dialogue. It was—Laura felt—an uneasy alliance: the musicologist, much taken up with his nervy administration of both the aural and visual aids required to illustrate the snatched musical phrases, seemed rather impervious to the psychoanalyst's insights. These comments, directed to the music specialist with the intention of generating a discussion, but being unreciprocated with any discernible enthusiasm, made it increasingly clear that the psychoanalyst was to have only a minor supporting role to play on this occasion. Laura wondered what the famously non-musical Freud might have made of the evening.

More aware of her own ebbing and flowing, Laura found it difficult to concentrate her interest on the establishment of the incestuous theme, let alone its inversion and recapitulation. She wondered somewhat ruefully if the man sitting somewhere behind her might have been at all disconcerted by his brief confrontation with a skeleton from the past. Or perhaps, since his interest in Rigoletto's theme was intense enough to record the lecture for later re-play, he might, in his fantasy, be assigning her the role of poor Gilda, dumped by her erring father into the river in a body bag.

When the interval arrived, her friend turned to her and said "Is it just me or are you finding this very boring? Do you want to go and eat somewhere?" Laura thought it a good moment to cut her losses, and they got up. As they passed the Doctor, who had been sitting not far behind them, Laura saw that his face was carefully averted to his tape-recorder.

Pink Mist

Zoë Fairbairns

Brief therapy. I like the sound of that. Bit of a contradiction in terms, though, isn't it? I understood therapy went on for years. That's why I never fancied the idea. I'm a busy woman and certainly not the sort to make a hobby out of lying on a couch while some overpaid stranger—no offence, and to be fair your rates are no more than I'd pay a decent plumber and a lot less than an auditor, but still it's a lot out of taxed income—sits there with their fingertips pressed together going "hm" and "ah" while I dredge up memories of events which may or may not have happened in my childhood and may or may not have some bearing on my current predicament. But when I saw on your website that you could fix me up in six sessions, I thought, great.

It may not be exactly six. Of course. No guarantees. Values can go down as well as up, past performance is not necessarily a guide. OK- if I leave here madder than when I came in, I promise not to sue. But we'll give it a try, shall we?

Did I say predicament? That's the wrong word, it overstates the case: it's not a predicament at all, it's just this little thing that keeps happening. I fall asleep. Well, not asleep exactly. More like passing out. No, that's not right either. I don't collapse, I don't crash the car, drop things or make wildly inappropriate remarks. To all outward appearances I'm functioning like a normal person, or at least no-one has given any indication that I'm not.

It's just that I'm not there.

It can happen anywhere. At work, at home. My little girl asks me for some milk, I get her some, or at least I think I'm getting her some, then suddenly she's saying, "Mummy, where's my milk?" and I realise I've been staring into the fridge for God knows how long, my mind a complete blank. It's such a waste of time. While I was staring at the fridge I could have been making phone calls or answering emails or putting the dinner on. Happens in meetings too. One minute I'm making some pithy and pertinent point, or at least I hope it's pithy and pertinent, I have no way of knowing because the meeting is over. I'll check the minutes to see if there's any evidence of me having made a total and complete prat of myself, but even if there's nothing, it's not exactly reassuring. They might have agreed to leave it out and circulate it via an amusing-anecdotes-about-the-boss email.

It's nothing medical, I've had tests. My doctor thinks I'm making a fuss about nothing, he says, "Look, if you've got no other symptoms and it's not affecting your life, why worry about it?" He thinks I should take a holiday. He thinks I do too much.

Speaking of which, I've got a meeting with a client directly after this, so could we get started?

We have started. Oh.

I've been thinking about what you said last time. What you asked me. You said the big difference between brief therapy and the lying-on-the-couch-for-weeks-on-end kind—you had a technical name for it—is that brief therapy doesn't waste time digging around for reasons for problems, it concentrates on finding solutions.

No, you probably didn't use the expression "waste time", that would be a very unprofessional thing to say about your colleagues in different disciplines, but for me that sort of thing would be a waste of time. Take my word for it, there is absolutely nothing in my past to explain why I should suddenly start taking little holidays from consciousness, if we can call it that. I just want to stop doing it.

I've done my homework. I didn't realise there would be homework. You want me to read it out? Do I have to? It was bad enough having to do it. I'm no stranger to assignments and deadlines, but this was hard. This time last week I thought therapy meant lying on a couch, now I'm about to give you a presentation. You don't happen to have a flipchart, do you? That was a joke, I don't really need a flipchart. I took some of the squared paper that we use for market forecasting analysis and divided each of them into twenty-four. Made me feel about six. My little girl is six. She said, "What are you doing, Mummy?" I said, "My homework."

"What sort of homework?"

"Well, I have to draw these squares and put red dots in them." I didn't tell her that the red dots represent times of the day when I don't have the faintest idea what I'm doing. When I'm not aware of anyone, not even her.

Sorry I'm late. Security alert on the tube. Bloody terrorists, I nearly rang you and cancelled, but then I thought, no, if we let them disrupt our lives, they've won, haven't they?

I was reading something about the US marines and the language they use. You know, "take out", "collateral damage", "friendly fire", that kind of thing. Bland phrases to cover unspeakable horrors. One of them said that if you get hit by a certain type of missile you turn into pink mist. It's probably not that different if you get blown up on the Underground. Fully functioning, then bang, pink mist.

Here are this week's charts. The number of dots does seem to be diminishing. Last week it averaged two or three per day, but this time there have only been four all week. None at all today. Today I've been fully alert and firing on all cylinders. I can't remember when I felt better. Just as a matter of interest, how brief can brief therapy be?

One session. You've actually had people come to you for one session and go away cured. The very fact of asking for help is sometimes enough to make the problem go away. That must be nice for the client, but not such good news for you as a businessperson. I mean, there you were, expecting to have someone for six sessions at least, and they're gone after just one. Or just three in my case. Because I don't think I need to come any more, do you, now that my dots are diminishing of their own accord.

Of course it's up to me, and I haven't to worry about you losing revenue, because for every crazy person you fix up, another ten sprout like dragons' teeth.

No I'm sure you don't use the expression "crazy person". Neither do I. I'm not crazy at all. I'm cured.

Thanks so much for letting me pop in without an appointment. I just happened to be passing, and I thought I'd take a chance that you might be free. Of course I'll expect you to invoice me in the usual way.

I didn't feel right about the way we parted last time. Quite apart from the professional relationship between us, which as I've said has

done me an awful lot of good, I really have enjoyed our little chats—
and it gives me a bad feeling to think that we parted on, well I won't
call it a lie, but an untruth. A white lie. It's nothing to do with the
therapy—I'm speaking as a human being now, rather than a client—
but I'd like to put something straight.

You remember I was late? And I said it was because of a terrorist
alert. Well, it wasn't. Poor old terrorists, they get blamed for everything. The truth is, I went into one of my dazes on the tube. I'd had
such a good week and then I was out of it and I couldn't bring myself
to mark it on the sheet, and as I hadn't marked it on the chart I couldn't
really tell you. But the truth is, I missed my station, Bond Street, and
went whizzing through to Marble Arch. The sensible thing would
have been to get out there and walk back, but I have a problem with
Marble Arch because that was where I see the angel of death.

Isn't that the funniest thing? Sensible old down-to-earth me,
haunted by ghoulies and ghosties and things that go whump in the
night. But I didn't want to see it again, once is enough for that sort
of thing, don't you agree? So I stayed on till Lancaster Gate then
walked back two stops, which is the real reason why I was late.

There's no need to write anything down. This isn't anything to
do with the therapy, we've finished with the therapy, I just wanted
to tell you.

I've done my homework. I've drawn the angel of death.

I used my daughter's felt-tips. She wanted to know what I was
drawing. I said, "Just a funny person I saw on the tube." She said,
"Is it a man or a woman?" I said, "I don't know, what do you think?"
She said, "I think it's a man-woman," so a man-woman it is.

It wasn't actually on the tube, it was outside the station, sitting
by the railings on Oxford Street, just opposite the exit. It—I'll call it
'it'—was sitting on a box or a stool, as if it was selling newspapers
or something, but it wasn't selling newspapers. It wasn't writing in
a book either, as I believe some mythological angels of death are wont
to do, or reaping or cutting thread. It was just looking. Choosing,
maybe. I don't know why I thought it was the angel of death rather
than just any old funny-looking person. I suppose with all the bombs
and everything I've become a bit jumpy. It might have been the face.
It was so white. No-one's face is that white. And you could see the
shape of the skull, only the bones weren't poking through the skin

in the way they do when someone's very thin or ill, it was more white and oval, like a white egg, smooth and polished and expressionless. I let my little girl colour its clothes in bright colours and only made them black after she'd gone to bed. Because it was black. The umbrella over its head, that was black too.

I bet if you put ten people in a room and asked them all to draw a picture of the angel of death, they'd all come up with something different. My friend Briony for example, she saw it as a bird. "Like a bloody great eagle or something, flying over me," she said, when she had her stroke. "Huge great swipe it gave me with its wing. If it had been flying any lower, it would have finished me off."

Amazing, that stroke. She was as healthy as you or me, then wham! Right out of it. But she came round and her doctors didn't seem too flustered, they said everyone's allowed one stroke, these things happen and usually there's a complete recovery and no recurrence. They were quite laid-back about it, so we all were too.

Well, that's it. This time it really is goodbye, and I promise there won't be any more return visits, raving on about angels or giant birds or eggs. You asked at the beginning which I'd prefer, to understand my problem or solve it, and I said solve it. But now I think I've done both. I'm not getting these blank-outs any more, and I understand that when I was getting them it was because I was practising being dead. I don't want to be like Briony who died very quickly and with virtually no warning. Not exactly pink mist, but nearly. Just because everyone's allowed one stroke, doesn't mean that one stroke mightn't be a sign of something more deadly.

So I've been practising. Testing what it's like not being here. Not feeling, not seeing. And I've been making sure my work is all up to date and my little girl knows how to pour her own milk. That's what gets to me when I think I might get blown into pink mist in an underground bombing. Every time she does it, she'll think, Mummy used to do this for me.

But I've practised enough. I'm going to walk out of here a fully conscious person, and remain fully conscious. I think we've achieved a lot in six sessions. So thank you.

What do you mean, it's been a hundred and six?

The Analyst's New Couch

Judith Harris

"You can't be serious about the new couch," his wife is saying in a near whisper. They are sitting in his red Audi, waiting for him to press the garage door opener. It is Saturday. The neighbor's water sprinkler is just beginning its rotation on the yard next door. The grass is emerald green and the hedges are shiny with wax leaves. The roses are exorbitant this year, having come out in all of their lush complexity, like the intricate coiling of the unconscious mind; they devolve, they materialize, they unravel, and shatter on the black topsoil. As they drive away, Neuman feels the warm September air mixing itself with the burnt ends of summer.

Neuman's glance dismisses his wife's concern. At sixty-five, he walks gingerly and retains a trim figure. In appearance, he resembles the dignified Freud in his late fifties, with sparse hair, and owl-eyed spectacles. Indeed, he is one of the orthodox Freudians under siege from the younger analysts claiming Freud is an antique. While sometimes seeking what Ferenczi called the "mental nakedness" of the patient, Neuman has strict guidelines about abstinence and anonymity. He feels as if didacticism is not appreciated anymore. Technique is an art to be admired. But if it's the patient who is doing the admiring, something is wrong with the therapy.

Joy, his second wife, is a part-time real estate agent, and something of a socialite. She is a decade younger than Neuman, and wears her hair curt, and is athletically slim. Although she never had children, she has been a sympathetic stepmother to Neuman's children, one now in law school, the other doing graduate work at Emory. She finds the idea of her husband's "new couch" amusing—something like a fairy tale object that grows bigger with the beanstalks. "This reminds me of that children's tale, *The Emperor's New Clothes*. Now you are an analyst with a new couch!" Joy pauses, bringing the visor down to shade the strong sun from her eyes.

Neuman merges onto the highway. He remembers that the Emperor did not want to be contradicted; the story is really about power and coercion, and it is also about misdirected pride. Joy looks through her window, and taps at it with her pinky finger nail, as if to test the reality of the glass. She is admiring the woody manors tucked behind gates, "That's a nice house, isn't it, Len?" Neuman nods; he knows that Joy is restless, even as a realtor; she wants a change, something beyond the signpost of being a psychiatrist's wife.

"Talking about real estate, Len, that acquaintance of yours, Charles Longchamps, phoned for you—but he talked to me—he's brain-storming about some funding for the Psychoanalytic Institute to get them some more real estate in the district. He also said he had some ideas for the Education curriculum."

"Ah-huh? He called at home? Did you tell him to try the office?"

"No, after a while I just hung up."

Neuman stops at a four way cross street, and waits for the other car to take its proper lead. He appreciates this polite aspect of driving; the moment that a driver must heed, or defer to the other driver—for no other reason than the fact that the other automobile arrived there first. It is a matter of boundaries, giving and getting them. Neuman suspects that Charles Longchamps is calling him on another pretense; what he really wants is to reassure himself that Neuman will not retaliate against him on Ruth's behalf. Charles, a Freudian literary critic, is one of the new academics joining the Institute on a research fellowship. Neuman is ambivalent about allowing lay analysts into the Institute, or training them at all. He recognizes the fact that Charles is playing coy, but wants to secure his ascendancy at the Institute. Just last month he had cornered Neuman at a Scientific Meeting and brought the conversation around to Ruth. He even suggested that Neuman officiate a session with the two of them as if Neuman were a judge in a county bake-off. Neuman was insulted and chastised Charles very harshly, "I can't discuss this case!" Only a month later, Charles showed up at another function—this one a film viewing and discussion—arm-in-arm with Helene Russ, a social worker training to be a psychoanalyst, and Neuman's own supervisee. Neuman was astonished, and introduced

Joy to the drab and underdressed couple, and they exchanged niceties over the cheese platter, while another analyst rumbled on about drive theory.

In Joy's view, Neuman should consider retiring from the profession altogether; he's already served as president of the Institute, and now travels around the country on an Executive Committee observing other analysts' techniques. A new couch, like new water skis, suggests a prologue rather than a denouement. Neuman explains he has begun working with a patient who is over six foot and the old couch can't accommodate his height lying down; the patient's large feet dangle over the end. While it doesn't bother the patient, it bothers Neuman—something like a drawer that won't close, or a carpet stain. He hasn't analyzed himself about why he feels he must be fastidious about the patient who may already feel awkward about being so tall he can't fit on the shorter couch.

Joy also worries that Neuman's Freudianism is too old-fashioned. Just last month, a classic portrait of Freud was displayed on the cover of *Newsweek* with the title: "Freud is Not Dead" with the "Not" highlighted in yellow as if a mischievous pupil had scribbled it on the blackboard.

Neuman responds by saying that he might be orthodox in his methods, but he has perfected his skills by allowing his mind to spin outwards, becoming finer and finer in contour—the way a hummingbird's wings sputter and jettison until flight is all that is seen. He is seamless as virgin cloth. Still, when colleagues make derisive comments about analysis, he feels prickled as if someone has just criticized his old fashioned clothes.

Neuman drives up to the shopping mall and Joy rattles her purse to make sure she has her house keys in case they get separated and she has to take a taxi home. Neuman says this is just part of Joy's catastrophizing, and perhaps she is harboring an unconscious wish they would get separated. "It's all in the wording; the wish is the wording, Joy." Joy laughs, "OK dear, get the couch, but don't most of the patients now face you in chairs? I thought this reclining position was obsolete."

The couch is, in fact, Neuman's preference. He's never liked the shift to the new face-to-face encounter. Freud was more pragmatic: he didn't want to be stared at all day—never imagined doing it any other way, except once it has been said that he analyzed a German novelist while they took long walks in a park. Only to Ruth would the couch position resemble the one the dead take in open coffins. She told him that in the first week of therapy. Ruth has a classic morbidity. Ruth sits up in her sessions.

On Tuesday, Ruth's appointment day, Neuman is in the office very early. He measures the diagonal between the chairs, and looks at the old couch which shows the weight of so much human misery. It sags, is a little nappy around the wooden legs, and has lost its honeymoon spring. When patients face him in chairs, Neuman really does get tired of being stared at hour after hour, and sometimes he feels like he's a Bernini statue: he can't sneeze without provoking some reaction in the patient; he can't close his eyes because he's got a headache; and he can't scowl. Scowling has become a luxury that Neuman sometimes does just to do it: like the imp of the perverse. "I don't want to talk about that," Ruth is saying, "Is it clear to you what "that" is? It's not clear to me.

"Why don't you want to talk about that?"

"Because you are scowling at me."

"How do you know that, have I done something that makes you think so?"

Ruth knits her eyebrows together trying to mimic him. She's over forty, now, but appears younger. She has a fragility that people often remark upon and a doll-like face that is obstinately over-rouged. She looks out through the slatted blinds of the window where the trees have laced their branches. Sometimes the upper branches are picked clean as bone, and sometimes there is that skin of ice on them. Sometimes the birds flutter there. Sometimes she says she hears them chiseling on the upper branches with their beaks and singing their sporadic songs.

Of all of Neuman's patients, Ruth scrutinizes him the most. She's well read in psychiatric literature and insists she is able to distinguish the real Neuman from the Neuman of her own transference. Neuman dismisses this as yet another layer of Ruth's resistance.

Because of her low self-esteem, Ruth won't talk about sex or body parts or about what body parts do. Neuman asks her how she views her body. Does she look at herself in the mirror? Ruth says "No." Neuman asks her if she sees herself naked, or if she sees her husband naked. Ruth recoils. "No, absolutely."

"That sounds very definite. Are you curious about why?"

"I used to draw the nude model in art school," she says, "I used to get up close. I was good."

"Good"? What would be 'bad'?"

"I mean I was a good draftsman."

"Why did you bring it up, is there any connection to anything you were just saying?" Ruth takes another sidelong look at him. He can almost sense her piercing through his veneer of evenly dispersed attention as if it were a beekeeper's screen. She takes in a long silence. "I just wanted to think about you," she says. "What about me?" Neuman understands that Ruth as wanting to impress him, her narcissism insists on making some impression on him although, like a handprint in sand, it is only a temporary pressure. She must be mistaking the doctor for the illness again. It's the story of the Emperor: she seems to want to be seen in the most marvelous, magnificent clothing and she wants him to tell her, even if it's not true, that this is what she is. "Why don't you just lie to me?"

"What would that accomplish?"

"I might feel better. Everything is subjective. I could persuade myself of any falseness if I thought you thought it was the truth."

Neuman is silent. He gazes at her. When Ruth sits in the chair, she looks too small and feminine for it, and she holds onto the claws of the arms like she's holding onto the levers that operate the hand brakes of a motorcycle. It is very slow, this business of gaining trust. Once Ruth pointed out that some patients were throwing their wadded tissues out in the bronzed umbrella stand near the doorway on their way out, thinking it was a waste paper basket. Neuman was unnerved. "And you feel superior to the other patients because you, unlike them, know the difference between an umbrella stand and a trash bin?"

"That's an unfair extrapolation of what I just said, Dr Neuman. The truth is you are a neat person, and you don't like the idea of people putting their sad sniffles and tears in your umbrella stand. It is so déclassé. But if I were to free-associate, I'd say rain is just another kind of wetness."

"Wetness?"

Ruth had thrown her head back. "I knew you would say that. That's just what Dora said."

"Dora didn't say anything about wetness."

"No, she said that Freud would interpret anything she did sexually, like playing with her reticule."

"And what's the problem in doing that?"

"I don't know, because I don't have a reticule to play with; but I just don't do those kinds of things." Neuman takes a theatrical pause, and looks at his own desk. "Do what?"

"I knew you would say that."

Ruth seems to be an interminable case. Who else would stare inside wasted umbrella stands, or rusted sink drains, observing the way things tarnish, scab over, or erode in order to draw some parallel with her own life? She sits in the white provincial chair with her head on her long hands, looking up and out of the window, or deep inside the twisted roots of the potted plant beside her. She likes being in the office because it's womblike, she says. She says she hears sounds which are predictable and comforting as the heartbeat of a mother dog is to her litter; there is the low hum of the air coming in—seasonally heat or air conditioning—the flopping of a flag on a pole outside, right outside her peripheral view, and sometimes the disruption of the telephone ringing which is followed by click and a long pause in which the magnetic tape is recording someone's voice. In this session, she hears the click and "zip" and asks Neuman if he is recording their session. "What makes you think that?"

"I heard a click and what sounded like a tape machine."

"That's the answering machine."

"My last psychiatrist used to answer the phone when I was right there. I listened in on her conversations."

"What brought your last psychiatrist up?"

"I don't know."

"Maybe you miss her. She took a direct role in your life. She told you what to do; I don't work that way. I think that is annoying to you."

"Are you trying to get rid of me?"

"How do you arrive at that conclusion?"

"Because if you say you don't do what I want you to do I'm afraid you're going to tell me to go find somebody else who will. Maybe you know a nice woman psychiatrist."

"Why would you say a woman? Does my being a man make a difference?"

"Only when you disapprove of me."

"That's a big leap. How do you know what I'm thinking?"

"Because you're scowling."

"I'm not scowling. This is what you have deposited in me—it's a fiction, it doesn't exist."

"No, you are not a fiction. You really are underneath whatever other you I made up . . . I feel like I love you. And you will say it is only the transference, so you don't really exist except in my own mind. You're a blank. That would mean I am in love with myself. That's sickening." Neuman lifts his eyebrows. "Why sickening? That's pretty strong language."

Ruth has a look of repulsion on her face. He decides to offer an informed interpretation. "Why, then, not consider that you know nothing at all about what I'm thinking—but its necessary for you to view me in a certain way—someone cold, and judgmental, and always rejecting."

Ruth becomes very quiet, her twisted-up seating position on the chair begins to unknot itself and her legs go straight in front of her. She confides that she is thinking about her mother, dead now, for only a year and a half. She is imagining her mother eavesdropping in the session, now that she is dead—she can be anywhere and it doesn't take anything more than a layer of air to cover her up. "Everybody rejects me."

"How do you feel about the fact that you can't know what I'm thinking about you."

"I read you the way that deaf people can read lips."

"Deaf people don't read lips in that way. They don't make sounds in their minds if they've been deaf; those sounds don't exist." Ruth appears not to be disturbed by Neuman's spoiling her analogies. She tells Neuman this: "Your factual world is boring. It's like living inside Plato's cave and believing in those shadows."

"Why don't you like such facts?"

"Because I can't make them up." Neuman sways in his chair. He's discovered that he's scowling, too, and quickly erases it. He clears his throat and his professional demeanor as well. "Would you agree that your idea of my scowling comes from a negative thought that originates not in me, but in your imagination?"

"I don't think it's my imagination. But how am I ever going to know if you can't tell me anything about what you are thinking. The scales are tipped in your favor. You can interpret me, but I can't interpret you. If you looked in a mirror the way you looked at me you could see you are scowling."

Neuman puts one of his hands under the other and lays his head down letting them anchor him. He feels like a charmed child listening to a bedtime story. Ruth surveys the articles on his desk again: Melanie Klein's Object-Relations Theory, the notebook pages with his delicate handwriting. She confirms that she doesn't think she has any negative thoughts about Neuman; in fact, she reveals how much she idealizes him. When she is with Neuman, she views the world outside as less relevant, and therefore less dangerous. "I want to live inside your head where it would be safe" she says. "Why would it be safe there if you think I hold such negative ideas there about you. Isn't that a contradiction?"

"But I would then be on the same side with my own enemy. That would be safest. If you're on the same side, the enemy can't hurt you."

The hour is up. Ruth departs without saying another word and closes the door behind her. Neuman is alone with his thoughts. He takes out Ruth's thickening file, and the notes he scribbled from their first meeting to the present. He remembers how she sobbed all the way through the preliminary interview until her cheeks were striped with clumpy mascara. She talked mostly about her job crisis, her anxiety, and Charles Longchamps.

Charles was well known in French philosophy and psychoanalytic circles, although he didn't know any French. He wore a scruffy beard that probably disguised a weak, or redundant chin. He was middle aged but tried to look younger by dressing in tight jeans with his Einstein hair always mussed up. Ten years ago, Ruth was a graduate student working on her dissertation when the brilliant Longchamps took a particular interest in her topic, something that he had long wanted to publish about. Longchamps also took a special interest in Ruth, as well, and invited her to lunch. She was married to a composer, and had just had a baby girl. She and Charles sat at a wooden booth at a Southwestern restaurant and Charles drank Mexican beers while Ruth sipped water through a straw. They talked about the unconscious, and when Ruth said something smart such as the unconscious may represent the totality of the internal body, Charles got visibly excited and wrote it down on a little notebook he kept in his pocket. He perched his near-sighted glasses on a folded cloth napkin, and stared deeply into her eyes with his very mesmerizing blue eyes. That was the beginning. When it was time for Longchamps to break off the ambiguous relationship, he did so very publicly. He told Ruth he didn't want to appear to be exploiting her now that he was publishing articles that she had collaborated with him on. But Ruth would not shake off. She stuck to Longchamps like a sticky patch of hitchhiker thorns stuck on a woody camper's Bermuda shorts. She did not budge from avowing her love for the hypnotizing Longchamps.

Ruth said in her first interview with Neuman that if he were a friend of Professor Longchamps, she shouldn't see him. Neuman did, in fact, have a professional relationship with Longchamps and admired his scholarship.

At this point, ethics may have dictated Neuman persuading Ruth to find another psychiatrist. But for multiple reasons, including an instant rapport, Ruth continued to see Neuman, despite knowing that Neuman and Longchamps were distant colleagues. More important to Ruth was the humming sound of the radiator, the silver color of the wallpaper, the matriarchal chairs in the waiting room, the knock-offs of Utrillo watercolors framed on the walls. Ruth talked about Utrillo and how he suffered for his art—his Parisian cafés and women figures crowded under black umbrellas. And so they had stayed, often with Ruth painfully reliving Charles Longchamps' rejection which had crippled her self confidence.

Recalling all this, Neuman leans back in his expensive, royal-red leather desk chair, and spins his pen on the table. His supervisee, Helene, is now in love with Longchamps, which is influencing supervision. Longchamps is always that elephant in the room. Now he is two elephants. Neuman thinks that it is indeed coincidental, to find that his two clients, one a patient, one a supervisee, are somehow both entangled with the same rather coarse man but he reminds himself that Freud did not believe in such accidents. Just then, he is interrupted by a phone call. "This is Dr Neuman."

"This is the Scan warehouse. We've got your couch to deliver somewhere in the next two weeks" Dr Neuman unscrews his pen top and picks up his folded reading glasses. He's got no time opening up that day until six pm. "Can you make it at six; is that too late?"

The next morning is bleak and gray, and everyone seems sleepy, irritable, and mildly uncooperative. His appointments go slowly and monotonously: Mitchell, the obsessive-compulsive, who arrives twenty minutes early, and who rattles the doorknob seven times after he's shut it, is still locked in a mute armor Neuman can't penetrate. In the afternoon, Ruth is coming in again, this time for a make-up appointment. He had to cancel her appointment last week due to a competency hearing. He typically enjoys a day off from Ruth; her effects on him are beguiling but also disconcerting.

By afternoon, it is pounding rain, fogging up the windows in Neuman's consulting room, blurring his view of the city monument in the distance. In the waiting room, Ruth tissues off the rain from her brow and passive-aggressively chooses a corner chair which will force Neuman to crane his head around when he opens the door for her appointment, calling out, "Good Afternoon" with his arm wide, so that Ruth can saunter in with a little compulsive sniffle. Typically, Ruth follows Helene on the schedule and the two women exchange glances, and greetings, as Helene swings her knapsack around and heads out from her hour of supervision.

Today, as the session begins, Ruth's eyes rivet around the consulting room, as if she's inspecting it for dust. She refuses to talk. Neuman asks her if there is something particular about today that is causing her to be silent. Or, for that matter, is there something she's looking for that she can't find? "I didn't see your supervisee today leaving your consulting room. I guess that is because I'm here on a Wednesday, a make-up session."

"What about my supervisee?" Neuman is using his acting voice; actually it is the tone that tough cops use when they are pickling their kindness in the vinegar of interrogation. It's a false voice, one that Ruth recognizes as not the real Dr Neuman. "I like to watch her come out of your office because she whistles. Real patients, however, are quiet as sand."

"Are you a real patient?"

"Well, I'm not a make-believe patient like she is."

Neuman considers that. He comes back to the metaphor. Ruth is fond of metaphors. He clicks his tongue on his teeth, which sounds salty, to Ruth, if things can sound salty. Ruth admits she is roused by his voice; she sometimes thinks of Neuman's tongue slipping between her lips, and travelling over her teeth. She puts forth that she has fantasies she never dares to tell him about and she has also had explicit dreams. She thinks it would be corny to tell her dreams to an analyst. "It's difficult for you to hold on to me between sessions;

it seems difficult for you to keep your feelings exclusively for the intimacy of our sessions."

"No, that's not true."

"Isn't it?" Neuman says as if he were an umpire calling a strike. She holds herself out as if waiting for someone to cut off her hands and feet. "You pull back, Dr Neuman. You must think I'm too needy; you must think I'm the person that Longchamps said I was."

"Now you're in my mind, again. It is astonishing to me how much more preferable it is for you to be in my mind than yours. You have no curiosity about your own mind."

"I do have curiosity, but if we jiggle me like a cracker-jack box, there's still no prize! I am waiting for you to say I'm acceptable, even desirable. But you never say anything to make me feel better."

"Make you?"

"I know. Nothing is supposed to make me feel or do anything."

Neuman widens one eye as if he's fitting on a monocle. "But if you could recognize that you can make choices and influence how you feel, you might find yourself being surprised. You might choose to choose, and make better choices."

Ruth looks intensely at him. To Neuman, each session is like a tour of Ruth's still furnished, but empty house of the psyche. In each room lurks some collection of her ashy secrets—envelopes upon which the ink has turned a stale sienna, toys, and fox furs with the jagged teeth. There is the nursery room with the flowery paper where she recovered from a life-threatening illness, and asked the existential questions that some have the leisure to ask when their natural lives are drawing to an expected, rather than unexpected, close.

And then there is the blank room, the room Neuman would label the unconscious, the place where Ruth mysteriously contributes to her own misery; the room with the wall of mirrors that she complains always disgust her, and the sunlight that gets immediately covered with blinds. This was the room in which the psychoanalyst accepts that his patient will be infatuated, even fall in love with him; just like a mechanic accepts that his hands will always be covered in black gasoline grime that can never be scrubbed away. This is the room where Ruth sits when she wants to convince Neuman that she falls in love with every man who doesn't want her.

After Ruth leaves, Neuman returns phone calls and marks his busy calendar. He is still waiting for the couch. Two hours later,

Helene is ushered in for supervision, having changed her schedule at Neuman's request. She doesn't know why he is now insisting on seeing her at a different hours, which means she has to shift her own patient's appointments. Irritably, she consents.

In this meeting, Helene is deeply absorbed in talking about her case. As a supervisor, Neuman had discussed the power of the transference. He had cautioned Helene about the necessity of titrating gratification, providing just enough motivation for the patient to work through resistance. On occasion, Neuman even talked about Ruth's case as an instance of someone whose desire for the analyst's self-disclosure would become insatiable. Now he finds his confidences to Helene about Ruth to be reckless.

Suddenly, and uncharacteristically, Neuman breaks in on Helene's chattering, and asks "How long have you been seeing Charles Longchamps?" Helene sits back in her chair, suddenly imperious, as if she's just won a battle. "About three months. He's divorced, you know." Helene resonates self-confidence. In contrast, Ruth's presence in Longchamp's life had been like a giant gnat bite. She continues, "We're moving in together. He's been really stuck with his first wife, and then—well, you know—the woman who almost cost him his reputation, a while back. God knows he deserves a good relationship."

Helene is overly cheerful, and oddly awkward today. They return to discussing her case, and Neuman makes recommendations. At the end of her appointment, she raises herself robotically from the chair, but then drops her unzipped knapsack, so that some of the notebooks and papers slide out. She retrieves them, with her face hot. "There, I got them all. I'm so sorry, Dr Neuman, I've been all thumbs lately." She seems miserable and happy at the same time. Longchamps seems to have that enigmatic effect on women. Neuman wonders if he isn't really gay. As Helene moves toward the door, she suddenly halts and turns around to Neuman who is just stretching his back and rotating the cups of his shoulders. "I know there's a little conflict here . . ."

"How shall we handle it?"

"I don't know, what do you think, Dr Neuman?"

"I should ask you the same question."

"Well, Charles tells me he has in every, every circumstance refused to speak to your patient. But she still pursues him so masochistically; she begs him all the time. We are all so disappointed for her sake!"

"All?"

"Aren't you?"

"You don't really expect me to answer your question, do you?" Helene stabs her toe in the carpet. She shakes her head, and opens the door to the outer room, half-expecting to see Ruth, who is not there. Helene looks at the vacant chair as if it is suddenly tragic.

A week later, Ruth is back in the consulting room, obsessed with death. The more she talks about death, the more Neuman is aware of how tenaciously she is trying to break through the boundaries, and on through Neuman's professional neutrality. She wants him to respond in a way that will make her feel like she really exists. But Neuman is exceptionally skilled at keeping his attention evenly dispersed. Every good poker player knows how to do that. "I see I'm boring you."

"You can't see anything," he rejoins, "But it's clear you would rather be in my mind, than your mind . . . you are not curious about the meaning of why you see things a particular way."

"But I do see. And you telling me that I am just seeing what's invisible, what's been sketched out of my own mind, not yours."

"It's just your imagination."

"No, it's in your imagination that I can't see what's in yours." Neuman is respectfully silent. She continues.

"I need something more for sleep. I keep thinking that if I sleep, I won't wake up again, so I can't sleep."

"That must serve a purpose."

"Like thinking that I love you more than I love myself serves the purpose of my not having to think about my life, and my death. I have survived neither one of them." Neuman's fingers scratch at his forehead. "To what do you attribute that?"

"Charles. I attribute it all to Charles. I am sitting in this chair just like that woman just before me, the one who always comes out of here smiling, with the knapsack over her shoulder. She reminds me of Happy, one of the dwarves in *Snow White*. And she is probably talking about somebody just like Charles, and you are probably telling her that it's all in her imagination, too. And she probably even knows what happened to me with Charles, and how bad I am."

Neuman is startled; he watches the minute hand of the clock. It is staggering like a drunk. He examines Ruth's expression, again. She is so credible; so genuinely sculpted. For the first time in a long time,

Neuman's assessment of Ruth's clinical depression is turning to pity, the one thing he knows he can't give her, even as a substitute for himself. Ruth turns her head to the clock. He watches her. "Have you ended the session?"

"Why do you always say that I do that?"

"So that I can't end the session. You won't give up that power. And in that way you take power for yourself."

The hour is up, again, and neither one have them have moved. The phone is ringing, probably Joy, or the movers with the new couch. Ruth had stood up as she always does. She is wearing her daughter's blue jeans and a lacy negligee shirt that teenage girls wear. Neuman always rises with the same Victorian bow. He can't understand why Charles Longchamps would mean anything at all to Ruth. As the door nervously closes behind her, he can hear her charm bracelet jingling as if she is just smoothing her hair. He allows himself a fantasy. He smells Ruth's honeysuckle perfume. The phone rings. It is the movers downstairs. They will have to tip the couch at a severe angle to push it through. They are coming up the padded elevator to the third floor. He tells them to wait a few minutes so he can help. "Sure"

"I'll come out and meet you in the hall."

"Okey-Dokey"

Together, they clumsily move the couch into the office now darkened with late afternoon; darkness like a pen stirred in an inkpot. They settle it with a thud next to the old shorter divan with the pillow at the bottom. Twenty-eight years of sin and redemption, twenty-eight years like a marriage that carries on out of duty, not choice.

The movers leave him with the new couch in its fresh coat of bubble wrap. Neuman thinks of his six foot three patient arriving at dawn with his 7/11 cup of coffee with the lid still on, and his moustache damp. For a moment, Neuman just looks at the new couch, the invisible looms of the original design and glowing colors that went into it. He thinks of the twin silk worms that worked to weave it together and apart. He thinks of Charles and Helene and what an unlikely couple they are; perhaps drawn together by their jealous rivalry—each seeking his attention—with Ruth being the obstacle. Then he thinks of Ruth riding in the crowded subway, and tries to free-associate. He then has an image of his mother smoking a Lucky cigarette on the porch.

She is waving to him at a distance, and suddenly her face turns into Joy's, which melts into Ruth's, who is smiling at the sun. He realizes he will have to return the call to Charles, that the power has now shifted just as Ruth predicted. He sits down on the plastic; he lies down.

Ancient History

Phil Leask

What could she say? How could she say it? The woman sat opposite her with her back to the window, waiting for her to speak. Some things are too awful for anyone to hear, she thought. And yet this woman wanted to hear them. Why? What good would it do? Wasn't it all too long ago?

The leaves on the silver birch shivered. One or two were yellow. Soon it would be autumn. She closed her eyes and for a moment was back there, back then, walking beneath the trees by the river. They would walk all the way to the North Sea, they used to say. On a good day, even now, she believed she could still walk for ever. She opened her eyes. This was not a good day.

She should speak. The woman was waiting. Patiently. Too patiently. Patience was irritating. Or worse, patience was an attack, pity dressed up as compassion. That much she knew without coming here. Why had she come? Because she had said she would, because they had arranged it, she and the woman, this week to get started and after that the next week and then the week after that and on and on and on, as long as she wanted until she felt it was finished. She reached for the glass of water the woman had left for her, along with a box of tissues. Was weeping obligatory she wondered.

On the wall there was a clock they could both see. Soon it would be too late, her time would be up before she knew why she was here. "Mein Mann . . ." she started to say, then remembered this was not the woman's language. "My husband . . . He died." The woman nodded, as if in agreement. "It was not my fault," she went on.

It wasn't clear whether the woman believed her. Did it matter? If she could find a way to say what she felt she had to say, did it matter what was true or what was false or what anyone else believed, as long as the story was out there: told, let go of, given up? She would tell the woman and the woman would listen because she was paid to. Then it was up to her what she made of it. She would have the money and the story and she—Regina—would be finished with it.

The woman smiled benevolently. Regina sighed. "It was before your time," she said. She felt old and dispirited. When she ran her fingers through her hair she could feel how brittle and lifeless it had become. Once it had been alight, blazing up like a forest fire. It had grown back darker and lusher than before like fresh growth on a well-watered hillside. How many years ago was that? Too long to think about. She was ancient now. Too old for it to matter any more. Her story was ancient history.

"Tell me anyway,' the woman said, gently enough.

"We lived in Hamburg, my husband and I. We were bombed, on and off. People died, but not so many. And then in 1943—in the summer—you set out to kill us all." She tried to smile, excusing the woman; it was not her fault, after all. "You cannot imagine what it was like. No one who was not there can understand how it felt . . ." She looked at the woman but the woman said nothing.

Regina sighed again. That was not where she had meant to start. The lamp in the corner grew brighter as the light faded outside. Dusk. She did not want to see it. "Could you close the curtains?" she asked the woman. The woman hesitated. She wants to ask me why and what it signifies, Regina thought and sat there, waiting. The woman gave what might have been a smile and turned to the windows and looked out for a moment—a moment too long, Regina thought— before closing the curtains and sitting down again, ready for her to go on.

"Thank you," Regina said. No one else would see her now. Or hear what she might say. "I like to think we were happy once." She stopped, reminding herself to breathe, to restore some life to her thin, old voice. "Before the bombing, we lived above a bar. I still dream about it now. I see us sleeping with the windows open, I feel the wind blowing up the river, rattling the shutters. In the morning, in my dream, we wake up slowly and lie there listening to the clattering of chairs and tables being moved on to the pavement, and people talking and laughing. Just talking and laughing. In the distance we hear ships full of passengers sailing to America." She tried to smile, to show it didn't matter, but could not. It had not been like that. Ever.

Not in real life. Growing up had meant being among men in uniform with their dogs and guns and the sounds of shouting and shooting and children crying and later of sirens that sent them down to the cellar where they huddled, waiting for the bombs to fall.

"Before the war," she went on, "he was an engineer in a chemical works. There was an explosion—a fire—the fumes burned his lungs. Afterwards, they wouldn't take him in the army. So we were together during the war."

That must have been a relief, for both of you, she thought the woman would say, but the woman still said nothing. "It was terrible," Regina admitted for the first time, even to herself. "We were so young. What did we know about anything? I even tried to forget there was a war on. I wanted to enjoy myself. I wanted to go dancing. He couldn't, or wouldn't. I wanted to be with other men, I wanted a life of my own . . . Away from him," she was shocked to hear herself say.

"Dancing?" the woman said, and there was surprise in her voice.

"Dancing was meant to keep us happy. It was our duty to the Führer to be happy. Or at least cheerful." She tried to smile, as if apologising for her levity. "Sometimes we were happy, despite everything. Mostly the bombs were somewhere else and not so dangerous. In his chemical works my husband concocted poisons that he said would change the world. To me he was just a boy playing in the school laboratory. In the evening he started to write. His first story was about the bombs falling and the people in the cellars laughing and sometimes growing angry. People were cruel, he said. He put the story away in a drawer. For after the war, when people would want to read about what it had been like and what we had endured. And then he wrote others and he put them in the drawer too. And a diary."

She looked at the curtains. The lamp picked out sombre tones—dark reds, browns, purples—and here and there a glint of light, of unexpected brightness. Outside, beyond the curtains, it was growing dark. She was pleased she could not see it.

"Were you working as well?" the woman asked, as if it mattered. Regina nodded. "I made lists . . . Lists of supplies that were needed for the U-boats. Before they went back to sea." The woman looked uncomfortable. She probably hated her for what she was saying. As if Regina was to blame.

"Your husband . . ." the woman prompted. "Kurt . . . 'Chemische Kurt', Chemical Kurt, they used to call him," Regina said and almost giggled, it sounded so strange now, something from a bygone era. "No, it's not what you're thinking," she added.

Still the woman looked uneasy. She crossed her legs then uncrossed them again. What did she want? Children's stories with happy endings? Where had she been all these years? "When the real bombing came, the one that started the firestorm—did you know your leaders called it "Sodom and Gomorrah"?—we knew the cellar wouldn't protect us. We wrapped ourselves in wet blankets and ran through the fire to the bunker. By the time we got there our blankets were smouldering and our arms and heads were burnt." She touched her hair, remembering. "We stayed there for three days. There was not enough water to drink and hardly enough air to breathe. When we came out our city had gone . . . You can't imagine what it was like. Street after street had disappeared. Where our apartment had been, the whole block had gone. Our neighbours were in the cellar underneath it all. We didn't know what to do. There was nowhere else to go. We sat on top of the pile of rubble that we thought was our rubble and called it home. Smoke drifted over us. Rats ran around our feet. That was how it was. And after all the noise, there was silence. Until the bombers came again."

Always the bombing, Regina thought. However she tried to escape from it, it was always there, waiting for her, this endlessly shifting pile of rubble, this chaos of images and feelings, fragments of thoughts that could not cohere and, somewhere down in there, things she only half sensed, that must be memories. She had never talked about it before. Kurt, on the other hand, could do nothing else. He had written about it incessantly, story after story that no one could bring themselves to read. They had to read them, he would say. They had to want to read them. They never did, but still he kept on writing them. "I couldn't bear it," she said.

She had wanted to go dancing. With the English officers. He wouldn't let her. It wasn't right, he said; they had to remember. Remember what? she would ask him. Nothing mattered but the years still to come: her life, waiting to be lived. He had suffocated her. Always the war, always the bombing, the ruins, death, all he could ever talk about. She could not bear it. "I couldn't bear it," she said.

And then, since she could not stop now, "One night when he was having trouble breathing . . ." The woman nodded, encouraging her. ". . . I put a pillow over his head . . . And held it there until I knew that he was dead." The woman tried not to look shocked. Or perhaps was not shocked. "Do you worry that he suffered?" she asked. Regina shook her head. "No, he didn't suffer. He was grateful." In the silence, she could hear rain falling and car tyres squelching on the wet street outside.

"Then there was the diary," Regina began. The woman nodded and glanced sideways at the clock.

"Perhaps we'll talk about that next time," she said.

Terra Incognita

Peter Heinl

Even a century after Sigmund Freud's discovery of the unconscious mind, the perception and diagnosis of unconscious
phenomena remains a challenge to clinicians and laymen
alike. Venturing into the unconscious has occupied my thinking for
many years and has never ceased to fascinate me. I therefore want
to describe an approach that I developed over twenty-five years,
which is designed to shed light on unconscious phenomena. I hope
that my account may inspire the reader to ask questions, and stir a
sense of curiosity about the fact that each individual we meet contains
a world of his own and, indeed, a largely unknown world. I would
like to describe a case that I carried out some years ago in which I
explored an early experience of trauma. In order to explain to you
the complexity of the process I shall make explicit reference to what
took place within my own mind.

One of my professional heroes—if I may put it that way—is not
a mental health professional at all but the famous astronomer
Johannes Kepler. He produced magnificent insights into the laws
governing planetary movements. He changed the way we look at
the world. Despite a miserable life his inner spirit was enlightened
and driven by an immense desire to observe and to understand the
mystery of phenomena surrounding us. One of his quotations has
become an inspiration for the way I look at the terra incognita of
unconscious early trauma. In a letter written in December 1610 he
wrote, "My eyesight is bad. I am, I fear, no Columbus of the heavens,
but a modest stay-at-home, an armchair dreamer. The phenomena
with which I am already familiar are sufficiently strange and
wonderful. If the new stargazers discover novel facts which will help
to explain the true causes of things, fair enough; but it seems to me

that the real answers to the cosmic mystery are to be found not in the sky, but in that other, infinitely smaller though no less mysterious firmament contained within the skull. In a word, my dear friend, I am old-fashioned." I hope my account will provide some evidence for Kepler's breathtakingly modern view of the immense world contained inside the skull.

A few years ago I conducted a five day seminar designed to explore these early experiences. A group of ten professionals attended. I started the seminar by introducing myself. Then the participants introduced themselves, giving their name, professional background and motivation for participating. When it came to Dr A there was nothing conspicuous in the manner in which she spoke. Her brief introduction was clear, concise, and to the point. I should emphasize that she made no reference to her early personal or family background. I should also mention that nothing in her demeanor gave me any reason to ask additional questions. With hindsight she may have appeared slightly anxious, but this would not have seemed strange considering the circumstances.

After Dr A's introduction I should normally have asked the next participant to proceed but, rather than taking the initiative, I seemed to slip into a state of mind where I remained sitting silently in my chair—without knowing why I remained so indolent or what my mind was preoccupied with. I was aware that my demeanour was not quite in line with what could be expected of a leader in charge of a seminar, but such was my frame of mind that this did not perturb me; nor did it worry me that I still did not have any insights. Rather —however unreasonable this may seem—a confidence suffused my mind and assured me that a deeper understanding would eventually emerge although there was no indication when this might be.

Suddenly something even stranger happened. Whilst still sitting silently on my chair I experienced a sense that my hands were assuming some kind of autonomous control. Without any hesitation or explanation, my hands swiftly opened my work box, which is filled with a curious collection of objects, and reached for a little pink koala bear from within it.

I presume anyone watching what I was doing must have started to wonder what was happening to me. It is true that I wondered myself. Without reflecting on the next step in a rational way, my right hand grasped the pink koala bear and threw it in an elegant curve across the seminar room towards Dr A, who found herself at the receiving end of my unusual intervention. I should not have been surprised had she responded with indignation but, strangely enough, she caught the flying pink koala bear with ease. Without saying anything she looked at it for a while. Then she got up from her chair and placed it on the carpet in the middle of the seminar room. I watched in silence. Had I been asked at this stage whether I could give an explanation for the meaning of this strange, even surreal sequence of events, I would not have been able to do so. All that occurred to me now, was to get up from my chair and place a sheet of white paper under the pink koala bear so that it would contrast more sharply against the colourful patterns of the carpet.

Only when bending down to do so did I register, for the first time, a change in the curious sense of detachment that had taken hold of me. I also noticed that the head of the pink koala bear had been turned backwards by some 180 degrees. Surely enough this may have been considered as an entirely irrelevant detail. I would, of course, have no problems in adopting such a view. Nevertheless, what I observed next was a rush of pity within myself for the little koala with its twisted head and then—suddenly, whilst standing up again—I noticed a painful sensation in my neck. Although it was immediately clear to me that this was not the result of a real physical pain I mentioned it to Dr A and invited her to turn the head of the koala bear back to its proper position.

I could only respect her cool response when she said that there was nothing to worry about the twisted head of the koala bear. After all, this was only a little bear. But her reply did nothing to lessen my worries about the twisted head. Again, and indeed twice more, I urged her to correct the position of the koala bear's little head. But she simply stuck smilingly to her decision not to do anything about its imagined plight. To make my position even more tenuous, she received support from another seminar participant. Smartly discovering a hole in my zoological knowledge he pointed out that koala bears may, indeed, rotate their heads back quite far.

It slowly dawned on me that whatever I was doing, without knowing why I was doing it, had not produced any brilliant success. To the contrary, whatever had occupied and guided my mind had started from nowhere and had led to nowhere. Still finding it difficult to accept this state of affairs I sat looking out of the window for some moments. However, the sequence of events made it perfectly clear to me that there was only one way to extricate myself from this situation and this was to put the pink koala bear back inside the box. Yet even now my mind, or at least fragments of my mind, still seemed to drift in a world governed by different laws, and I realised to my surprise that nothing had dented my confidence that a meaning for my behaviour would eventually emerge. In fact, my confidence had now grown into virtual certainty. I believed that the seemingly surreal flight of the pink koala bear was not the product of pure phantasy but a mysterious reflection of Dr A's true life experiences. Proof remained all that was missing.

Maybe a stubborn refusal to concede defeat in the face of overwhelming evidence prevailed. Maybe my mind was split in two, as if the connecting bridges between the left and right hemispheres were blocked. Had someone asked me at this stage whether there was any hidden meaning to the surreal sequence of events I would have said yes, without hesitation. However, at this point I needed to be pragmatic, and I therefore asked the seminar participants to continue with their introductions. Over the next hour or so the episode with the pink koala bear faded into the background like so many inexplicable occurrences in life. Then, when I was just about to announce the break for lunch, I saw Dr A raising her hand as if she wanted to say something. I noticed that she looked agitated and restless and as I realized immediately that there was something urgent on her mind, I allowed her to speak. She said that something important had come back to her mind—that the surreal interlude with the pink koala bear had reminded her that she herself had suffered from a kind of twisted head. At the age of two she had accidentally fallen from a balcony and fractured the atlas bone—the uppermost part of her spine; this resulted in a brief loss of consciousness. This serious condition had a substantial mortality rate. She had required hospital admission and inpatient treatment that meant being stuck inside an upper body-plaster for more than a month. A more detailed analysis in the following session revealed the full dimension of the traumatic accident. The atlas fracture healed within several weeks without any lasting movement restriction affecting her head, but the circumstances surrounding the medical treatment had been highly traumatic. There had been a lack of emotional care, loneliness and isolation. When she had returned home her family had appeared to be more concerned about the effect of their child's accident on themselves, and had not understood her need for psychological care.

In the weeks following the seminar Dr A became aware that she had always consoled the other family members. This had made it impossible to mourn her misery. Suppressing her wish to cry had become second nature. But due to the seminar experience she was now able to overcome this problem. Soon after the seminar she had a dream in which, for the first time, she experienced her body as a whole organism. This dream made her aware that the lengthy immobilization of her head and shoulders in plaster had suppressed the formation of a whole-body image. This psychological side effect of the treatment had produced what might be described as a de-coupling of the head from the body. At last this was becoming reversed.

Having been trained in a wide range of psychiatric, psychological and family therapy approaches, concepts and principles, and psychological research methods, it was also obvious to me that I would not have been able to detect such trauma by relying on a conventional or conscious approach to information gathering. At the same time I did not have a conceptual framework that would allow me to explain the nature of the phenomena and the processes that occurred in the course of the pink koala bear episode. But this did not deter me. It became evident that an intuitive approach was capable of assessing early and often unconscious trauma with surprising speed and accuracy, and carried considerable therapeutic potential for the accurate perception and diagnosis of unrecognized, unresolved and unmitigated early traumas—a prerequisite for their resolution. By the mid 1980s, this spontaneous and seemingly bizarre approach had enabled me to detect the unconscious pain caused by the losses, separations, abuses, and family problems of many patients. It has been crucial in detecting the lasting damage caused by childhood experiences of war, which has been virtually overlooked in post-war Germany. It has been central in detecting unconscious Holocaust trauma.

A whole spectrum of technologies is available for diagnosis in medicine by visualizing internal body structures but there is not a clear looking-glass available to assist a psychotherapist to see into the mind and history of an individual who has no conscious knowledge of what has traumatized her in infancy. This is the challenge and having developed an approach to enter the unconscious space, I became eager in my pursuit of an explanation.

I have always resisted attempts to link the intuitive approach to magical powers. I believe that the dynamics underpinning this approach are rooted in brain processes. Just as I did not believe that my heartbeat was following different laws from that of any other human being, neither did I believe my brain was functioning in fundamentally different ways. If there was a difference, this might be due to an inclination for observation and perception, to experience and to wait in order to allow ideas to ripen, rather than to reject impatiently unfinished contemplations on the basis of seemingly rational judgments.

Initially I also found it virtually impossible to make statements on the nature of the processes taking place in my mind in the course of such explorative work except to say that they appeared to be of an intuitive nature. Insights that emerged in such unexpected ways so puzzled me that I initially felt as though they had been implanted into my mind. This was, of course, an unlikely explanation but it reflected my perception of the marked difference between insights that appeared without any conscious effort, seemingly produced by themselves, and those that were the result of a painstaking process of rational thought. I gradually realized that such intuitive processes were, in fact, originating within myself and that they could be seen as self-organizing processes.

Although this may seem a rather uninspiring conclusion it took me some time to truly accept this view, as it undermined the supremacy of logical thought. Yet the reality and intensity of such intuitive processes have left me in no doubt of their power and sophistication. They are perfectly capable of assimilating complex information transmitted by another person, of discriminating communicative patterns relating to past experiences, synthesizing such information and then producing diagnostic insights that pinpoint the nature of an early trauma. Finally, 'intuitive diagnostics' appeared the appropriate term to describe this vital instrument for venturing into the cosmos of the unconscious space.

Avoiding the Toads

Annie Macdonald

I think I will always remember the client I was unable to help. One reason I will remember her is that, strangely enough, I forgot her completely after her first session—erased her from my memory. So that when I checked my appointments diary at the beginning of the week as I habitually do, I saw a name that I didn't recognise at all. 'Melanie. Tuesday 9am' was written in my handwriting, but as I sat there on Monday morning with a cup of coffee, feeling perfectly awake and alert, I had no idea who Melanie was, what she looked like, what her problems were, or how she had come to me.

She must have come for the first visit last week when I was indeed quite busy, but I had never forgotten a new client so totally before. What was going on with me? Well, I would soon find out when I read the page of notes waiting in my top drawer. I always made notes during the first session: background, family details, phrases or words from the client describing their situation, their own feelings, why they had come, what they wanted from therapy. I made notes every time and had done for years. I had a careful system for keeping the pages in the top desk drawer until the third or fourth session when I filed them alphabetically in a separate cardboard folder for each client. I opened the drawer and pulled out the six pieces of paper that were in there, feeling curious and only slightly alarmed at my amnesia. My diary confirmed that 'Melanie' had come to see me last Tuesday at 9am. A telephone number was written next to her name. But the six pages in the top drawer related to three other new clients. I searched the filing cabinet, just in case, feeling distinctly uneasy. Nothing. It seemed I had seen a female—apparently a female—last Tuesday morning and had not only forgotten everything about her but had also failed to write down even a single sentence.

As I sat there puzzling, the postman arrived with a travel magazine and some kitchenware catalogues. I started reading about a jazz cruise in the Caribbean in order to distract myself from troubling recollections of a conversation with a much older colleague who said she was going to have to start taking less clients because her memory was beginning to let her down. Could that already be happening to me? I looked at pictures of some cast-iron saucepans in one of the catalogues, deciding that the dark green would look rather good in my kitchen, but there were too many of them in the set and really my old pans were still serviceable. There was nothing I could do about Melanie until tomorrow morning, so I would just have to trust that whatever she had talked about for an hour last week would come back to me when I saw her again. But still I was puzzled by the absence of notes.

By seven o'clock that Monday evening I had seen four clients: one in the morning, two in the afternoon and the last one at six. I felt I had been as alert and focused as I usually was. In one case we had made quite a breakthrough. No sign of any impending mental deterioration there.

I felt quite good as Tuesday dawned, as I went for my early morning walk in the park and finished a light breakfast. At nine o'clock the doorbell rang. Melanie. Even in the split second of the door opening I still had no visual or mental image of the person coming to see me. The worrying thought flickered through my mind that maybe I still wouldn't recall meeting her after she had come in. But as soon as I saw her, her story fell into place. Of course. She hadn't been in London long, had come from Australia, worked in a University library and shared a flat but felt shy and lonely and couldn't seem to make friends. Quite unremarkable. And so was she. Pleasant looking, dressed in a pleated skirt, a brown polo-neck sweater, a short cream trench coat and well polished brown leather shoes. Nicely cut dark hair, slightly curly, and a little make up.

While part of me was listening to her telling of the events of her week, another part was still trying, unsuccessfully, to work out why I had blanked her so completely. "... I had to leave that flat," she was saying. "So now I'm flat-hunting. I just hope I find people to share with who don't treat me like that. I couldn't bear to stay there another minute. I left all my things." I seemed to have missed something here. "Tell me what else they did," I asked carefully. "Well, apart from talking about me like that behind my back, there was the time they were mocking me over my dog getting run over. That was bad. I was up in my room feeling homesick and just looking at some photos of my childhood I keep locked in my trunk. Well I have my collection of pressed flowers at the bottom and they're fragile. I like to keep my things private."

"Of course," I said.

"I was looking particularly at one photo of me standing next to my dog's grave. Then I put the album back in the trunk. I went down to the kitchen for a cup of cocoa. The others were all in there laughing and I heard one girl saying 'she shouldn't have thrown the ball so hard, then Rory wouldn't have been run over. That was a stupid thing to do.' And they were all agreeing. They even knew my dog's name. There were lots of things like that. I found them talking about the birthday party I'd had when I was seven. 'That conjuror with the moustache wasn't any good,' someone said, 'and how ridiculous having a birthday cake shaped like a musical instrument.' In fact, my cake was shaped like a guitar and I thought it was great. They had no right to make fun of me like that."

"Melanie, let me get something straight," I said. "Did these flatmates know you as a child, back in Australia?"

"Oh no. They're all from England. I'd only been living with them for a couple of weeks. I didn't even have a photo of that birthday party, but they found out all about it and were talking about me every night."

"I see," I lied. "That must have been difficult for you . . ."

"It was impossible. That's why I couldn't stay."

I nodded, fixing a sympathetic expression on my face to cover the fact that I was floundering here. I'd never had a case like this. To benefit from psychotherapy a client needs to be to some extent 'psychologically minded', able at least to think about their problem. But here I felt I was in the presence of a young woman who was convinced of the reality of what was sounding increasingly like paranoid delusions and I didn't know what to do or say next. So I decided simply to listen.

Melanie had a lot to tell me. As well as her flat, she was leaving her job. The work was all right, she said, and one of her colleagues, Judy, had initially befriended her. But last week she found out what had really been going on. She'd been out shopping at the weekend, tempted by some pale green silk pyjamas and matching French knickers. She had bought them and they were still in their wrapping paper in her room when she went into work on Monday. There she found her colleagues talking and laughing together about some woman who foolishly thought she'd be elegant if she bought herself green silk underwear.

"It was obvious who they were talking about," she said, looking at me for affirmation. I just sat, hands folded, and looked at her. "I wonder," I ventured, "Why all these people were talking about you in this way?"

With anyone else I would have suggested we unravel the logic and explore the hidden feelings behind these apparent criticisms, but I felt that Melanie was not going to be able to join me in questioning her own story and may react to my probing as yet more criticism. She would then follow her pattern and walk out. Yet she obviously needed to tell someone about it and had chosen me. "Good question," she replied. "I wonder too. What do you think?" I stalled, asking "What do you think they have in common?"

"Just this one thing: that they want to upset and humiliate me. But there are more of them. Yesterday, after I'd heard them talking about the green underwear, Judy came and asked me if I'd like to join her for lunch in a pub. She hadn't been in the room while they were talking earlier and she sounded friendly, so I said yes. I thought she might turn out to be my friend after all. We went to a pub I'd never been to a few streets away . . ." She paused as a bell rang but it wasn't my bell and she relaxed again.

"The pub was quite crowded but we found seats at the end of a table. Judy went up to the bar to order, and then I heard that the people at the table were gossiping about someone—I couldn't believe my ears. They were saying, 'Just imagine, she keeps a whole lot of silly books of pressed flowers at the bottom of her trunk.' I couldn't stay in that pub. I just ran out. I didn't care that Judy had ordered lunch for me. She'd brought me there to be laughed at. She was in it with them too. So when I got back to the library I handed in my notice. And I'm not going back." There was a pause and I looked at her. She seemed composed and sounded quiet and matter-of-fact as she outlined her predicament. "And I'm not going back to Australia," she added, calmly and firmly.

"Would you like to tell me why?"

"The toads," she replied. "Do you know about the toads—the Queensland toads? They've got as far south as Brisbane. They'll reach Sydney in no time. Well, I won't be there. I'd rather be in London. Even if people are mean to me here, at least I shall be avoiding the toads."

I gazed at her, by now slightly stunned. What could I do with this young woman? She needed help: she was ill. My first thought was to refer her on for psychiatric assessment, but how could I suggest it? She would certainly see that as persecutory. At least I realised now why I hadn't made any notes during that first session: if she'd seen me writing things down about her that would have surely made me part of the great conspiracy too.

And although she had appeared unremarkable at first, I must have picked up the paranoia without being consciously aware of it. "OK Melanie," I said, "Let me get this straight: you haven't a job, you've given up your flat, so where are you sleeping?"

"I'm staying in the Youth Hostel. But in fact I'm not actually sleeping. I can't seem to sleep."

"Ah . . . you're not sleeping. You must be feeling worn out." At last I could see a glimmer of light.

"That's true. I don't feel too good."

I'd got my cue. "Well, it might be an idea if you asked your doctor for something to help you sleep. You don't want to get ill, and winter's coming. You could tell your doctor about the stress you've been under and the reasons for it. Doctors, as well as therapists, have a strict code of confidentiality, you know." She looked at me blankly. "I haven't got a doctor," she said. "Oh!" The expression on my face betrayed the shock and concern this information produced. It was certainly not a professionally detached response. My eyebrows had shot up and I must have looked and sounded as dismayed as I felt. "Well, um, it's usual to register with a doctor when you move to a new place, so maybe you should." I said lamely, though what I really wanted to say was, "You need a doctor and a referral to a psychiatrist, so get one now."

"I see," she said, looking thoughtful. "But I'd really like to come back and see you. Next Tuesday, if that's all right."

Melanie had her diary out, waiting for an answer. A great weariness came over me. I found myself, in her presence, almost unable to judge or to think. It was as if she was showing me what it was like to be inside her head. It must be a lonely place in there, I mused, as London was for her now: no friends, no family, just the sense of people letting her down and ganging up on her everywhere. She wanted to come back and although I hadn't helped her, I hadn't let her down yet. Also, I reflected, I had a meeting with my supervisor between now and then. Perhaps together he and I would be able to work out some ways in which I could be more effective with her. We made the appointment for the next Tuesday and she left, looking perfectly cheerful and with a grateful smile. I had never felt so useless. It wasn't a comfortable feeling.

The next Monday morning as I was preparing to go to my supervision, the phone rang. It was Melanie. She sounded different, quite light and upbeat. "I'm sorry but I won't be able to come to see you tomorrow. I'm in St Mark's hospital, the psychiatric wing. My doctor got me in. They're looking after me here. I think I'll be staying for a few weeks."

"Oh, good." I breathed relief. "Do you like it there, Melanie?"

"Oh yes, it's lovely, much better than the Youth Hostel—and the food's OK too. Thank you very much for all your help. I wouldn't have made it without you."

After I had told the whole story to my supervisor I said, "But what I can't understand is how exactly did I help her?" My supervisor sometimes had subtle ways of communicating. He just looked at me and then he raised his eyebrows. "That's what you did, that's how you helped her. Simple," he said.

Criss-Cross

Anna Fodorova

She read somewhere that a psychotherapy session is when two anxious individuals meet in a room, the therapist hopefully being the less frightened of the two. Right now this seems a sensible concept to hold on to. Gael looks around Norma Roman's office, compares her watch with the hospital clock on the wall: twenty minutes to go. There is a note on the desk from Norma Roman: 'Gael is welcome to use the room but not to interfere with the window.' The window sits too high to reach. A potted plant with shrivelled leaves occupies the filing cabinet underneath. She sprinkles it with mineral water. Behind her, computers are being switched off, doors locked. Voices call "see you tomorrow", feet hurry. By the time she inspects a small grey box on the wall the outside sounds have died off. It dawns on her that this must be the panic button.

She glances again over the form in which Mr Geoff Edge pleads to be seen after hours; were he to ask for time off work, he argues, his job could be in jeopardy. Evidence of a paranoid-schizoid position? She stops herself: too late to start revising theory right now. Why did she choose this man from the pile of referral files passed on to her by Dr Chang? Perhaps it was his name, it somehow matched hers: Geoff Edge—Gael May. There were one or two other things with a familiar ring to them.

Somewhere the clock strikes half past five. And indeed, she hears footsteps. She darts back to her chair, the one with the better view of the clock. Once there, she adopts an expression she had tried out beforehand: not too soft, not too tough. Serene. The steps recede; there is the whoosh of the lift. Only now she fully takes in that she will be completely alone here with her new patient—the first one ever.

She checks the waiting room but there is no one there, only magazines scattered on empty seats. How different this place looks when everyone is gone. Suddenly she is aware of noises she had not noticed before: the hum of the air conditioning, the crackle of the strip lights, and then something else—a tap, forlorn and persistent: tap, tap . . . tap, tap. At the far end of the corridor she makes out a small figure, his head in a helmet, the rest concealed in a leather jacket, rolled up jeans. The boy, for she is convinced that it is a child who has wandered in by mistake, seems to be tapping on an office door with his forehead. "Excuse me," she calls, "Are you looking for someone?" The apparition slowly turns to reveal a middle-aged face framed by oversized glasses: narrow beaky nose, hollow cheeks, grey stubble.

"I'm looking for the Ho-no-ra-ry Therapist," the man announces. To her surprise, standing next to him, Geoff Edge turns out to be the same height as her. He double-checks the name on the office door then, each step accompanied by a squeak from his old trainers, heads straight for the chair she has allocated to herself. There he unzips his leather jacket and places it on the floor, the helmet beside it. His hair sticks to his scalp in greasy streaks, a mixture of sweat and engine oil emanates from his fleece. Everything on him, including his specs, looks as if on a loan from someone larger. "I'm the department's senior audiovisual technician," is Geoff Edge's opening gambit. "Sorry, not quite accurate," he quickly rectifies, keen for her to know that his true expertise lies in old time film cameras, film splicers, and picture synchronisers. She endures the entire inventory before managing to ask about the rest of his life. She is told that after work Geoff does the shopping in the local supermarket—at times they stock tuna in brine, at others tuna in sunflower oil—and since he cannot carry as much as most he needs to make three, four trips and so—

"What about your spouse?" she interrupts him. "Crime fiction writer of e-nor-mous potential," he states simply. Then, searching for the most precise, most judicious words, Geoff Edge confides in Gael that as his wife requires maximum time on her laptop he offered to vacate their bedroom. His wife's teenage son, on the other hand, needs the 24/7 company of his mates instead of looking for a job. Her elderly father, who inhabits their basement, only foul-mouths Geoff. On the few occasions Gael succeeds in interrupting his tirade Geoff Edge politely waits while she has her say, then carries on as if she hadn't spoken. He never brings up his parents' death in his teens—the boating accident Gael read about on the form. When she asks about his reason for wanting therapy he shoots her a look of disbelief. "To be of greater use to all. Isn't that clear?"

Before they part he lets Gael wait through his slow-motion zipping-up ceremony, the headgear replacement. By the door his hand emerges from his sleeve to find hers. Instinctively she pulls back and then is embarrassed by her refusal. She allows some minutes for him to reach the lift, and to steady the sudden tremor in her knees. She turns the lights off and locks the room. After groping for the light switch in the secretaries' office she drops the key in Norma Roman's pigeonhole, as instructed. At the end of the corridor she has a choice of lifts. But first she must use the toilet. How odd it would be, it occurs to her then, if she were to open the door to find Geoff Edge waiting for her there.

He stays with her for the whole week. He is in her mind while she shops. While watching the news she remembers his thinness. Choked by a surge of pity she even thinks of him while letting in her cat. In bed she wonders if Geoff Edge and his wife ever have sex.

At supervision Dr Chang yawns listening to her notes: film kit and erratically stocked supermarket shelves hold no interest for him. It is what Gael felt during the session that he wants to know about. What was her counter-transference? Gael, who finds the idea of emotions transferred from one to another still hard to tolerate, says she felt sorry for Geoff Edge. Anything else? After further search she admits to feeling like a victim. Bravo! Dr Chang claps. Gael has just described her patient's projection. All she needs to do is to interpret it back to him. Her therapist, however, advises Gael to let herself and Geoff Edge become comfortable with each other first.

The following Tuesday Gael makes herself at home in Norma Roman's office. She waters the plant from the mineral water bottle to which she had added a few drops of *Baby Bio*. She transfers it to the window ledge to catch the rest of the daylight. Next to it she props up a post card of Dufy's blue sea painting. At five-twenty-five, hearing some movement outside, she opens the door to find her face inches away from Geoff Edge's myopic gaze. "Is your real name Norma Roman?" he asks. As he readjusts his thick lenses Gael notices a bruise in the middle of his forehead. It transpires that Norma, alias Ruth Roman, was a famous Hollywood star.

Today Geoff Edge, who now refers to himself as Geoffrey, is more specific about his predicament: his award-winning prolific novelist wife, his stepson whose IQ is no less than 130, his elderly father-in-law, a man of tremendous willpower despite his near blindness—all fully rely on Geoffrey to leave something in the fridge for them when he goes to work. Or the freezer, depending on individual requirement: his wife prefers to scorch her meals under the grill, her dad zaps his in the microwave, the son melts them in frying pans.

Faced with such problems Gael limits herself to pointing out that everyone around Geoffrey has complicated needs, while he himself seems to have none. She nearly says that he exists on the edge but stops in time. The question is—she makes a guess—who then is to feed Geoffrey? Is this why he came to therapy? "Good God!" he rejects her metaphor. "Actually all Geoffrey needs is simple food. Mostly boiled," he assures her. "To expect more, so to speak, would be nuts. Sorry—a wrong expression! I meant 'childish' or rather—'presumptuous' . . . In fact 'fatuous' would be more precise."

She puts it to him that he polishes words to run away from what he feels. It may be, she suggests, that the words that come to him first cause him discomfort—even pain. He silently peers at her throughout her speech and she is suddenly worried that she had only repeated something she had read in a book. But they move on. Geoffrey is now keen for her to know that, although physically weaker than others, he possesses a robust knowledge of cinematography. Is Gael aware that Ruth Roman acted in Hitchcock's *Strangers on a Train*? Quietly he summarises the film's premise: "In our life we all have someone we want to kill." This time he could hardly be more succinct. His mouth twists with sudden mirth and Gael takes this as a veiled warning. On his way out Geoff Edge presents her again with his hand. He holds it near her breasts, thin and quivering. When she avoids it he grins with sad triumph.

The first thing she does is to take a sip from her bottle—her mouth suddenly feels so dry. Then she realizes she has just swallowed some of the *Baby Bio* mixture. She runs to the toilet where she makes herself sick. She rushes the key procedure, turning the lights on and off in confused haste. In the lift she becomes afraid she might land in one of the subterranean floors with no exit. Outside the rain is falling in long silver streaks; she is glad to feel it on her cheeks. As she crosses the street she spots an old Nike trainer flattened by the passing traffic and for a split second has a fantasy that Geoffrey's scooter had skidded on the dark wet road and that he is dead, or at least not coming back.

That evening, while searching for a tape, perhaps not entirely by coincidence Gael's eyes fall on the shelf with Hitchcock's thrillers. The opening shot of *Strangers on a Train* is a close-up of two sets of male feet. Two strangers sit on a train. They both have someone who makes their life hell. Bruno, the madman, comes up with the idea that they will kill for each other so that there won't be an obvious motive. "A perfect murder. Criss-cross," Bruno laughs. He sets out to strangle the other man's wife. As she tries, in vain, to force Bruno's hands from her throat her over-sized glasses fall on the ground. Her murder is seen in their cracked lenses. Norma alias Ruth Roman plays the good guy's true love who lives to witness Bruno's miserable death. While she watches the film the harmless, down-trodden Geoff Edge undergoes a transformation in Gael's head. He is now a dangerous psychopath.

She passes the week in mounting dread. Everything startles her. A crow gliding past the window is enough to make her shriek. When asked why she is so jittery she barks that jittery is an imprecise term for how she is. A voice begins to gnaw at her: it was a fatal mistake taking up that training, Gael. You should've stayed a teacher. Next time she lies on her therapist's couch she mentions the fear that has suddenly grown inside her. The therapist's interpretations have become a little slower over the years, but today she is alert. In her opinion Geoff Edge is angry and terrified by his own fury, which he got rid of by projecting it on Gael. She needs to digest it and give it back to him. But that's mad! Gael wants to protest. A thing transmitted criss-cross from one to another? Why doesn't the therapist realise that it is not Geoff Edge's fear? It is hers!

In the supervision with Dr Chang she raises her worry, hoping he will order her to stop Geoff Edge's therapy. He says nothing of the sort. Strictly speaking, Gael shouldn't be working alone. Nevertheless, she has the phone, and the reception staff, only three floors down, are aware she is seeing a patient. The main thing, he reminds her, is to talk to him about his rage that she picked up in her counter-transference. Criss-cross? She checks. She can never tell if Dr Chang's eyes are smiling or serious.

Fear spreads in her like a disease, unchecked. She is convinced she is in mortal danger, that her life is about to end. She enquires in Boots what to buy for self-protection. Do they sell some gas spray or an electronic shocker? Illegal, she is told. How is one to disable an attacker then? Ask the police.

She considers phoning in sick. Every night she dies while waiting for her husband Richard to come to bed. About how Geoff Edge would murder her she is not clear; he is so frail, his body smaller than hers. But every night she sees him stealing down the corridor, leaving behind her corpse slumped in the chair and his signature— his scent. She sees Dr Chang and her therapist questioned by the police, preaching to them about projection and counter-transference. Once she had tried to clarify these terms for unconscious communication to Richard. But as soon he tossed back at her words like 'the paranormal' she stopped. From then on she bore her doubts by herself. Now she feels alone with her dread, alone and abandoned, as when her parents died in a space of months. Why did they leave her so alone? Alone and pitiful as Geoff Edge.

Next Tuesday, before setting out, she chances upon the penknife her father gave her when she was a girl. She slips it in her pocket as a talisman. There is a note from Norma Roman asking her to refrain from bringing in her artefacts. Next to it Norma has put the Dufy sea postcard as an alibi of Gael's crime. The plant is back in its dark spot. At quarter to six, with no sign of her patient, wild scenarios start chasing around Gael's head. What if Geoff Edge is playing a trick on her; is he spying on her? She stands on her toes to glimpse the darkening courtyard; people are milling around there, laughing. She longs to be one of them. Today Norma Roman's room reminds her of a prison cell.

Geoff Edge strides in twenty minutes before the end of his session, not wearing his helmet. His scooter broke down, he explains. He had to run errands for his father-in-law, to take his wife's manuscript to the post office. He is sorry he let Gael wait though. In his experience, people in hospitals are no more than numbers. Is it that he thinks he is just a number for her, she asks? He shoots her a furtive glance that makes her wonder if she herself is no more than a room fixture for him, a thing he would have no qualm to dispose of. "With respect," Geoff Edge says, "I was referring to the operation I had on my ulcers, aged seventeen, shortly after my parents had drowned. I was on a ward with men in their fifties. I suffered internal bleeding. If it weren't for this I would have accomplished far more in life."

Feeling somewhat brittle Gael attempts another tactic. "Was it perhaps your parents' death that made you become fifty when you were only seventeen?" She lets a moment pass then, willing her voice not to waver, she adds "You couldn't digest your sorrow. You bled." He studies her for a long time through his lenses. "When I was young I believe I was good at scripting comedy. Although I admit, now I'd loathe figuring in my wife's biography as someone who had stopped her from writing—this would be a tragedy."

"You do not seem to have a biography of your own, Geoffrey," she remarks. He silently studies her again, his stillness disturbed solely by the movement of his Adam's apple, sharp as an elbow. Was this a cruel thing to say? What if he gets up and attacks her? She tries to avoid his specs, afraid of what she might glean in them. The knife in her pocket presses hard against her thigh. And then, without warning, Geoff Edge suddenly rattles with a madman's laugh. "Geoffrey!" he screeches, then mocking her accent, "The lady just told you that you're a loser. A loser, Geoffrey!"

"Not the lady but Gael," she blurts out, feeling absurd but not knowing what else to say. What is left of their time together that day they spend in icy silence.

Tonight he zips up with his back to her. At the door he attempts again to offer her his hand, yet immediately pulls back. She listens for his footsteps in the corridor but hears nothing. No sound of lift doors. Half expecting to see him waiting for her, smiling his meek smile, she peeks out cautiously. But he has evaporated. She grabs her postcard, plonks the plant back to its dark hole. Then she pulls out her pen-knife and flips it open. Like a mouse she scurries to the secretaries' office. She drops the key in the tray, turns the light off, and heads for the door. Suddenly she hears a click behind her. She freezes. Clutching the knife she slowly turns to see that one of the computers' screens came back to life. Not until she is on the street does she feel safe enough to hide the knife inside her bag.

"Have you interpreted to your patient his rage yet?" the therapist asks Gael next time she lies on her couch, her tears wetting the pillow. These days her therapist is reduced to feeding her paper hankies. The supervision with Dr Chang passes in a blur. Gael scribbles notes about incomplete mourning and impotence. Worryingly, and for reasons she only vaguely understands, Dr Chang has taken to referring to Geoff Edge's penis as both defunct and a murderous weapon.

She feels a wreck. For the whole week, as if by chance, she carries the knife open at the bottom of her bag. Only once when she accidentally touches the blade does she think of Geoff Edge. Tuesday arrives. Humming to herself she goes through her routine, placing the sea picture back on the window ledge, the plant nearer the light. She positions her bag next to her chair. She pulls it slightly open, enough for her hand to be able to slip in. Her plan is quite simple: she will leave the room alive, just as Ruth Roman did.

Even before spotting his trainers she catches the whiff of his unaired flesh. He is perched in the waiting room, fully clad, his head protection in place. "Father-in-law threw the pilchards I bought for him at me," he announces after the habitual unzipping. "I had to get something else and was late for work. The stepson was sleeping off a hangover; my wife mustn't be disturbed."

This is the moment Gael decides to test the long overdue news on him. "I think Geoffrey is . . ." she pauses for emphasis. "Angry." she completes. "Very very angry." He directs his spectacles at her, his eyes monstrously magnified. "No, she's wrong", he says. "Geoffrey is not angry at all. Not a bit."

"You feel you're being used . . ." She keeps on now that she had made a start.

"Not used—useful," he puts her right.

"Your needs are ignored," she persists.

"Ignored? Not ignored—uncredited."

"You are also angry with me,'" she finally dares. Have their eyes locked? She cannot tell through the strip lights in his glasses. He pulls off his fleece. Not angry, he repeats, his tee shirt releasing another whiff of his perfume. To his knowledge Geoffrey hasn't been angry with anyone for at least two decades. "What happened twenty years back?" He cannot remember. "Isn't this when your parents died?" He peers at her, his lenses ablaze. She musters courage. "You were angry with them for going out on that boat, for leaving you behind, for drowning. Maybe that's why you let me wait the other day—to make me miss you like you have missed them."

His feet start to slosh around his dirty trainers. Driblets of sweat run down his nose. The air has become dense, the window above them pitch black; the world has shrunk to this room and its two inhabitants. "Geoffrey," he pipes up after he lets some time lapse, "If Miss Roman is right perhaps her treatment could externalise your discomfort in a civilised way."

"Gael," she offers, in spite of herself. "What other way could there be for you to externalise your anger?"

"Not anger. Discomfort," he corrects her again. Then, slowly cracking his fingers, he hesitates. "My discomfort could get out of control, that's what could happen."

"In what way?" she probes, her voice thin as a hair, her neck clammy. And then he is up. She backs into her chair, her hand shooting to the bag. If she were to stand up now their heads would crash. From close by his face looks as if it had been folded in the dark and only recently uncreased. He points to a mark on her armrest—a knot in the wood that mirrors the bruise on his forehead—an ill omen. "You mustn't touch that Geoffrey!" he tells himself, his finger trembling over the dark blemish. "Do you know what would happen if you did?" What else is she to say to distract him from her arm now dangling in her bag? Which part of him would she go for? Where would she sink the blade? His heart? His groin? Geoffrey must not touch," he repeats. "There must be no contact."

Keeping her breath shallow not to ingest his smell she slowly shifts her hand to establish contact with the knife. But the moment has passed. Squeaks of his trainers escort him back to his chair. His jeans, half-mast, reveal the beginnings of his bony buttocks. He fishes out a tissue, buries his nose in it and blows a lonely call of distress. "If Geoffrey touched the knot things could get out of control," he murmurs. "How?" she asks. He points to his forehead, "I bang my head."

"To stop yourself thinking thoughts you believe are bad . . . ?" He lets some time pass, searching her face. "Do you think bottled-up anger leads to depression?" he enquires, but instantly retreats into his chant about the good-for-nothing stepson, the crippled father-in-law, the scribbler wife whom Geoffrey suspects of secret guilt for thinking her papa an insufferable burden.

Perhaps it is Geoffrey himself who feels guilty, Gael proposes. "Tssss . . ." He expels air through his teeth as if she had jabbed a festering wound. "It may be you envy your stepson's carefree youth?" she advances carefully. "There was no one to worry about you when you were that age."

"Tssss . . . tssss . . ." he squirms.

"You may even be jealous of your wife's success or that she still has a parent while you yourself . . ."

He stops her, his face contorted, his lenses steamed up. "The truth is I often wish to come down in the morning to find the old bastard— tssss . . ."

"Dead?" She samples the word on his behalf. "You wish your father-in-law dead?"

He nods. "Him and her son both. Gone. Not there. And even her— my wife. At times that's all I want. Can you understand?"

It is from the part of herself that knows misery that she talks to him. She speaks about the thing Geoff has been hauling inside him since his parents' death—or perhaps even before, for who is to say when someone decides they aren't worth much? The secret thing that had hardened in him till it was no bigger than a knot. She calls it despair that became rage—a terrifying, murderous rage.

He takes his specs off, brushes them against his sleeve, lays them in his lap. His naked, out of focus eyes make him look like a night creature. She feels aching pity for him. They sit out the rest of the time mute. Today, she promises herself, she will not refuse his touch. When the hour is over he puts his glasses on, briefly taps the wooden armrest, gathers his outfit. By the door he says thank you without attempting to shake her hand.

She closes the door after him, fishes the pen knife out of her bag and snaps it closed. Her madness is over. She removes the postcard from the window sill and as she is about to put the plant back on the filing cabinet she notices that a tiny green lump, a life bud, has appeared on the trunk, between the grey leaves.

Stones

David Herbert

A s we got to the door, he turned to me and he stuck something sharp into my side. I thought it was his nail. He had a grin. I thought it was a joke after a rather intense first meeting. But as it became uncomfortable, I put my hand down and moved back. He moved closer. "Hey!" I'd cut my finger. It was a very sharp knife.

"You tell me this is all in confidence," he whispered, very close to me. "So, if you say one word of what I have told, if I hear that any of what I have told you has leaked out, I shall come back for a second session, since you have invited me graciously, and I will kill you."

"This is uncharted territory for me," he had stated an hour earlier, staring into the garden, reluctant to sit. "My name is Edward Gilchrist. I am thirty-nine. I have come here to honour my mother. I gave her a promise as she died. She wanted me to sort out a certain problem. I was given your name by a colleague . . . or was it the Rector . . . St Jude's, Wickham, Norfolk . . . No, I have not done this before . . . No, I am not on medication. No, I haven't any questions to ask you . . . not yet, Sir." He looked away from the windows, sat back a little in the chair and glanced gingerly round the room, pausing a while on a picture of a path through a forest, then on a vase of drooping mauve tulips.

"Nice," he said, almost looking at me, scratching his wrists and pushing at his flannels. Then bending down, he rubbed at a little stain on his beige, suede desert boots. He checked his fingers and cleared his throat.

"Shall I begin?" he asked. "Have you got children? Grandchildren. Am I permitted to ask questions? Did you teach them about that?"

he indicated the picture of the forest. "Bluebells . . . naming the names of flowers and the ways not just through the woods but how to survive there is much more important, I'm sure you'll agree, than the mastery of the computer. We need to know how to deal with Mother Nature in all her moods and manifestations. Do you know Wordsworth? That tranquillity he talks of that inspires poetry. It is not a given. It has to be achieved . . . You did not ask me if I was a graduate? East Anglia. Biology. I have handed it on when I can to my boys. The mastery of the forest is the mastery of oneself, I have taught them."

"Your boys?" I asked, surprised at my intervention, wondering what my supervisor would have to say. "Intervention is the thief of theme," is her favourite adage—"let them tell their story till they stop."

"There are books we recommend they read but reading is not a strong objective, important though it be, today," he continues, "Observation, the power of observation, is the skill we most instill . . . and alongside it appreciation,

For, what is this life if full of care
We have no time to stand and stare
Or, what is this life if without love
We have no time to look above . . .

at birds, at trees, at canopies and, of course . . . to look down . . .at ferns and what's within them . . . Walt Whitman . . . Do you know his words? 'I believe a leaf of grass,' he said, 'is no less than the journey-work of the stars.' And then there are stones. Stones. Humble, timeless stones. Observe in wonder stones that are not stones . . . what we call pretend stones. Seriously. They are plants that mimic pebbles. What we botanists call Lithops that come in a variety of shades and shapes and sizes in order to protect themselves from grazing animals, and if only these ruminates knew . . . the sweetness that hides under the disguise . . . So . . . living stones. Of course the boys have never seen them, not here in England. They're to be found in the Karoo in the Cape, for example . . . But we look for their equivalent, for the ingenuity of Nature. We call the business 'Woodcraft' and of course it keeps the boys away from modern imagery, computers, etcetera. Idle thoughts, idle hands, etcetera.

'What are you doing in the woods? What do you do in the garden in your tent?' My mother's constant questions to which there was no reply, she understood. 'And, why's my bright boy gone into the bank?' 'Money!' she understood this superficial answer but would continue, 'An idealist isn't interested in money!' 'My idealism is expressed through the movement!' I might reply at the risk of her snorting contempt, 'Huh!' She could be harsh! Oh yes!

The fact is she very much wanted me to leave the movement. 'It gets in the way of your meeting women! Aren't you interested in meeting women? Don't you know what they say about Baden Powell?' Oh yes, there were gentle little digs and there were blows aimed quite far below the belt. You see she wanted to have a grandchild even if it was to arrive posthumously. She was a woman of staunch faith who could see herself looking down from above to witness her son and her grandson playing in the garden. Hence the deathbed pressure, the promise extracted that I come and speak to someone like you. And what would be her request of you? I can tell you quite precisely: 'Get my son to come in from the garden, i.e., to give up tent-life, and find him a wife before it is too late.'"

He paused briefly at the sound of a car pulling up nearby but came in quickly as I began to frame a question: "Talk about contradictions!" He half laughed, reaching towards his belt. "Who do you think gave me this multi-purpose Swiss knife for my thirtieth, which I found wrapped in a newly knitted scarf at the foot of my bed? You have to laugh." He stopped and held up a hand. With the other, he withdrew a handkerchief from his inside pocket as I offered him tissues for I thought I saw tears welling up in his eyes. He shook his head. "I am not sure that I should have told you all that; loyalty and all that. The woman meant well. When you only have one child and have been widowed from the word go . . . Well . . ."

Suddenly he stood, this tall, thin man beginning to reveal considerable agitation, turning his back to hide a rising feeling and moving to the windows. "Excuse me!" he said, folding his handkerchief and returning it to his right-hand trouser pocket beneath his knife and keys which hung and now clinked from his belt.

"I like it here," he said, surprising me and seeming calmer. "Do you ever do your counselling in the garden? The shade, the shrubs, apple trees, lavatera, yes, I would like to come again. Thank you. I think I could be much more forthcoming out there. OK," he turned back but looked towards the picture of the forest, "I confess," he licked his lips, "I have spent most of my life in the garden, so to speak, under canvas . . . and she certainly had a point because I went to cub-camp, I went to scout-camp, to jamborees, and overseas, time and time again, as often as I could. Not, I hasten to add, because I disliked her entirely, she was my mother, and she paid for it all. And she introduced me to it all, took me by the hand and introduced me to Akela when I was seven and I was immediately hooked. All the tasks, tying knots, sending signals, making fires, camping out. *Robinson Crusoe, Captain Courageous, Captain Blood, Brigadier Gerard, Treasure Island, Jock of the Bushveld* were the books we were persuaded to read by our Patrol Leader, Patrick, and I read them in my tent in the garden by torchlight which contributed, I daresay, to premature specs and to my eczema.

I was so engrossed in these stories I hardly noticed the insects biting away each summer, just scratching away, reflexively, and not even telling my mother about the encroaching rash. Look!" His palms and wrists, the sleeves pulled up, were held before me. "Blotches! And on my scalp! And elsewhere!" He pulled at his flannels. Then he dropped his arms and looked at the clock, "How long have we got left?" Not a question he wanted answered for he sat down and looked at me for the first time. "About twelve minutes," he estimated. I nodded. "Good! I have decided I can trust you. Be prepared to trust, is my variation on the scout motto. Secret! I tell you that in confidence. Yes . . . I believe I am ready . . . Are you ready?"

His gaze was hard to hold. When I looked down at last, feeling quite uneasy but long-trained to be ready for anything, he started sotto voce, "Firstly, my name is not Edward Gilchrist. Secondly, I have no religion. I would never speak to our Patrol Pastor about anything, certainly not about this because he knows everyone in our Village, which is not in Norfolk, and he sneaks religion into everything, even our sing-songs round the camp fire and my whole troop dislike him, not just me. He thinks things go on in the tents. It does not! Not in my tent. I would not permit it! Thirdly, I have no degree. I am an autodidact or an ignoramus who needed to speak to a stranger: you; who, fourthly, did not come recommended by anyone . . . found you, as they say, on the internet via your association. Easy. London. Far away. Anonymous. Near the Heath. Lots of letters after your name whose dates told me you were old enough to have seen and heard it all and old enough not to be shocked. And, lastly, old enough to have some historical and philosophical sense of the scout movement."

He sat back at last and found my gaze again, this time looking less hostile, "I am not what I have told you, except a scout-master. I am not what you see, not what my mother, old Patrick, the Rector, the scout troop, neighbours, villagers have seen round and about. I am not. Under this sports-coat and flannels and scout-belt, under these ostentatious church keys and Swiss knife is not gentle James. My name is James. My mother told me that they christened me in honour of what she called Jesus' gentle disciple, James. 'You were such a good baby!' she said a thousand times, 'You never cried.' And I have tried, desperately, to live up to this image . . . of one who is understanding, patient, gentle . . . But I'm not! It's a lie!"

His mouth was dry and I indicated the water but his eyes were on the clock. "Sir, the truth is I am consumed with the desire to hate and to hurt. But seriously! I have fantasies that take me to the edge of . . . the very edge of . . . Believe me, I have been this close . . ."

Right forefinger and thumb thrust out were all but touching and tears once again had leapt into his eyes. He shook his head. "My hope, Sir, my hope is that by telling someone about it at last, by telling you about my constant temptation to erupt into violence, it will go away . . . that as I leave here today I will become what I have pretended to be . . . a gentle man."

Mustard therapy

Alexandra Wilson

Have you ever wondered what it's like to be married to a psychotherapist? If you thought life would be one free therapy session you'd be wrong. Take the party Jocasta and I went to the other night. "And what do you do for a living Lewis?" asks a guest. "I'm in computers," I reply and wait for the fixed smile, the glazed eyes looking over my shoulder to find someone more rewarding to talk to. It doesn't take long. "How interesting," the guest replies, "And what about you Jocasta? Are you in computers too?"

"Oh no! I'm a psychotherapist," says my wife. "A psychotherapist! How absolutely fascinating! I must tell you about this strange dream I had the other night." This is the point at which I slope off to the kitchen where the other sad nerds hang out. For some reason this infuriates Jocasta. "You have never resolved your Oedipus complex Lewis. Why don't you see a therapist and sort yourself out."

"Maybe I will," I lie.

There are other minor irritations I could tell you about, but in the end it's not the knowing smile when I make a so-called Freudian slip or the feeling that I am an open book and probably more of an airport read than a Proustian masterpiece. No, in the end what really gets to me is that my wife is behind closed doors with a constant stream of other men.

The first significant 'other' in our relationship was Mr Ellis. In the heady days when Jocasta still laughed at my jokes and we held hands—in fact we couldn't keep our hands off each other—we went to see the new Woody Allen film. As we stood innocently queuing for our tickets the colour drained from Jocasta's face. "My God! It's Ellis," she cried clutching my arm. "Who?"

"My analyst, Mr Ellis. Look, in front of us! No don't look!" I look. Mr Ellis is a short middle-aged man with dark curly hair wearing a green corduroy suit. "And he's with another woman!" Jocasta exclaims. I couldn't help noticing a hint of hysteria in her usually calm personality. "What do you mean 'another' woman?" I ask but she ignores my question. "We can't possibly see the film now Lewis. I'm sorry we'll have to see the Bergman instead. '*Wild* something'."

"*Strawberries*, but I don't see the problem. I'm in the dark here."

"That's just it," cries Jocasta. "I'm not sitting in the dark knowing that Mr Ellis is snogging some floozy in the back row."

I take another peek. Mr Ellis' floozy is a pleasant plump woman with short grey hair, actually she looks a little like my aunt Nelly. Mr. Ellis himself reminds me of a benevolent dentist but I keep this observation to myself. "It's probably his wife," I point out but it wasn't the right thing to say. "You don't understand do you Lewis?" Jocasta says in a new cold voice, taking her arm away from mine, "And I couldn't possibly explain."

When we moved in together Jocasta's consulting room was upstairs and my office was in the basement. All I heard throughout the working day was creaking floorboards followed by the door of the consulting room being shut. From my troll habitat in the basement I watched as various pairs of trousers and an occasional skirt mounted the steps to the front door. Once when I needed a book I'd left upstairs I met a pair of trousers on his way out of my wife's inner sanctum. "Excuse me," I said in a pleasant but definitely 'I am the man of the house' voice. The trouser legs man looked at me startled and, muttering something I couldn't catch, fled down the stairs. As the front door slammed shut I found myself trembling. Which one of us was the intruder? I was suddenly unclear.

At tea-time Jocasta would emerge from her room blinking as though she had been deprived of light which she probably had been since she kept the blinds permanently drawn. Her eyes held a far off look as though she'd been visiting far off places I knew nothing about. "I've just heard the most extraordinary story," she'd say shaking her head. "Extraordinary." I soon learnt that to express curiosity was interpreted as being voyeuristic and the safest option was a detached "Mmmm?"

"Of course I can't talk about it, confidentiality issues etcetera."

"Of course."

By our fourth year of marriage I was beginning to feel redundant. Jocasta was making more money than I was and we'd started to bicker. You know the kind of thing, 'you said you'd put the rubbish out', 'you're behaving like your father', and so on. By April things had got so bad that I'd started to circle the bedsits in the 'to rent' column. We were drifting apart and I didn't know how to stop the downward slide. If Jocasta hadn't been a therapist I might have gone to see one but somehow that felt like her territory.

One Monday morning a call came from Bristol. Jocasta's elderly mother had fallen over and been taken to hospital. For once Jocasta couldn't handle it. "What am I going to do?" she wailed. "You're going to pack a bag and go to Bristol," I said. "But what about my patients? Oh Lewis!"

"Go upstairs, telephone them and when you've done that I will drive you to the station. You should be in Bristol in two hours." My voice was slow and steady. This was the me I like: masterful, controlled. Half an hour later Jocasta was ready. "I've cancelled everybody except my twelve o'clock—Sam Carter. I can't believe some people don't have answer-phones."

"Don't worry, leave me Carter's number and I'll phone later. Now let's get you on that train."

I drove home from the station playing Van Morrison loudly, something I haven't done for a long time. For once I had been needed and I had risen to the occasion. I even remembered to try phoning Carter but there was still no reply. The house felt strange without Jocasta. I went up to her consulting room and sat in her black leather chair. It was rare for me to go in that room. "Now, er," I said out loud and then stopped. Did she call them Mr? Or would it be Bill or Fred or whatever? I got up and looked curiously at the small square of clean white tissue spread neatly over the back of the couch, That's where they put their greasy heads I thought. I stretched out on the couch and lay with my hands folded on my chest. "I want to tell you about an erotic dream I had last night Mrs Hart. You were lying on the bed naked and . . . At that moment the doorbell rang. I looked at my watch. Damn! It was Sam Carter. A young woman stood on the doorstep. She had kipper eyes and a mass of red curly hair. "Oh," she said, "I've come to see Mrs Hart."

"I'm afraid Mrs Hart has been called away on urgent business. Can I help?" I smiled; she was extremely attractive. "But she can't."

The girls eyes filled with tears.

"Would you like to leave a message?"

"Tell her Sam came but she wasn't here," said the girl.

"So you're Sam Carter! I've been trying to get hold of you!" To my dismay she burst into tears. "I think you'd better come in and sit down," I said. She nodded her head and followed me into the kitchen where she sat at the kitchen table. "I'm sorry but it's the last straw Mrs Hart not being here. I've had a dreadful week and I've been holding myself together until today."

"Mmm." I said. "You see, the man I love has been promising to leave his wife for two years and I believed him, I am such an idiot!"

"Mmm." I said again. "My father left when I was seven and I think I've spent my whole life not trusting men. When I met Brian," she paused to blow her nose, "I thought he was different." She looked up at me. Her eyes were a marvelous shade of green. "Mm." I said. "And then I saw him on Saturday and he was with a girl laughing and holding hands."

I tutted sympathetically. "He'd said he was visiting his father. And the worst thing was it wasn't even his wife." We sat in silence for a minute. "Would you like a cheese sandwich?" I asked. "I was just about to make one."

"Perhaps I will," she said with a faint smile. "Mrs Hart says it's all to do with hating my mother," Sam Carter said. "Oh! Why is that?"

"Trying to get Brian away from his wife—revenge."

"I see. But you're an attractive young woman Sam, if I may say so. And quite frankly I don't know why you're wasting time on someone who is obviously a jerk. In fact," I said warming to my role, "If I were you I'd go home right now and give him the old heave-ho. I forgot to ask would you like mustard in your sandwich?"

"Mustard?"

"I do think it gives a sandwich that extra little something."

"Perhaps I will then."

I opened the cupboard door. "English or French? Grainy or smooth? There's a choice. You could say it's like life, it depends on how hot you like it or whether you go for a smooth or a rough ride." Sam Carter looked thoughtful. "Yes," she said slowly, "I suppose it does."

"You poor little thing," I said leaning over the table to squeeze her hand. Her red hair reminded me of one of the Pre-Raphaelites, a period I am particularly fond of. "Have you seen the new Woody Allen by any chance?" I asked. "No, I haven't. But I must go, My fifty minutes is up!" She laughed. "When is Mrs Hart back did you say?"

"Probably Thursday, I'm on my own until then," I said, "A lonely old bachelor."

"If only ..." she began with a wistful smile. "Yes?" I asked eagerly. "If only I'd had a father like you," she said.

When her mother had been settled-in Jocasta returned home. "I missed you Lewis," she said and then we kissed for the first time in months. "I missed you too." And it was true I hadn't looked at the 'to rent' ads since she'd been away. The next day she came into my office holding a letter. "I've had the strangest letter from one of my patients. Do you remember I asked you to ring Sam Carter?" I nodded. "Well, she says she doesn't need therapy any more, her life has completely changed and she's happy for the first time. She's broken off her relationship, chucked in her job and she's going travelling. It's funny, I didn't think we'd got very far, I found her very resistant."

"There you are darling, a miracle cure."

"Then again," Jocasta looked thoughtful, "It could be a sort of revenge."

"Revenge?"

"She was so angry that I was away that she's turned me into the mother she hates and now she's got rid of me."

"That could be one theory," I said.

"Oh, and she says say thank you to you for some reason." I smiled. Jocasta looked at me. "So what do you think Dr Freud?"

"Well," I replied, "I think it may have something to do with the mustard."

CHILDHOOD

Fragments

Ella Landauer

My friend Luisella sees each moment of life as contributing to a larger whole and a wider story. Thus any event which might be important, interesting, or just amusing, is turned-over and enjoyed many times and in varying company, so that it can gradually take its place in the accumulating narrative. I have known Luisella for twenty-seven years and have always greatly envied this capacity of hers, even though I have never been able to find it within myself to construct life in this way. But here, now, on this stony, pine-scented Croatian island where we are spending a holiday together, these thoughts come to me again sharply, just as yesterday, swimming in a pale-turquoise bay, the surface ripples suddenly calmed and I could see the pebbles, sea urchins and sea cucumbers far below as if through a polished magnifying glass.

I arrived in Trieste three weeks ago, the last Italian city before the Croatian border. I was due to meet Luisella the following afternoon at the Caffè San Marco, before travelling on together to the island Lošinj where we are spending the summer. After a good night's rest and a fairly early breakfast I made for the centre of the city and my favourite church there: the Serbian Orthodox Church, with its golden mosaics, its short, domed towers and rounded, welcoming appearance. The musky smell of incense hung in the air even though there was no mass being celebrated. At last relaxed after the intense effort of the journey and its preparations, I started to remember the two times I had visited Lošinj in the past, once with Luisella seventeen years before and the first time, with my parents at the end of the 1960s when I was ten. The feeling of a soft receptiveness created by morning light falling on the mosaics suddenly vanished as I went back in my mind to that earlier holiday, and at the same moment remembered that the town where Luisella and I had booked rooms was where I had spent that holiday with my parents: Mali Lošinj. Why did I suddenly feel slightly anxious and uncomfortable deep inside me, as if I had remembered an unpleasant fact? What had that holiday in 1969 been like? I could not remember clearly anymore. I recalled going into the local shops each day to buy food for our picnic lunch and returning with bread, perhaps a couple of tins of sardines and a little fruit, sometimes fresh, local figs; the food back then had usually been scarce and unappetizing. But that was not it. Had there been an accident during the holiday, or illness? Had the hotel been welcoming? Our room on the top floor had been filled with large, cumbersome, dark furniture: a wardrobe with a key; white, embroidered fine-cotton curtains over the windows even during the day, to keep out the hot sunlight. Then I knew, and I felt shocked that I had not connected in my mind the place that we were about to visit with the events of the past.

Before that evening in July 1969 I had felt strongly that there was a family story in which I was playing my part, an important part in fact and one which carried many responsibilities as I was the only surviving child of my parents and their siblings. Both my parents had lost their fathers at an early age, and had then been clung-to by their mothers, desperate not to lose them too. The symmetry appeared to end there because my father adored his mother, whereas my mother was frightened of hers and escaped from her as soon as she could to move from Northern England to London. My father, on the other hand, fled with his mother from Nazi Austria to England in 1938, living together with her until she died ten years later. When my parents met after the war they recognized each other instantly for what they had in common: that each of them was a survivor of many different sorts of tragedy. But they were prepared to be resilient and enjoy life if possible, even try to make sense of it, and when I was born the stories were told to me, people from the past brought to life, not for my consideration but for my information. I was willing to take my place, helping the stories to be validated but also fade into the distance where they caused less pain. In addition to everything else, my parents had lost a daughter shortly before my birth. I believe it was my mother who decided against final despair at this point and there was only one other option. When I was born I knew from early on that it was essential we all clung together. No one and nothing of any great importance seemed to exist outside our family. It did not matter though because it all made sense and because we were everything to each other. But the evening in the hotel in July 1969 changed my view of this in a way that could never be reversed.

We had eaten at a local restaurant earlier in the evening. My mother must have drunk more wine than usual and on the way home she was emotional and talkative. This worried me because most of the time my mother was collected and predictable—'sensible' or 'decent' in her eyes—in any given situation. But after she had had more than a certain amount of alcohol my father and I would fall silent knowing that to say anything might provoke a sharp reply. We waited quietly, tensely, whilst she talked and laughed, my father and I each too alarmed to support each other.

We ascended to our room in the small rickety, wood-panelled lift. Once inside my mother fell back on the bed, exhausted and now becoming distressed. As her mood turned I tried not to listen to what she was saying. My father stood near her, concerned and silent. I began to get ready for bed, but as I undressed realised that in between her sobs she was describing something I did not understand and had not heard about before during any of these episodes: ". . . she looked just like you, the baby looked just like you . . . you showed me the album, I knew immediately . . . We'd only been married for one week . . ." My father looked over to me at the other side of the large room; I was sitting on my bed, watching, not at all sure what I was witnessing. He looked back to my mother who was crying quietly now—I had only twice seen her cry before—tears running backwards over her cheeks, sinking into her hair and then the bed cover. He remained composed and looked serious, concerned, but still did not speak.

I knew about my sister Michaela who had died aged three. My mother would occasionally mention her, trying to tell me about her brief life and the awful events leading up to her death, believing it was right that I was informed. She placed the facts (or some of them) clearly but very succinctly before me with the aim of protecting me from the greater part of the continuing confusion and agony of it all. To this my father, if present, would murmur "No, no, . . . please Cara." It was still too painful for him to hear these things spoken out loud and it always remained so, even later. But this time my father did not respond like that, he just looked on. I waited for more to come, but there was nothing that made what she had said any clearer, though with tears still flowing onto the bed and sobbing quietly, she repeated different phrases of her original uttering. Eventually my mother fell asleep. Later, I lay in the dark with my eyes open wondering what I had just heard.

The hotel dining room next morning was calm and quiet as usual, with its small selection of holiday-makers and a few elderly Austrians who still visited Mali remembering its former glory days. My father had chosen the hotel because he had remembered it from the time he and his family used to come to stay in the town before the First World War. At that time the islands had belonged to the Austrian Empire and the Austrians considered them part of their 'Riviera'. He and his family had been in Mali in late June 1914 when the Archduke Franz Ferdinand was assassinated in Sarajevo, to the south west. Austrians were advised by the government to leave the area as soon as possible in case there were further developments and my father's family had returned to Vienna. I imagined the high-ceilinged dining room grander and also somehow lighter in those days, as it probably was. There was little money for redecoration now. We drank the rather bitter coffee as usual and ate the bread thickly covered with quince jam. Afterwards, my mother said she was returning to our room to get her things for the day. My father and I found ourselves alone. "Mummy said things last night that she shouldn't have said," my father stated gently. We looked at each other for a moment. I wondered if there was going to be more, but also knew there would not be. He had done what he considered to be the right thing, to answer the unspoken question he realized was in my mind, but he did not want me to know more and glancing into my eyes could see that I did not either. We never spoke about the subject again.

Woken each day since we have been here by the half-hourly ringing-out of church bells starting at daybreak, I have been turning over this sequence of events in my mind as it gets light; it is always the same. But yesterday, at Punta Kriza, I told Luisella this story as we dangled our feet in the water. I did not exactly remember ever having told her about these events, but somehow expected that she would know about them all the same. I glanced at her frequently to see if this was the sort of story she wanted to hear. She listened quietly, apparently forgiving me immediately for the fact that I had omitted this important account until then. "And how did you feel when you discovered you had a half-sister?" she asked eventually. This seemed a good question, an interesting one, but one to which I did not have an immediate answer. "I'm not sure now . . . it's such a long time ago . . . thirty-five, thirty-six years", I replied. But driving back to Lošinj, along the narrow roads flanked by holm-oaks and low walls of thrown-together rocks, I started to think how I could explain to Luisella and also to myself my real reaction to the discovery that I probably had a half-sister living somewhere, almost certainly in Europe. Luisella had said she would have wanted to try to find her immediately if she had been in my place. I had always wanted a sister, or a brother for that matter, more than anything else in the world that I could think of, as companion, play-mate and someone with whom to share the great responsibility of being alive and staying alive handed to me at birth.

Once over the short bridge and back on Lošinj we stopped at a village to buy cold mineral water and to drink an espresso on the square in front of the small, white, flat-fronted church, now turned to a fiery orange-pink in the path of the setting sun. "The thing was," I announced my train of thought without an introduction, "how I felt or how I might have felt depended on things I did not really want to know about. I had to put straight-forward feelings about the discovery, strong feelings, on hold, because I had to wait to see if there was more information and then put it all together in my mind." Luisella, sitting opposite, quickly put down her espresso, leant her crossed arms on the small marble table and found my gaze again. "Yes, I wanted a sister, desperately really," I went on, "but the most important thing in our little family was stability and sticking together after all my parents had been through."

"Yes, I can see that," Luisella reflected supportively. "You see, they didn't say very much to me, did they?" I continued, trying to make a point which I still felt unsure about.

"All my father did was confirm something that happened between him and my Mother a long time ago, in fact it was just after they got married in 1952. He showed her the album with the picture in—or maybe there was more than one picture—because in a way he wanted her to know. It was a dreadful moment for my mother. For her it confirmed all the bad things her mother had said about my father before they got married. Her mother had told her he must be married already, at his age—he was seventeen years older than my mother. And she said he must be a war criminal! That was probably because of his Austrian accent, which she wouldn't have been able to tell from a German accent: lots of people were like that after the war in England. And so on. So my mother suddenly had serious doubts about this handsome Jewish foreigner she found herself setting-up home with. She managed to get through that, though I think it was touch and go for a bit. The really dreadful time was when Michaela was born, with all her problems, my mother knowing that there was this other child elsewhere, with no problems. I think she felt she'd failed again."

Luisella nodded attentively, then pushed herself backwards and relaxed into her chair. Still holding my gaze she slowly let out a chest-full of air through her pursed lips. "So that was the past," I continued after a few moments, "At least it appeared to be in the past. I think that was the thing I didn't really want to think clearly about: was he still in contact with the mother and daughter and if he was, what did that mean? I knew what an affair was and I knew it was something wrong. And actually, the reason I knew it was wrong was that for a long time before that my father had been telling me it was. He'd always told me as a child about a relation of his called Sigmund Freud—I had no idea he was famous—who made his wife very unhappy by having an affair with her sister, Minna. He was clearly extremely angry with this person and disliked him intensely. His anger was a bit alarming, because it was puzzling: I felt there was something I didn't understand."

"So your father knew Sigmund Freud in Vienna?" Luisella asked. "No, it was my grandmother really. Her grandmother and Freud's mother were cousins, but it was Martha—his wife—that she was friendly with. When they met up Martha would pour out all her unhappiness about this affair to my grandmother. Martha was pretty miserable apparently, over a very long period. My father said all the wider family knew about it. The sister lived with Freud and Martha. My grandparents detested him; there were other reasons too. Anyway, that's how I learnt about affairs. And that morning in the hotel, when my father confirmed what seemed to be a story about a half-sister, I think I began to wonder what else it confirmed. In other words, I began to wonder whether his anger with this person called Sigmund Freud was to do with his anger with himself over something about himself or something he was doing that really he found unacceptable. Aged ten, of course, I didn't think of it quite like that; it was more as if I'd stepped suddenly into a whole unsafe area that I didn't want to go any further into and in a way I felt I'd known something of it for a long time."

I looked into Luisella's face to check whether she had been able to follow what seemed to me like a dislocated and unsettling account. She was evidently thinking over what I had been saying and seemed unperturbed. I was relieved. The setting sun had disappeared behind a house whilst we had been talking and had cast a shadow over the village square. With our hair still damp from the sea it left us suddenly feeling chilly and less at home. So we paid for our coffees and left to resume the winding drive down to Mali.

We fell silent for the first few kilometres of the journey. I tried to reflect on why during my many years of working as a psycho-therapist and during my own training therapy I had not worked in any great detail on this story of my half-sister and what it meant for our family. I had not really felt interested and now my lack of curiosity interested me. Luisella broke the silence: "I heard once that Freud did something bad to someone in his family, I thought it was a daughter. Did he have a daughter?"

"Yes, he had three. He had a daughter called Anna, who worked with him later on. They were very close and she was extremely protective of his reputation. And he had a daughter who died in the flu epidemic after the First World War. He was absolutely grief stricken about her death; he referred to her as his favourite daughter, which must have been very painful for the others. And there was Mathilde, the eldest. But you might be thinking about this question of the affair with his sister-in-law, Minna Bernays, which lots of people have wondered about over the years. They were very close and they used to travel together, so I guess people wondered what it amounted to.

"My father wrote a letter in the 1970s to Anna Freud to clarify some of his memories about the past. He particularly wanted to discuss Mausi Graf, who was a niece of Sigmund Freud's, the daughter of his sister Rosa. Her real name was Cäcilie. She used to come on holiday with my father's family to Bad Ischl sometimes. My father was very fond of her, so were his parents. Her hobby was making dolls houses. She committed suicide when she was twenty-three, whilst she was working for Freud as an assistant, I believe. My grandmother was angry with him in relation to this, apparently, although I'm not really sure why. Mausi had recently discovered she was pregnant—she wasn't married. I know he tended to act as head of the family; maybe had known about the pregnancy and given her a hard time over it. Perhaps she felt he should have taken better care of her, I'm not clear, though I know he was very distressed about her death—he'd been very fond of her too. Anyway, Anna wrote back a very defensive, short letter to my father (we still have it), rather unfriendly—his letter seemed quite reasonable, from what I remember. But maybe she hadn't liked his parents. Or may be she felt there was an implied criticism of her father. I don't know."

"So your grandparents really didn't get on with Sigmund Freud!" laughed Luisella.

"No, but I'm not sure how much they needed to. I don't know if they all met socially. I never asked my father, I don't think. He died just before I might have got more interested in all these details. I know that my grandfather went to the same café each day as Freud. They probably avoided each other, hid behind their newspapers on those frames, puffing at their cigars! Anyway, they were very different, that's why they didn't like Freud much, I'm afraid. My grandfather had a silk factory near Vienna in Unterwaltersdorf. They were hard-working, practical business people. His father had been a doctor, a physician, in the Dutch Navy—he'd written some books himself—and my grandparents would have thought Freud was throwing away his medical education doing the kind of work he was doing. They would have had views about how much he earned for his family too and would have felt he should be carving-out a reputation for himself as an established Viennese doctor, who lots of people would go to, not developing his odd ideas about the mind!"

Returning from the trip I sat down on the cushioned wicker armchair near the open window and my mind raced over the various conversations we had had that day. I was beginning to feel engaged in the whole question of my half-sister in a way that I had never been before. There was something about the way Luisella listened that made it possible to talk about the most difficult things. She was not more or less interested in my accounts of my grandparents' relationship with the Freuds than the discovery that I had a half-sister. To her, it is all important.

I had begun to have a new thought about their relationship to Sigmund Freud during our conversation in the car although previously I had not imagined there were any new thoughts to be had. I reflected that the few times my mother and I had discussed it in the past, we had both tended to characterise my father's parents as lacking imagination in their apparent disapproval of Freud's deviation from the more conventional career paths within medicine. We saw them as bigoted, even stupid. But now I was not so sure what the evidence for this was. I remembered my father telling me once that his brother Wilhelm went through a period of stealing their father's neck-ties; this might have been around 1912. My grandparents were concerned about this behaviour, but rather than seeing it as cause for punishment, sent him to a therapist, whom my father described as a 'psychologist', not previously known to the family. My father did not know about the details of the advice given, or treatment, but said it centred around resolving a difficulty between father and son, the neck-ties being a symbol of male power. This has the mark of a practitioner at least influenced by the new psycho-analytic ideas around at the time.

I had also wondered, for the first time ever, whether my grandmother would have talked with Freud's collaborator Josef Breuer about the treatment they were developing. Breuer had been my grandmother's doctor in his capacity as physician and he had also been their family doctor when she was growing up. I had learnt recently from my mother that my grandmother had felt very fond of her doctor and also his wife, Mathilde; she kept a photograph of the couple at home in their flat in the Kaiserstrasse. She described him as a very warm and fatherly person and considered him an excellent doctor. I could visualize them now, after one of his house calls to his patient, talking amiably over coffee and cake about this new area of his work. She would sound engaged and warm as she questioned him—keeping his cup and plate well-filled throughout—and to be honest, much more interested in his views and in hearing about his contribution to the new treatment than in getting information that could be held against her relative in future conversations in other social settings.

This picture of my grandparents as more open-minded and interested in innovation would fit with other things I knew about them. I was aware that they enjoyed art and literature and had a small collection of art in their flat, which had to be left behind when they fled the Nazis. Three languages were spoken in their home: German, French and Czech, and this would have opened them to different cultural influences both in Vienna and when they travelled. My grandfather must have spoken some English too, as he made business trips to England. Like many Austrians he was a keen mountain walker and he had been one of the founders of the Ottohaus, the imposing lodge on the much-visited Rax mountain near Vienna, which opened early in 1893. (It was in August that year in the Ottohaus that Freud happened to get talking to Aurelia Kronich, the daughter of the inn-keeper, and learnt about the sexual abuse that appeared to have lead to her present state of anxiety, with accompanying hallucinations. The treatment proceeding from this exchange was carried out over the course of that afternoon, in the lodge. The case took its place in his *Studies on Hysteria* where she was named Katharina.)

I was beginning to prefer this view of my grandparents as people who were culturally open and aware. It fitted more coherently with my picture of the sort of family in which my father would have been raised and by which he would have been influenced. He was unendingly curious about life, open to new ideas and solutions and loved art, literature and history. It was only in areas of his experience where he felt frightened and confused that he became mistrustful, rejecting and sometimes bigoted.

What was more likely to be true about my grandparents, I reflected, was that they felt that the Jews who were newcomers to Vienna, albeit in the atmosphere of Emperor Franz Joseph's liberal attitude to minority groups, ought to feel grateful that they were safe and tolerated and should get on with leading their lives quietly and industriously. My grandmother's section of the family had migrated from Freiberg in Moravia at the same time as Sigmund Freud's. Vienna would have offered more opportunities of all sorts for ambitious, hard-working Jews and would have at least potentially offered the opportunity for them of a closer integration with the non-Jewish community. My grandparents had grasped the opportunity with both hands. When they moved into their flat in the seventh district of Vienna as a young married couple in the 1890s there was a Frau Seufzer living in the same building. (*Seufzen* means to sigh; 'ein Seufzer' might be translated 'a plangent sigh'.) Her constant plea to them was said to be "Komm zu Jesus! Komm zu Jesus!" ("Come to Jesus! Come to Jesus!") delivered in exactly that plangent sigh, as demonstrated by my father for me many years later. And this is exactly what they did, converting as a couple to Catholicism, which they practiced from then on in a committed way. This was one of his favourite stories of his Vienna days and although it has the ring of a dream reported by Freud in his writings I suspect that this is exactly what happened. At least on one level. On another, the impetus to assimilate culturally and to convert was probably very much present before this event. Essentially, I think they saw it as being to do with survival, potentially a question of life or death in the ever-changing political climates of Central and Eastern Europe. My guess was that Sigmund Freud's determination to develop his ideas and gain a reputation at the cost of also gaining some notoriety would have irritated my grandparents who would have felt he should have fitted in more quietly. They themselves took nothing for granted and like their famous relative, when their presence in Vienna was no longer tolerated because of their Jewish heritage, my grandmother and father were deeply grateful for the welcome they received in Britain.

So, I decided, I had no real evidence for thinking my father's family detested Sigmund Freud, even if they did not particularly like him, or approve of his behaviour. The powerful, somewhat frightening anger towards him was my father's own; I had no reason to think the rest of his family had felt like this. A casually held but secretly important family myth was in the process of being undermined and I realized that my train of thought was rejoining the place I had left it more or less undisturbed for well over thirty years. Had any information been added since then? Well, yes. But as with Sigmund and Minna one did not know precisely what it meant and therefore what to do with it. Maybe it was better to leave it as a fragment than a possibility, with all the danger that a possibility can bring to good, sustaining memories.

It was one summer's afternoon when my father was in his late seventies and I was in my late twenties. He stayed at home that day and my mother and I drove to a local village in the West Country to attend a concert in the church there. We had already been talking about family matters, about the past, and as we walked towards the church she turned to me. "There's something you need to know about Daddy," she said clearly and calmly, as if she had been planning this moment for a long time. "I already know," I said. I had sensed immediately what she wanted to tell me. "What do you know?" she returned with sharp surprise in her voice and looking into my eyes more directly than I was used to. "I know about my half-sister." It was one of the few occasions in my life that I have seen her shocked and nearly lost for words. "How do you know that?" Her voice was louder and less controlled now, in spite of other concert-goers making their way in the same direction as us. "You told me yourself, when I was about ten."

"I told you . . . ? No I didn't. I thought you didn't know!"

Evidently my father had never referred to the incident, they had never discussed it and she had completely forgotten the events of that evening in Mali. I described for her the sequence of events, in outline. "So you've known all along . . . and you didn't say anything!" she commented when I had finished, which was clearly true. My mother tried to describe to me the struggle she had had with herself when she had found out about my father's first daughter. She had discovered letters at the flat that we owned for a time in London, postmarked in the German town where she knew the girl's mother lived. She had felt enraged. My mother does not speak German so there would have been no point in her opening them, even if she had wanted to: to discover the details of a betrayal would have been the final, pointless injury.

So my father had stayed in contact with my half-sister or her mother. At the very least he must have given them the address of our flat in London. And the most? This was much more painful to think about: not only the betrayal and secrecy, but also the loss of something perhaps immeasurably good, that might have been there for the taking, but was never offered. It is possible, I conceded, that my father remained in contact with my half-sister and her mother for forty-five years, until he died. Maybe he sent them money regularly. There was not much extra money available in our family, but I knew he had sent money regularly to his brother in France, to my mother's great annoyance. And my father used to travel quite a bit on business: to Africa, in Europe and sometimes the Middle East.

This would have offered opportunities to visit them if he had so wished. Since childhood I had always wanted there to be another explanation for my father's fury with Sigmund Freud over his alleged long-standing affair with Minna Bernays, but the more clearly I thought about all the evidence the further this possibility receded into the distance.

Another family, alongside ours, waiting quietly in a different room. A big sister for me, perhaps thirteen years old when I was born. I wondered what they looked like. Maybe the girl looked like me—maybe very like me. I thought of an afternoon in Vienna twelve years before, shortly after my father died. I was visiting with my husband David and my mother, but was spending a few hours alone. The skies and buildings suddenly darkened and a typically Austrian deluge of rain began. Although I was next to the opera house, right in the centre of the city, when I looked round everyone had vanished from the pavements: the entire city appeared to be taking shelter. I walked out into the rain and over to the Jewish monument behind the opera, which commemorates the suffering of the Jews of Vienna during the Nazi era. A few moments later a woman a bit older than I appeared there. I was crying and it was raining very hard; there were just the two of us in the square. But I recognised her, or I felt I did. We looked at each other. My heart began beating wildly and painfully. I began to move over to where she was standing, to speak to her, although I did not know what I was gong to say. And then suddenly I could not and I turned and ran away as fast as my legs would go to the safety of a nearby café, tears and rain streaming over my face. I was appalled that I had fled from what had felt like one of the most important moments of my life and I returned to the square after a minute or two, but she had gone. Maybe that was her: my half-sister. But then again, almost any woman in her mid-forties, on a city street, could have been her.

I lay back on the bed, exhausted by the day and the workings of my mind, but determined not to fall asleep on another day without taking my train of thought a little further on. The sadness that I felt welling up in me was for our little family, alone and struggling, but mainly alone. And for myself, as a child, desperately needing a sibling to share life with. I did not feel angry with my father. It was much too late for that. I could see that to bring the two families together in some way might have destroyed both of them.

Several years ago my mother told me that she was planning to write down her memories, write an account of her life. She repeated her intention a couple of times. I did not hear anything more. But then, in passing, last year she told me she had started to write the narrative but had had to give up the project: it was too painful for her. I understood this. Her life has been too painful. I wondered, would it help that I had begun, with Luisella, to lay the different parts of this particular story side by side, forced myself to think them through and had started to imagine? Would that make it better or worse for her, for us? I had no idea of the answer to that question, and allowed myself to close my eyes.

The Process of Healing the Fish

Mary Steel

We walk together through the hallway of the old Georgian school house, past the magnificent stairway, and turn to the left down a narrow corridor with a patterned tile floor. When we reach the Art Therapy room, John rushes in and starts taking sugar paper from the shelf. He seems a lot more relaxed now that he is getting used to the routine; it has taken him ten weeks to begin to feel safe and at home. "Can I do a painting?"

"Yes of course. The paints are just here, and here is the apron to help you keep your clothes clean. Can you push your sleeves up please? That's it."

He is small for his age, and thin, with black hair and dark brown eyes. He is sensitive, articulate, forthright, passionate, anxious and sometimes aggressive. He wears his school uniform grudgingly; his sweat shirt with the school logo above muddy trousers and his shoes laced but not tied up. He will take his feet half out of them when he sits down.

He chooses pale green paper, and sits at the table, his small figure surrounded by a sea of washing-up liquid style bottles of paint. He takes a fine bristly brush from the pot of brushes, and begins to work very fast. At first, he is silently intent on his image. As the elements appear and evolve, he begins to describe the drama in his emerging painted world.

"It was a peaceful morning," he says. His first mark on the paper is a round yellow sun. "And then a volcano went off." He splashes red paint upwards in long strokes to obliterate the round yellow sun. "Then an ambulance came along, and then a fire engine which filled the volcano up with water. The good thing was, it was near a pond and this water could be used to fill up the volcano with, the bad thing was there were fish in the pond and they got put in the volcano too."

"Oh, good," I say, "that the water put out the volcano, but bad that the poor fish went in too." He pushes a deep blue forcefully into the paper until it wears a hole. Red fire and blue water mix with the yellow to create purple and brown ripples. "The hospital, here, was set on fire by a spark from the volcano. Then an aeroplane came and sprayed all the world with water."

The oblong architecture of the white hospital and the white dart of the aeroplane appear, clearly visible for a while until they are obliterated during the eruption of the red spark from the volcano and the shower of blue water from the aeroplane. "One thing was wrong though, the plane went too fast and crashed. When it crashed it made a big bang and then the tree went on fire."

More red fire, and more holes appear in the paper until the table begins to become part of the painting.

"Another rocket went past spraying everything with water from the pond, making it a little puddle. It put everything out except the volcano."

He adds deep blue again, this time by dripping paint directly out of the bottle, making a swirling spiral. By now, most of the other colours are mixed to a brown and grey puddle. He sits back and reflects on the scene of destruction. "A magic raindrop can do all sorts of damage, but a fish can travel in it." John adds orange spots to represent the fish, then mixes them in until they are lost again. He takes some black paint as he expands his thoughts on the magic raindrop.

"It can make earthquakes, thunder clouds, floods, dents in the runway to make planes crash. It can split the world in half and kill anyone, even God and the Devil. The magic raindrop kills the people who kill the fish."

Black dots are banged onto the page using the brush on its side in his fist, like a drum stick. The brush brought down so hard that splashes land on the table and one or two land on John's face. "No one likes the fish so it needs some healing," he explains, and looking at the soaking page with its holes he tells me "This picture's finished now."

"Would you like to have a new piece of paper?'

"Yes, I'm going to paint the fish."

We put the painting on some clean sheets of paper to support it, and then lay it carefully on the drying rack and clean the table together. The palette now contains mainly shades of brown and grey, and it is washed and replenished with clean brightly coloured paint. For his next image, John takes brown paper and begins again. "There was a big fire and a lake."

Red again. A fire in the centre of the image, but not as large as the volcano had been, and more carefully delineated. Then pale blue for the lake. For the moment, he has forgotten that he was going to paint the fish. "There were some people by the lake." Four stick people appear, standing in a line, two large and two small, like a family of two adults with their two children.

"A fire engine came to put the fire out." White paint, applied in smooth strokes with a fat brush across the page, washes away the fire, and then the lake, and then the people standing by.

"Oh, the people John!"

"Fish from the lake went in the fire and got cooked."

Orange dots dabbed gently into the muddy red, brown and grey fire.

"Oh, the poor fish!"

"There was a volcano again." Red again brushed on top to dissolve the marks of the orange fish. "And a magic raindrop, and big waves came. The biggest of all the oceans in the world and a whirlwind sucks everything into the fire."

Blue. At first curving waves across the paper and then circles made with the whole length of his arm that mix all the colours on the page together into a shining wet pool. "Then a huge hoover comes and hoovers it all up."

He folds the edges of the paper towards the middle and the paint runs together and pools in the centre, pouring out at the edges. He takes more paper and wraps up the folded picture, in one, two, three layers, and then puts it to one side.

"My next picture is going to be the fish."

"OK John. Help yourself to the paper that you would like to use."

For his final image John takes a sheet of white cartridge paper. He makes the outline of his fish in black, large, in the centre of the page. He carefully adds some white scales, and an eye. He keeps the brush with the black paint in one hand, and takes another brush, dips it in the red paint and trails it tentatively underneath. He puts the brushes down and looks at me anxiously. "It's blood. The fish is hurt."

"Oh, the poor fish is hurt."

He scribbles out the fish with white paint, until there is no sign of it remaining. "Shall I get it back? What would be a good colour to heal the fish?"

"I'm not sure. What colour do you feel would be good to heal the fish?"

"Blue."

He takes a clean brush, and blue paint, and finds the fish again in the wet sea of paint, re-outlining the shape, carefully restoring each scale and its eye. It looks quite different this time. Now it swims in a background of blue, grey and pink and is looking more solid. John too is beginning to change, and is working and talking more slowly, as the tension drains out of him into the painting. He sits back in his chair for a moment and gazes out of the window.

"This fish is on his own," he reflects. "He had parents but they didn't treat him nicely and they hit him and shouted at him and left him alone for ages."

"Were the fish's parents like your parents John?"

"Yes."

"But he's not being hit now."

"No, he's not being hit anymore . . . he's safe now." We sit together in this understanding for a moment. "What do you think the fish needs John?"

"He needs to go in a safe pond where he won't get sucked up and put in the volcano."

John stands up and takes a cardboard carton from the shelf and some scissors. It takes him considerable time to trim down the edges, until he has created a deep rectangular tray. He then puts the picture into the bottom of the tray and looks up at me. "Done!"

"It is finished now. Do you feel that he will be safe in there?"

"Yes."

"Where shall we put him? Will he be safe on this shelf to dry until next week?"

"Yes, but he must be here near the window so that he can see out."

The art materials are washed and put away and the table wiped. The apron is hung back on his hook behind the door, and we use a damp tissue to clean the black splashes from John's face. As we walk back through the school, over the patterned tiles, past the stairs and out into the hall, he tells me that he is looking forward to football practice, and to visiting a friend for tea, after which they are going to the cinema. When we arrive in the hall, his foster mother is waiting and she smiles. He runs up to her.

"I did healing a fish!"

Jigsaw

Barbara Hillman

It is like an invasion. The laughter and chattering of mothers and children is abruptly drowned by the oncoming roar of an engine, the crunch of car wheels and screech of brakes as a cloud of dust gradually subsides around an old, open-backed truck skidding to a halt on the dirt track. A baby dressed in pink and wearing a bonnet is crawling towards one of its front wheels. In those seconds, when everyone including her mother seems paralysed by the spectacle, the truck reverses with a whine, catching and dragging the baby by the arm, swallowing her into a swirl of dust and fumes.

Unable to bear it, I turn and rush towards a red brick wall and, flinging my arms up against it for support, bury my head in my chest overwhelmed by feelings of cowardice, shame and horror at the way I am turning my back on this catastrophe. Simultaneously my mind whirrs into overdrive as I prepare to turn and help, visualizing the scenario behind me. I know what I have to do: free the baby; stem the bleeding and try to save its life; save its arm; comfort the mother who, like everyone else, has receded into the shadows of the bush. In short, I have to bring some semblance of control to the chaos and suffering before me. In the appalling silence I race towards the baby.

And then I wake up. I can feel my heart pounding as I drag myself from sleep. Still gripped by the nightmare I try to detach myself, to look at the scene as if it were a film. But that is worse. Alarmingly, I still feel part of that familiar scene, where a dirt track ending in a clearing of sparse, khaki grass surrounded by eucalyptus trees in scorching heat with the incessant shrill of crickets was part of the backdrop to my childhood in South Africa. But why the dirt-encrusted brown truck? It doesn't make sense.

I open my eyes. Sunlight slices through the curtains revealing the comfort of familiar objects. My eyes settle on a large black and white photograph, hazy in the half-light, revealing a group of children clustered around a woman. They form a triangle and at their apex a slim girl stands as if guarding her family. That provides the trigger. Only then do I make the connection: the driver of that old brown truck was Father Griffin, a Jesuit priest who used to visit our family frequently around the time that photograph was taken. Both relieved and shaken by identifying this piece of the puzzle, I sit up to draw the curtains and stop to gaze for a second at a silver haired woman reflected in the mirror, with a slightly fuller face but the same definite eyebrows framing anxious eyes, with the same high cheekbones and strong jaw as the girl in the photograph.

Leaning against the pillows while sipping tea, I relate the dream to my husband, Michael, hoping to lessen its impact. "I don't know what it's all about."

"It's obvious. You're the damaged baby and you're the woman facing the brick wall. I mean you spent half your life denying what had happened to you."

Taken aback by his insight and my naivety after years of psychotherapy I hurry away to my appointment with Stephanie, a twice weekly occurrence, which at first Michael had heartily endorsed, but then complained that it had gone on too long and was becoming a way of life. Driving my familiar route, unusually oblivious to the beauty around me, I cross an ancient bridge on the Thames without a sideways glance, my mind centred on my dream.

One aspect that Michael did not interpret was that I took it upon myself to look after everyone, just as I did when a girl. But someone had to look after us, I muse, remembering the desperate strait my mother was in when my father abandoned us when I was ten. By then, the eldest of five with the youngest newly born, I was proud to be my mother's 'right-hand girl', as she spoke of me to her friends.

Once again I am back in South Africa. The day before I had felt rooted in England. This propulsion from one period of my life to another, one country to another and one emotional mood to another, with extremities of despair interspersed with periods of equilibrium and creativity, had been the norm throughout my psychotherapy; yet it still took me by surprise. Perhaps this is what occurs when someone has repressed abusive memories so deeply that they are recalled spasmodically, I decide, remembering early days in psycho-therapy. Then my memories had been veiled in a flimsy film of disbelief and confusion. I had kept them such a secret that at times I only half believed what I was saying to Stephanie. They seemed so preposterous that I sometimes wondered whether I was making them up and whether she even believed me as, at my own pace, I began to revisit my childhood.

Then two years into the therapy, one afternoon in May, my life seemed to turn upside down without any warning. Crouching against a backdrop of wisteria, potting clumps of lobelia and a shell pink geranium, I beckon my husband. "Michael, could you hold this in place while I plant? I've already snapped one of the stems, they're so brittle." Michael saunters over and holds the plant while I position it, filling the hole with soft soil, gently firming its roots. "Isn't it a beautiful?"

"Ssh" he hisses placing a finger over his lips and I notice he has earphones on as he moves the plant inadvertently, listening to the radio, not concentrating on the task.

"Careful, keep it still."

"Ssh," he replies more urgently, frowning, his eyes staring vacantly into space. "It's a Catholic priest. I'm trying to get the details."

"Another one!"

"Yes, but this one's a Jesuit. That's what caught my attention. A Father George Griffin has been convicted of sexual abuse of both boys and girls. A priest in his eighties I think. Here in England. He's to be imprisoned."

"Father Griffin! So . . . it's true . . . I didn't imagine it . . . I wasn't the only one . . . he's still alive."

"No you certainly weren't the only one."

"But that's amazing. Are you sure you got the name right?"

"Yes, definitely. We'll try and hear it on the nine o'clock news. Is this done? You look a bit pale. Are you alright?" and he puts his arm around my shoulders.

"It's just a shock. I haven't heard anything from him for almost thirty years."

"Shall we talk while we prepare supper?" and he walks away to gather his tools.

Alone, I wonder at this almost umbilical connection pulsing between abuser and victim. Is it always like this, I ask myself. As if waking from a trance I hear the comforting cooing of doves, the hum of a lawnmower and notice the lengthening shadows of the silver birch imperceptibly fingering a path across the lawn as I brush the soil from my grimy fingers. My teeth are chattering uncontrollably. The sun is sinking. I am in shadow.

Important new evidence has been found about Jill Dando's murder so there is nothing more about him on the news that evening. We go to bed. "We'll look in the papers tomorrow, get the facts, then you can put it all behind you."

"Yes," I reply uncertainly, knowing that I have been trying to do this most of my life. Now it is different: Father Griffin has returned in a way I had never expected. Soon Michael is breathing heavily. Alone, my mind spins out of control. Images flash by dizzily: images of an old priest in the dock before his brave victims, before a jury, before a judge. How did he bear it . . . the shame? Where is he now? I doze, I dream. I waken. It is not a dream. My memories, like a can of worms, jostle for space, restless. All night my relationship with him hurtles from scene to scene: his frequent visits to our fatherless home, coinciding with bath-time; him taking my brother and myself on picnics, lighting camp-fires, boiling billy cans for tea in enamel mugs, sweetened with condensed milk to wash down charred boerewors between thick hunks of brown bread; the afternoon he started a veld fire on sugar loaf hill; cuddling into bed with us to read Rudyard Kipling's *Jungle Stories*; his long absence and reappearance one night on a motorbike when he slept in our house then dedicated it to the Sacred Heart after saying Mass on the dining-room table, my mother beside him like a shadow; and bathroom scenes . . . their doors always without locks. I jerk and sit up.

"Are you alright?"

"Just a dream," I mutter as my mind continues to sift through a conglomeration of images like a jumble of jigsaw pieces in my half awake, half child, half adult, half in England and half in South Africa state.

Somehow I arrive at my session the following morning. "The most extraordinary thing happened yesterday. Last night Michael heard on the six o'clock news that Father Griffin has been convicted of child abuse—here in England." Stephanie listens quietly and calmly as though it were the most ordinary happening in the world that the day my abuser is convicted in court I hear about it in a slot of the nationwide news we seldom listen to, after being incommunicado for thirty years. "My first feeling was pure relief. But the more I think about it, the more guilty I feel that I didn't speak out about him when it happened. It might have stopped the abuse of the other children."

"There was no-one for you to trust enough to tell," she reminds me. "The only way you could cope at the time and in that climate of public denial was to bury it. That is what you did, like many other children."

I swing from feelings of triumph—that what I had always claimed had proved true, to feelings of disbelief—that perhaps my husband had heard it incorrectly. I turn to another topic. Too much has happened too quickly. It is less painful to avoid it for a while. "I'm going to buy some newspapers when I leave you. I have to hear or see for myself that this is true."

"If you can't find anything, you could search the web for the BBC news", Stephanie suggests. This is a novel idea to me, but we have a computer and I'm determined to try after I scan the newspapers—every column. But there is nothing about him, only a copious article and photograph of a younger priest who had re-offended for child abuse after a prison sentence. Secretly I wonder if Michael had confused Father Griffin's name with this priest. Furtively, before my daughter comes home, Michael shows me how to search the web, but he is still a novice. Then we find it:

PRIEST JAILED FOR ABUSING CHILDREN
An 87 year old Jesuit priest who sexually abused children over a nineteen year period has been jailed for two years. Father George Griffin pleaded guilty to 30 offences of indecent assault and gross indecency against 5 boys and 4 girls aged between 7 and 16 at the time of the assaults. He pleaded not guilty to another 17 similar offences.

Stunned, we read the lengthy report as his crimes and grave breaches of trust of parents and children are described and explained. "I wonder if anyone in court knows that although his past in Britain has caught up with him, he committed similar offences earlier on in South Africa?"

"Probably not. Well, apart from a fellow priest, or his Superior. The Church just shielded and moved them." Michael replies.

We print out the report. I place it in a box of cuttings I keep beside my bed. I feel as though I am concealing a guilty secret, as if I am hiding a part of him beside my bed. Exhausted, I am again unable to sleep. My mind is on red alert, a cesspit of images and memories as I digest the facts. This report fits him like a glove made up of the very fabric of his tactics and behaviour. The sun-worn texture of his skin, his muscular hairy arms, its creases and even his smell permeates my heightened sensitivity. I toss and turn and eventually slide out of bed and creep downstairs as I will do for nights to come. I find pen and paper. My tears merge with the black ink as I write. That first night I decide that I need to contact him, to confront him, to bring him to account for the damage he inflicted on me and maybe others in my family. As darkness dissolves into dawn I creep upstairs, glad that I have reached a decision and soon slip into the oblivion of sleep.

I wait for my next session with Stephanie. It is like hanging from a cliff waiting to be rescued. "It's as if it is happening all over again." I sob.

"Yes, it must be very painful for you."

"But why now, years afterwards?"

"It was not possible or safe for you to feel the pain then. You internalised it instead. Only now are you feeling what you should have felt when you were a girl."

"But why now? Now that I know he's been found out. Now that I know my memories are real. Now that I know I'm not the only one ... those other children ..." I sob, as if drowning in my own tears. "I feel so guilty ... If ... if only I had told someone then."

"There was no-one for you to tell, to trust," she reminds me for the umpteenth time. "You must remember that you and the rest of your family were in an extreme situation, had been for years. In times of such extreme stress it is as if there is no right and wrong. There is only survival and you did the only thing you could do at the time: you did nothing. But don't forget, when your younger sisters needed protecting, you spoke out. You did all you could to protect them."

"But it's unbearable ..." My sobs gradually cease. I lie, exhausted. "Let us find a metaphor for this experience. It is like an abscess or a carbuncle that has been opened up. It needs to drain. You need to re-experience the pain and when you have finished weeping you will heal from deep within you, but it will take time. You have contained this trauma for most of your life. Allow yourself time and rest to heal." Reassured, I lie peaceful. "I've decided I have to confront him as I did my father. But as I can't see him, I have to write to him."

"That sounds a good idea."

"I'll write this week." My midnight thoughts are feasible. Perhaps I've not gone mad, I think. "Take your time. There's no rush. Write when you are ready." I leave my session with a mission.

One morning I wake and find the courage to telephone Leeds Crown Court. With a trembling voice stifled with emotion, I explain my mission. A sympathetic voice gives the prison telephone number. I ring them with a little more confidence and am given his identity number and the address of a special prison he has been taken to. I am advised to check that he is indeed there as prisoners can be unexpectedly moved. At the next prison I meet with resistance by being told that I need to obtain the governor's permission before I write. This throws me into further turmoil. I cannot cope with the idea that it may not be granted, or that it may take weeks for a letter to reach him, so vital is my need to confront him. I decide for once to flout authority and begin to compose the letter in my head, writing several drafts until I am satisfied.

Dear Fr. Griffin,
Last week I heard of your conviction on the 6 o'clock news.

Perhaps I need to remind you who I am: the eldest daughter, Clare, of Elizabeth Hill; her younger children being Paul, Rosemary, Joan and Veronica. We lived in Williamstown where Paul was a pupil at Saint Edmund's College where you were a master.

In the late fifties we were a vulnerable catholic family abandoned by our father. As our mother was unable to support us unaided, we were reliant on charity for our survival and education, principally from the Church. You befriended us, visiting more and more frequently and fulfilling some of the needs of a fatherless family. My mother and I held you in awe and trusted you implicitly when you began your abuse of me in our home, violating my trust and innocence.

No words can describe the misery and pain your actions have had on my life and the anger and abhorrence I feel for what

you did to me and your other victims. I hope you understand
something of the anguish that you have caused us.

I do wonder what happened in your childhood. As a survivor
I have come to the realization that it is only by facing the
past, painful as it is, and achieving an understanding of why
we behaved as we did in our unique situation that we are
eventually able to go forwards and so find some peace in our
lives. This I sincerely wish for you too: that you eventually find
peace.

I place the letter into the mouth of the box and watch as it is
irrevocably swallowed. I step back, inexplicably frightened as though
I have released a timed explosive. As I walk home along the lane
decked with elderflowers and roses tumbling over fences and
hedgerows, I am seized with panic. What if the letter was too
aggressive or vindictive . . . ? What if he hangs himself alone in his
cell faced with my words . . . and I have not obtained the governor's
permission! All day I panic; admonishing myself, justifying myself,
forgiving myself; just as I did when I was young. But I don't make
the connection. Caught in this web, my fear that he might take his
life corresponds with my own fragility when destructive feelings
suddenly overwhelm me   when I am driving alone down the
motorway, or when I consider the concoction of medication I could
drink when Michael is out all day. I feel so fragmented that I feel
only my skin is holding me together.

Two days later I tell Stephanie what I have written in the letter.
"You would not have written a vindictive letter. You are not that
kind of person. It would be out of character." And I know she is
right. I leave Stephanie feeling calmer as though I have woken from
the nightmare. Twice a day I pour my feelings into my journal. It
tells of my survival. Like a life-belt it keeps me afloat between
sessions when I dive into my deepest, darkest depths.

Then one morning, dazzled by the bright sunlight, I walk through
my front door into the contrasting gloom. Before my eyes properly
adjust I see a white letter on the doormat and I know it is from him
before I even read my name or scrutinize the postmark. Like a rat
with a stolen titbit, I scurry upstairs and open it with trembling
fingers.

Dear Clare,

Thank you for your letter. It reinforces all the contrition for the harm I have done. I am protected by my failing memory of all that past except for a few blurred images. Otherwise it has all gone. But you have been left, it seems, with a damaged psyche. God forgive me! All I can do is keep you in my prayers.

I could not have endured myself the agony of the 15 months of waiting for my trial if there had not been a great support from God. He died for sinners.

I now follow the urges of my fellow priests and friends, to leave all these thoughts behind me. When my imprisonment is over I shall put a permanent MEMORIAL in my Mass—for you and all victims of my unaccountable behaviour.

NO. I had a serene childhood. My family, like yours, was a very solid Christian one. No excuse there. The punishment will be salutary. I have only one ambition now: to use this shock to get closer to God.

With love and shame
I wish you well in Jesus Christ

This is the reply I received from a man with barely a memory of his past. A man who cannot bear much reality. I have been left it seems with a damaged psyche . . . ? Maybe. But I am no longer imprisoned by denial and gripped in the vice of Catholic Dogma.

The whole experience is a dose of shock treatment, but instead of numbing it had the opposite effect. Although I had begun to scratch the surface of my childhood, this plunges me into a crevasse of memories and pain. There is no way out but to cling on and climb painstakingly up—sometimes in total darkness—hoping for a glimpse of light followed by a period of daylight, always with Stephanie's voice in the background guiding me forward. My writing becomes a constant refuge and companion; sifting through the debris of dreams, often of my childhood and how it continues to affect my relationships and choices in daily life; sometimes writing letters to myself as a child, sometimes to my mother or father as if they were alive. Here I face their betrayal. At my therapy sessions I begin to understand why and to attain some degree of acceptance. But the big single question I have to ask myself is why I feel so worthless that I have this habitual need to look after everyone else: my alcoholic father, my dying mother, my vulnerable siblings, Father Griffin, my own family, my friends, my pupils; the list is endless. Yet in my bad moments I feel that I have failed as a mother, am failing as a wife, am useless, unlovable. I am not good enough and I cannot, will not look after myself.

Then one morning I stand up and keel over. The room is revolving and the floor tips up to meet me. It feels as though I am once again a teenager in the Bay of Biscay on my way to England after my mother's death. At last I am rendered helpless. My husband and my children have to look after me and themselves—a learning experience for us all. Unable to travel to my psychotherapy, I have telephone sessions for months. Unable to earn, Stephanie suggests a token fee until I have recovered. I am not used to accepting an unconditional offer of love. It is not easy for me. That period is my darkest. It takes me six months to recover physically.

Gradually I am learning to love myself. I can vividly recall the memories. I still feel the pain at times. I have begun to share some of my experiences, to write about them, unpalatable as they are. Hopefully they will help other survivors too. I am finding the courage to bridge the chasm in my life, with secrecy and shame on the one side and freedom on the other. For me, the present and the future are contained in time past. I am learning that although past memories seem at times to be all-engulfing, they belong to the past. I am gradually letting go.

Finding the Four Year Old

Katherine Justesen

For as long as I can remember I have hated space invaders—those people who think it perfectly permissible to actually touch me within minutes of meeting. A handshake is fine, thank you very much, and if—in weeks or months to come—we find ourselves at that juncture in our relationship where I think it is acceptable for you to come within a foot of me, I'll let you know. But not before—understood?

This intense dislike of physical contact was not my reason for seeking therapy but when the sessions began recurring themes kept coming up: for instance, my need for total perfection, unceasing demands on myself and overwhelming sense of impending failure, and I was interested to find out why I did the things I did and felt the things I felt.

Over the course of about two years, I had started to identify patterns of behaviour in myself that manifested whenever I felt under attack, criticised, undermined, embarrassed or ashamed. My reactions would be strong, swift and in most instances inappropriate. With the help of my therapist, I began to understand that when I felt those emotions, I went back to being four years old. The child that reappeared was scared, lonely and unheard. With unbelievable skill and gentleness, my therapist guided me through my feelings and emotions until I reached the point when I could determine where the feelings originated. From that position of greater self-knowledge I was then able to recognise that those feelings belonged to the past. When they arose, I could acknowledge them, and then choose to respond from a more adult frame of reference.

Perhaps it is all a matter of perception. From the earliest age with big blue eyes and my hair in Baby Jane ringlets I was passed from lap to lap like a doll. Despite trying to impress upon my parents how I detested the attentions of whiskey-smelling business men and their bosomy wives—all cleavage and long gold necklaces—my protestations fell on deaf ears as I was handed another bowl of stuffed olives to pass round and told to "Sparkle! Sparkle!". My parents did an enormous amount of corporate entertaining and, as part of the team, I was expected to charm, giggle, recite and perform from about three years of age. Whilst there was never any question of impropriety, I hated being the centre of attention. But my discomfort and shame were ignored and, worse, ridiculed by my parents. Failure to comply would meet with derision and exclamations of "Spoilt, horrid girl!". The image of the perfect family was the illusive dream my parents sought, just as long as everyone outside our home believed in it.

Therapy is an extraordinary thing. In the year that I have been seeing my current therapist so much has been uncovered, so many pieces of the puzzle have started to fit. The process is undeniably painful and intense, but it brings with it those exquisite moments of understanding when I make sense of myself as a thirty-four year old woman, and ultimately start to like what I find. It has enabled me to understand my own reality, and to challenge those that would deny it. This strength to challenge has proved difficult for many, particularly my parents, but it is vital to ensuring my continued personal growth. Done with respect and care, challenging my mother and father has made my relationship with both of them more adult and equal.

My father rang me some weeks ago and said that he had been sorting through some documents and had found a press cutting from some twenty-five years ago. I was pictured in the local paper with a write up about an antiques fair that had opened at the weekend. The photo showed my face in profile looking into the blank eyes of a marble bust. As Dad waxed lyrical about how wonderful it was to find it, I was transported back to that day and I could feel the shame and embarrassment rising up. The photographer from the local rag had been walking around the fair and had asked my parents if he could take my picture. I said I didn't want to. My parents said they'd be delighted. The photographer asked me to bend over and stare at the marble head in front of me. I looked imploringly at my mother. She told me to hurry up. The photographer asked me to look like I was enjoying myself. I could feel the lump in my throat and tears pricking my eyes. My father joked with the photographer about working with animals and children.

As gently as I could, I told my father that far from having fond memories of the day I had been humiliated and embarrassed. Dad could not comprehend that his version of events could be so at odds with my own, and became defensive. "Well if it was so bloody awful for you, I'll throw the thing away then", he huffed.

"That would be a shame," I said. "You loved me having my picture taken, and you like the photo, you should keep it if it makes you smile. Just because I hated it, doesn't mean you have to. We can have different memories about the same event Dad". And he couldn't argue with that!

I have a son, and I struggle not to make the same mistakes with him that my mother made with me. I avoid her pitfalls but dig plenty of my own in the process. Because I was made to perform for the grown ups, to sit on laps, to kiss moustachioed women who all seemed to demand the prefix of "aunt", I am adamant that my son will not be required to do the same. He is required to treat everyone with respect and politeness, but I have not and will not force him to kiss anyone with whom he does not feel comfortable.

One day my mother came over for tea, and brought with her a family friend, an elderly lady whom we see once every six months. Whilst I have known this lady all my life, my son who is three did not remember her, and on leaving she embraced me and then turned to him. "Come and give your Aunty Joy a kiss then", she said and bent down towards him. He looked at me with huge imploring eyes that I recognised at once and hung back behind me. "Oh come along and don't be such a silly boy," said my mother, adopting her authoritative tone that makes my hackles rise. I looked down at my son and said quietly "Sweetheart, you don't have to kiss anyone you don't want to—its fine", and I smiled. He smiled back at me with a look of relief that broke my heart and make it sing at the same time.

I looked at my mother—I had stood up for my little boy—and finally for myself.

By Bread Alone

Antoinette Marshall

I know what it is to truly feel all right, to feel OK, contented, to feel happy, all together in soul and body. I know it because I experienced it once. Only once in my twenty-seven years of life. It's what I felt that day when I was four years old.

I close my eyes and I see a road in the west of Ireland. It goes through my village. On each side the white cottages are small, like nests. I can see the last red rambler roses in the gardens. Beyond them, the blue hills, and haze above them. It is a clear, very fresh autumn morning, and the yellow and purple leaves hang still on the trees. Our house is not far from the red-brick police station, next to the General Stores and Paddy's Bar. At the end of the village street my uncle has the Bakery. It is a Friday morning when my father puts the still warm round loaves in his big black car (the only taxi in the village), and takes them to farms and houses beyond our village, as far as the next village about ten miles down the road. A golden day. With golden loaves.

Today I am allowed to accompany him. The Bakery door is open and I can see the orange flames blazing in the oven at the back of what seems to be a deep cave. Some brown loaves are already lying in neat rows on the large wooden trays, and my uncle's white hat bobs up and down above them. He winks at me through the white flour, a fine film of dust smoothing out the lines of his round face. I help my father to cover the seats of his car (which he keeps always very shiny, like a hearse) with the long white sheets kept for this purpose. We then pile up the bread till the back window becomes invisible. I clamber on to the passenger seat in the front and we depart in a cloud of dust. The road in front of the Bakery was never repaired. My uncle always joked that the deepest hole in the ground could be used as a grave! He was very kind to me. He never beat me like my father and elder brother did when I was bad. He used to give me little brown pancakes to eat after he had finished baking. He could make me laugh, pretending he was a clown when his face was covered with white flour and he rolled his almost black eyes. He died of a sudden heart attack when I was nine. He was fifty-four and had never married. My parents took me to see him in his coffin. He seemed to have shrunk. He was lying very neatly, wearing a dark blue suit, a starchy white shirt with a red-spotted tie. He was not wearing his white hat anymore, and his skull was too shiny. No more flour on his face, just a blank expression. I felt numb. He was the first dead person I had ever seen.

Now I can see the dry-stone wall at the end of the village, and through its gaps, a small patch of green oats. A little further along, the turf is built into coarse ricks to dry. Sometimes I help my older brothers to put it into large black bags and carry it home for fuel in the winter. It is work for the lads; my sisters stay at home and help our mother with housework. Behind the hedges there are a few sheep nibbling whatever they can find. We reach a turn in the road where Our Lady smiles down on us from her stone face. Her statue looks gigantic, and there is a rusty vase at her feet with a few dry flowers in it. In the summer the hedges seem to bleed, the fuchsia flowers are called "Deora Dia" (tears of Christ) and I think it is a lovely name for Our Lord's Mother, a beautiful feminine name . . .

I hear barking dogs in the distance. My father drives on and does not talk, but I am sitting next to him and feel happy. I can smell the warm nourishing smell of bread around both of us. The wheels screech, my father stops the car. I am allowed to help unload the bread and carry some loaves very carefully to people's doors. I feel as if I am carrying the Holy Sacrament. Angels are smiling all around me, when farmers' wives open their doors and gratefully receive my offering. I hear them say, "What a big wain you've turned out to be, Tom O'Driscoll! The spitten image of your Da, aren't you?" I blush, swollen with pride and embarrassment. All morning, tottering up and down lanes, ignoring dogs barking, babies crying, I carry the bread from my father's black taxi to the villagers' front doors. My father exchanges news and gossip as well as loaf-bread and money, but he is a conscientious worker and generally does not like to waste his time with too much "idle talk". He never accepts any hard stuff to drink when he works and people respects him for that. I have learnt to keep my greed in check, to say "no thank you" when I am offered a delicious-looking scone or a glass of milk.

The air is getting very nippy. The range of mountains is brooding over the horizon. My nose is dripping and my hands start feeling numb. I had mittens knitted by my mother when I was a baby but I am too big for them now. I am glad to go back home after a long morning's work with my father. The car is now empty of loaves, apart from a few crumbs on the white cloth. I'll give them to the birds in our yard later on.

We arrive back home by two o'clock in the afternoon. The cold wind now blows the autumn leaves around; dead, crisp leaves fall on the road, on top of hedges. I am now looking forward to sitting in our warm kitchen again.

The fire is blazing in the hearth when we get home. My mother is on her own, busying herself by the stove. From her back, I guess she is in a good mood. I avoid looking at the picture of the Bleeding Heart on the wall. My mother's smile is comforting suddenly. I don't remember ever seeing her look so relaxed. She helps me take my coat, bonnet, scarf and brogues off and says there is a big platter of chips waiting. I sniff the sizzling potato-chips ready for us on the range. A fatty, earthy smell.

"Tom was a good helper. He deserves a good dinner," my father says to my mother. My father praised me! They both laugh and I feel so happy: for once I am not a disappointment! For once, they showed their love to each other, and there was enough love left for me too. That day I felt I was their child. The three of us were snug, a happy family in our warm kitchen, drinking strong tea and eating golden chips around the family table. This was my home—no rough brother, no bossy sister, no mocking lodger, no treacherous rival to share it with. That day they had all vanished!

I was at home, between my mother and my father, do you understand? Can you really see what it meant to me when I was four? My father was praising me for being his son, a very good worker like himself. My mother was feeding me my favourite food. They were both approving of me. That once. The once only, as far as I can remember. And my good uncle, the baker, was alive and we were eating his best bread! Once upon a time, my needs were completely fulfilled. You cannot take this away from me now. No one can, never.

My space . . . my own space. I did not have to fight for it then, just that once. That day in autumn, when I was four, my parents found time for each other. And time to spare for me as well. Time for love, wouldn't you say? So I knew it, just that once.

Tom's shoulders were now moving up and down in his rhythmic sobbing. He started rubbing his eyes with his two closed fists. "Sorry, sorry, sorry . . ." he moaned softly. The therapist pushed the box of tissues towards him. Tom's tears were now flowing quietly down his face. The therapist had never seen him crying in this spontaneous way before. She said gently, "Good to cry, Tom, tears can help you heal. Don't say sorry! We both know you'll feel better soon." They were both aware something momentous had just occurred. Some memories could be healing. "Are these tears healing?" the therapist asked herself, as Tom bravely smiled, his weeping receding.

A November day in London. The fog was gathering outside the tall windows. A bell rang from the bowels of the building. An institutional cabbagey, starchy smell reached their nostrils. The therapist cleared her throat, sighed and said softly. "Come, Tom. Your therapy's over for today. Your dinner's ready downstairs." She smiled. "See you again very soon."

They stood up and she opened the door.

LOVE

Dream On

Phil Lapworth

Cheryl's problem? Aged thirty-eight and single. My diagnosis? A delightful romantic. Her belief? One day her prince will come. My prognosis? He won't. Her hope? That therapy will help find him. My therapeutic objective? Get real.

It wasn't that Cheryl was short of suitors. They'd practically been queuing up at her door since she was a teenager. This tall, lithe, dark-haired, sultrily beautiful woman could have had her pick from hundreds of adoring men. Her physical beauty was equally matched by a warm and attractive personality. She was witty, intelligent, thoughtful, fun-loving, considerate, responsible, well-read, socially and occupationally successful and, despite all this, remained modest. She was well liked by all who came into contact with her, including me. And yet, she was one of my most challenging clients. Her belief that somewhere in the world was Mr Right—no, that's not quite it, more her belief that somewhere was the one and only Mr Right for her in all the world—was as intractable a conviction as I have ever met.

A formidable business women, an articulate host, a sensible and trustworthy friend and yet, in her relationships with men, Cheryl was totally unrealistic. Brought up on fairy tales, the Disney versions at that, her romantic dream of the man she would meet and marry was, as I so often told her, as likely as learning to fly. Inevitably no man she met came remotely near to her ideal. How could he? This was a fantasy man. He didn't exist.

"No, he wasn't right," she would say in her naturally sensual voice. "I know you think I'm stupid, but I could tell from the moment I met him that he didn't fit the bill. I just knew it."

"I don't think you're stupid," I would reply. "Far from it. It would make more sense if you were. But you have just described, as so often

259

you do, a handsome, intelligent, articulate, considerate, caring, eligible man whom you dismissed within the first few seconds of meeting."

"That's when I'll know," she would insist.

The fairy tales were, of course, an expression of a much deeper longing. They provided a loom around which Cheryl could weave her desperate fantasy: a fantasy that contained all her yearning for her lost father. He had died of cancer when she was four, an age rife with oedipal wishes to usurp mother's place and marry father. Winning the oedipal battle can be disastrous, but losing it before it can be lost with dignity can be even more profound, as I believe it was for Cheryl. She had few actual memories of him but naturally had formed an idealised picture of what he was like. Certainly, he was attractive, as evidenced by the photographs she showed me. Tall, dark and handsome would describe the father as equally well as the daughter. But as to his being the all-powerful, all-loving, all-giving prince of her fantasy, I could only try to disillusion her by making him real, by making him human, with human frailties.

Rationally, she could accept this but it did nothing to shift the idealised fantasy she clung to on a more emotional and primitive level. I realised this shift may only come about if tackled within the transference and I attempted to explore this with her one day when she asked me if I liked classical music. "I know your father liked classical music," I replied, avoiding the surface level of the question. "I wonder if there's a wish on your part for me to be like him?" Cheryl smiled. She hesitated before saying anything as if she was choosing her words carefully. "I know what you're implying," she said, still smiling. "You think I may see you as my father. But I have to be honest . . ."

"Yes, do," I encouraged. "It's just that you're not handsome and you're too old." She was not smiling now.

The first judgment I had to accept. Handsome was not a word I would use to describe myself. I had long ago agreed with my partner and friends whose description of me as 'interesting looking' seemed more accurate. I had few illusions on that score: I *was*, however, about to challenge her second judgment when it occurred to me that she was right on that score too. I was chronologically old enough to be her father (although certainly not *too* old!). But her actual father had not grown old at all. He had remained the age he was when he died. He would always be the thirty-something father of the photographs.

"Your father remains young in time for ever," I observed. "You are about his age now. But you will age, while he will not."

"That's right," she said, now smiling again. "I'd better hurry up."

"To find your father?" I asked.

"No, to find a man as good as my father."

"That's a tall order," I said somberly. "But it will happen," she replied with her usual optimism.

And so we continued. My challenge to disillusion her, to help her get real and engage with a man who was not based in fantasy was becoming more urgent as time went on. We had already worked together for two years. I had my own rather negative fantasy of Cheryl growing old without a partner. Perhaps she was more influenced by her mother's chosen path of a long widowhood than her espoused desire to have a man in her life.

Then she had a dream. This was significant in itself as Cheryl rarely remembered her dreams and never in such detail. Usually they were impressionistic shades of shapes and colours, wordless but full of feeling and longing. This was quite different in its narrative structure and its clarity—at least its dream-world clarity of story, if not of meaning. "I'm out in the countryside walking with two people, a man and a woman, along the banks of a river," she told me. "I'm carrying a picnic basket full of food and wine. When we come upon a field of red poppies, we sit to have our picnic. We're laughing and joking and having lots of fun but I'm aware of being watched. I think I hear someone in the long grass, and I jump up. As I do so, I knock over the picnic basket, which spills its contents on the ground. I look in the long grass and find a large green snake looking at me. I realise this is what has been looking at me all along. It turns and disappears into the grass. As I repack the basket, I notice there's a letter addressed to me on top. I start to open the letter—but I wake up before I can read what is says."

"How did you feel on waking?" I asked, noticing there was a marked absence of feelings in her reporting of the dream. "I guess I felt disappointed," she replied. "I would have liked to know what the letter said. It's a bit tantalising, like the dream was leading to this point and then didn't come up with the goods."

"That sounds familiar," I suggested. "Well, yes, I suppose so," she concurred. "It feels similar to how I feel about the men I meet. I'm hopeful, then disappointed."

"Tell me what you make of the dream itself," I encouraged her. "What do you think it's saying to you?"

"I'm not sure," she said, reclining further back in her chair to ponder on this. "Apart from the ending, I enjoyed the dream. I think I felt happy in it. I think it was saying something positive."

"So how are you understanding it?" I probed. "For example, who are the two people? What do they represent for you?"

"In reality, I don't know them. They're not people I recognise," Cheryl explained. "I know we've talked about my masculine and feminine aspects. I suppose they might represent those. I felt very in tune with them, enjoying them. I felt very safe. Do you think it's something to do with feeling balanced?"

"That's possible," I agreed. "But what also occurs to me when you say you felt safe is the safety a child might feel with her two parents."

Cheryl instantly looked tearful. "Oh yes," she cried, a tear trickling down her cheek. "That feels right. Yes, it was a lovely feeling. It felt like this is how it should be." I waited for her to cry some more. This interpretation seemed to have moved her deeply and I did not want to interrupt her. In a while, she sat up again and wiped her eyes with a tissue, clearly signalling she was ready to go on. "We're in the countryside walking along a river bank," she recounted. "It's very beautiful."

"What about the river? Do you notice anything significant?" I asked. Cheryl closed her eyes, the better to recapture it. "It's flowing away from us. It's quite fast and there are bends where we can't see where it's going until we turn a corner. It's deep in places while in others I can see the bottom. I guess it's life really. I think it's my life stretching out ahead of me. And, of course, I don't know what's coming until I'm there, until I'm round the bend!"

I laughed with her at her Freudian slip. We could have taken it as a serious suggestion, perhaps explored the 'madness' of her Prince Charming quest, but it felt more like a moment of intimacy between us as we shared the humour, rather like she did with the two others in the safety of her dream. "So it may be that your dream sees you walking through life with your parents and you feel that this is how it should be," I summarised so far. "And the picnic basket?"

"Oh, that's full of goodies!" Cheryl exclaimed, apparently delighted by the thought. "Goodies?" I repeated. "Yes, it's full of good things!" she continued in her excited fashion. "It must be saying that life is good. At this point on the journey through life, everything is good and as it should be. And then we see this beautiful field of poppies, bright red, masses of them and that's where we stop." She hesitated as she seemed to realise what she had just said. I wondered aloud if she meant that's where the 'we' stops—that the family is ending there. She nodded in assent.

"But no," she revoked emphatically, quickly contradicting her nod. "It doesn't stop there. We have the picnic. We laugh and we joke and we have a wonderful time."

"Surrounded by a field of poppies," I reminded her.

"Yes, those beautiful poppies," she sighed. "Those blood red, danger red, death red poppies."

"And . . . ?" I urged her on. "And, despite the fun, I have this feeling of being watched," she said softly. "There is something lurking, something waiting in the long grass." She paused for just a moment and then with certainty stated, "The snake is death."

I let the words hang in the room between us. I felt this was so important for Cheryl. It seemed to me that, after all this time, the dream was bringing her to the reality of her father's death and, maybe for the first time, to feel the full impact of that loss. Perhaps, after this, she could really grieve and move on into the reality of living with human partners rather than an idealised ghost. But then she seemed to doubt her interpretation.

" 'The snake in the grass'!" she laughed. "But it wasn't threatening. There was nothing devious about it. It was just looking and it did me no harm."

"That's true," I confirmed. "It did you no harm."

"Don't you shrinks think that snakes are sexual symbols, phalluses?" she suddenly asked.

"Cheryl, these are your symbols," I replied. "There are many possibilities. What makes most sense for you?"

" I think that's what it is," she said, but seemed to be convincing herself rather than sounding convinced. "It's sex. It's something to do with a relationship."

"Maybe it is," I said. Having assured her of her ownership of the dream and its symbolism, I did not want to impose my own conviction of her first interpretation—though, I must admit, I hoped she'd return to it and was relieved when she did. "I guess I just don't want to see it," she said. "I think I'm wanting to hold on to the positive feelings I had about the dream."

"Those came later," I reminded her. "Your initial feeling was disappointment. Maybe you are trying to avoid the disappointment of your dream—a dream that seems to be merely emphasising the reality of your loss. We're both avoiding the upsetting of the picnic basket even before you see the snake."

"Yes, you're right," she said, now looking sad again. "It was upset. Everything spilled out. All the goodies were spoilt!"

She wept profusely. I suspected the profundity of the dream had hit the reality of her childhood and its impact was devastating. I could do no more than sit with her as she sobbed. We were nearing the end of the session and, though I was curious about the unopened letter of her dream's pre-waking moment, I considered it more important for her to stay with her grief. After she'd gone, I went over the dream again in my mind. It contained all the elements of her young life, the pleasure, the hope, the future, the security she had had and still craved—and the dashing of that hope, the frightening destruction of the family through the impending death of her father. It seemed to me that Cheryl's unconscious mind had considered the timing right to let her feel the despair of her loss and be done with fairy tales. Like the ancient tribes who would have seen the snake, and its shedding of skin, as a symbol of rebirth, I privately held the view that this would be a major transformation for her.

I was prepared for Cheryl to enter a period of mourning, even of depression following our session on the dream so I was surprised when she returned for our next meeting looking cheerful, indeed, looking radiant. There was something about her that sparkled. Her already beautiful presence had now an extra intensity and passion. I sat and waited as neutrally as possible but I was immensely keen to learn of this sudden—too sudden?—transformation of energy. I was also concerned. After all, it is not uncommon for people to avoid painful feelings by fleeing into health. "It's happened!" she announced even before she had sat down, almost beside herself with excitement. "I can hardly believe it but I've met the love of my life!"

My heart sank. This news confirmed my worst fear that Cheryl might again avoid her grief by hiding in her childhood fantasies. Now, it seemed she was deluding herself further in the belief that her prince had really come. I wondered how to approach this. It's hard to have the task of disillusioning someone who thinks they have just fulfilled the quest of a lifetime. I hoped something might present itself in the session that would enable me to gently instil some reality. For now, I was curious about what had happened, and I knew I was about to be told.

"It's all so amazing really," she laughed, the words just tumbling out. "I nearly didn't go and if I hadn't, well, I'd never have met him. But I did and we met and, gosh, he's so right. Oh, and by the way, the snake must have been sexuality. He's very sexy!"

At least she had remembered the dream. There was some hope in that but I was none the wiser about what she was telling me. Her euphoria had totally obliterated her usual eloquence. She may have seen my puzzlement as she took a few deep breaths and calmed herself. "My friend John had invited me to go out for a meal with some friends of his," she explained in a more moderated tone. "In the event, John was ill. I was going to cancel but John insisted I would like this couple, Simon and Catherine, and persuaded me to go ahead anyway. So I did and they were lovely. I felt really at home with them, as if I'd known them all my life. We went to the Café Rouge on River Street and had a wonderful meal and we talked and laughed and joked. It was such a lovely time."

Her delight in her story could have been infectious but it was not delight that I felt as I sat and listened. I had a strange sensation, which I find hard to describe. Anxiety? Fear? I'm not sure. I was already surmising that she'd fallen for the man of the couple she dined with—and all the complications that might entail, not least the Oedipal triangle she might be re-creating. But it was more than this. There was something in this story—so far positive and innocent-sounding—something that left me feeling uncomfortable. I noticed the hairs on my arms were tingling. But I couldn't understand my strange reaction. I could only observe it as Cheryl continued. "Well, we got to the end of the meal and I'd fumbled about in my bag to find my purse. But, sweetly, Simon insisted they would treat me. I needed the loo so while they were waiting for the waiter to come, I got up— quite forgetting my open bag was still on my knee. God, I felt so embarrassed! The contents spilled all over the floor, just everywhere. I really shouldn't carry so much junk around with me. Anyway . . ."

But I did not hear what followed. The hairs on my arms were standing almost erect from my skin. The falling bag had fully alerted me to the cause of my previous subconscious disturbance. I reran Cheryl's story through my mind: a meal with a couple she didn't know, River Street, Café Rouge, the fun and laughter, feeling at home. She was telling me the dream all over again. "Are you alright?" she was asking me, sitting forward in her chair with a look of concern. "Cheryl," I faltered, struggling to bring myself into the room. "I'm so sorry. I was distracted by several thoughts in response to your story. I wonder . . . well, I . . ."

"You mean the dream," she interrupted. "Yes, your dream," I said, rather surprised at the matter-of-fact way she referred to it. "Have you, I mean, do you see . . . ."

She interrupted me again as if to save me from my hesitancy, "Yes, it's the dream come true. You seem surprised."

"Well, it is rather uncanny. The couple, the river, the poppies." was all I could think to reply.

"Shall I finish the story?" she asked in a somewhat teasing manner. She was clearly as unfazed as I was disconcerted. She went on anyway. "I knelt down to gather together the contents of my bag, which of course is the picnic basket. But no, I didn't feel that everything was spoiled. It was just an accident. No big deal. In fact, I was laughing as I packed the bag again. Then someone was helping me, someone who'd been sitting at the table behind me all evening. I looked up at this green-suited man, into his green eyes—yes, the snake, the beautiful snake—and I knew. I knew in an instant, as I've so often predicted, that this was the man I would live with."

"You discussed this possibility together?" I asked, probably sounding as tetchily disbelieving as I felt. "No," she replied calmly. "We didn't talk at all."

I was tempted to say, "I suppose you just walked hand in hand off into the sunset!" but I stopped myself from losing my professionalism in such a swipe. I had, however, lost control of my feelings. Why was I so irritated? Why did I want to destroy the very thing my client had come to therapy for in the first place? Was my agenda more important, correct, therapeutic? I think not. I realised quite simply that I was jealous. The realisation was salutary and I managed to return my attention to where it rightly belonged. "You didn't talk?" I enquired. "No," she replied, a smile spreading across her face. "You're forgetting the letter."

"Ah, yes," I said, well aware of the omission. "The unopened letter."

"It wasn't quite a letter," she explained. "It was a small envelope. Maybe that's what it had been in the dream, but that doesn't matter. When I got back from the loo he'd disappeared. You'd have predicted I might have felt that familiar sense of disappointment, but I didn't. I just knew everything would be fine. And then I saw the envelope."

"And this time you opened it?" I asked, now myself excited in anticipation. "Yes," she confirmed. "His business card was inside with his name and telephone numbers and a hand-written message. It said 'We are such stuff . . . please call me'."

It transpired that the same evening she had called him. They had since spent the week together in what Cheryl described as magical bliss. Of course, being realistic, it may not last. Like many instant attractions it may be doomed to failure. And surely Cheryl will need to grieve her lost father before she can create a real partnership with a man and not a dream prince—won't she? But for now, having identified and tamed my own hidden emotion, I was pleased that Cheryl was basking in the pleasure of this man. I congratulated her and encouraged her to enjoy their meeting. As she got up to leave at the end of the session, I still had one remaining curiosity. She had mentioned the man's business card but not what his business was. As if she had read my mind, she turned in the doorway.

"By the way," she said. "He's a flying instructor."

Taking an Afternoon Off

David Herbert

A gentleman came to me because, he said, he wanted to love his wife—wanted, he gradually revealed, "To make her feel happy," especially, we eventually drew out, when they were making love, "In that intimate time when we are close."

Mr S. would look at me (when he looked up) with the trust and tenderness of one who believes the other has the answer. "I want to make love!" he declared, clearing his throat. "I want truly to make love, for her, to make her happy, as I am, in this way . . ."

Some background was sought from this tall, dark, handsome, finely-dressed thirty-year-old gentleman and at the end of this first session he sat back with relief, unfolded his hands and said, "You didn't ask me my religion, Doctor, and although I am observant, perhaps, in this matter, it is not relevant."

Three days later, at the same time, four o'clock on the dot, the bell rang and there he stood with a half-smile and a hand out-stretched to shake mine. A mirror of how I had greeted him on his first visit. "I cannot talk to my men friends," he began, "although they might be very well-informed and worldly . . . out of loyalty and respect for my wife, you understand . . . I do not want them to think she is unsatisfied, or insatiable. I do not want them to think about her at all, not even my best friend in New York, who is most sophisticated and experienced and we e-mail each other from our desks. He is also a Leicester-boy, same school . . . because, well, out of my own shame . . . and pride." He drank water and dabbed his mouth with a handkerchief.

He liked to look around: three pictures on the wall, the curtains either side of the French windows, the desk, the coffee table, the two small Isfahan carpets, the flooring, my shoes, my hands and, when he did look up at me, it was briefly, with an intense, almost pained stare. He looked mostly at his own hands, at the fingers extended, at the turned-up palms lying on his thighs. Once or twice the hands came together to stretch the fingers a little, once or twice he rubbed the flattened palms together, but there was no agitation in these actions, no tension that was apparent in his body. The voice, however, with little resonance, betrayed his nerves and he poured and drank water not infrequently.

"Mr S., may I ask you if your wife is unhappy?" I ventured after one of his longer pauses. "Oh, no!" he replied, "not in the generality!"

"And in this specific?"

"This specific?" He cleared his throat and found his voice. "Well, I have to tell you that she never smiles when we are close. She has never smiled, and she is silent."

"Her eyes?" I inquired. "Her eyes? . . . Oh, her eyes! They match her skin. Gold!" He paused. "Her eyes are closed." A slight cough, then he continued, "I thank you that you do not laugh. If I told my best friend, he would say something like 'Does she close her eyes and think of Kashmir?' and of course I do not know what she thinks or feels in this matter . . . in some ways, although we share our lives together in complete and peaceful harmony, I know as little about her as I know about you, Doctor. I cannot ask you and, for very different reasons, I cannot ask her!" His hand reached for the water and he glanced at the clock.

"My family found her for me in the Kashmir where we still have connections and, of course, our roots. My family took their time for I am their only son. They could not have chosen better. A well educated and refined lady from an exemplary family with four 'very beautiful daughters' according to my mother, who made the final choice and, of course, yes I have to say to an Englishman even of, or perhaps especially of, your profession . . . she was completely and absolutely pure . . . in other words, a virgin. For the first four months, when we were married, when we sat close, I would stroke her arms . . . I stroked her arms, her forearms, with my fingertips, and she would look at me lovingly, I am sure . . . Eyes wide . . . Then, when I kissed her arms one day, passion overcame me and Nature took its natural course with an abundance of delight and amazement . . . for me. But . . ." A long pause whilst he searched for words and perhaps controlled his tears. "The veil descended, her eyes closed."

As he stretched his fingers and looked directly at me, a vibrant voice returned and he told me, "We are blessed. God is good. We have a daughter. I love them both with my whole spirit and to the last breath in my body . . . . And you know, Doctor, my wife seeks my company when I am home. She comes into my study, she watches me at my computer. She comes onto the verandah, sits beside me whilst I read, especially when our child sleeps . . . But what does she want? More than to make love? Is it more from making love? Can I ask her? Will you help me?" He raised his hands and clapped them with relief, and stood up. "She is so charmingly silent and my experience, despite my English education, is no more than skin deep."

This was enough for one day. He had paled and required the bathroom. "I never wear a hat," he said as I handed him his handsome new cap from the hall-stand near the door. "I wear this because I do not want to be recognised by anyone, oh not because I am famous in any way but because I am supposed to have the answers, of course . . . as a Muslim . . . and I parked my car far from your house near the Heath . . . It's a nice walk. It's a nice afternoon . . . and it is my shame . . . or my pride."

Finally, in our last session—our third—as he wiped his hands on his handkerchief, which he folded and shaped and returned to the top pocket of his deep-blue linen suit, as I opened the French doors to cool the room on a balmy early August evening, he said "I don't want to ask you any questions, Doctor. You are the expert. You know my situation. Will you very kindly tell me every thing you can about the subject . . . about the subject of how to love her in a way that will help her to smile, with open eyes. Please teach me. I trust you."

Thus I was granted permission to give my predictable and presumptuous little speech, once again, but treading gingerly in hushed tones and watching his hands and his eyes for their reactions. "This is about taking an afternoon off. This is about you seeking her company in order to spend time with her . . . sitting where she sits, walking alongside her, holding her hand, following her glance, listening to her, asking her . . . 'Do you like the Heath? Are you getting used to London? Do you miss home?' hearing her answers and all the while rendering an atmosphere of romance with little touches . . ."

"Little touches?" he looked up. I mean it literally of course . . . fingertips touching a hand or a shoulder or moving a loose curl back into place ... but also an unexpected text, a call from the office, a note by the bedside, a favourite confection, flowers out of nowhere ... all sending messages which accumulatively invite her to receive the big message: I hold you in reverence ... which you do! Without doubt!" I paused. He nodded. "You will sense, as you watch—always taking time—soft movements from her body. They are signs. They are responses to the touches that are asking what a woman wants ... tenderness, male tenderness, your tenderness."

"Yes," I heard him sigh.

"But you know all this," I muttered. "Yes," he smiled and opened his eyes.

I noticed later, after we had shaken hands and thanked each other, that he had left his fine new cap on the hall-stand and that I had forgotten to give it to him.

It Takes Two To Tango

Stephanie Elliot

When I hear of student therapists struggling to understand their own emotional responses to their patients, I realise again that from time to time a patient can come along who can teach a student a great deal about the struggles we face in being human in intimate relationships. In particular, I remember Liam. This, then, is the story of our relationship. It occurred during my training.

At the time of seeing him, Liam was detained in a prison, where I was undertaking my clinical training hours. At the age of thirty-seven, he had been residing in various prisons for the last twenty years. His offence was grievous bodily harm, which he had committed at the age of seventeen. His memory of the offence was that for a few minutes he was overcome with a violent rage, "lost it" and wanted someone else to feel the pain he was in. The day following the offence, he walked into a police station and confessed.

As a young child, Liam grew up in a household of extensive emotional and physical deprivation. When he was three, his father left the family home and he could clearly remember watching him walk down the lane and calling out, "I will never forget you, Dad!" From the age of ten he spent five years in a children's home. During this time, he and many other children were victims of a well-organised network of child sex abusers, where they were forced to submit to the most obscene, degrading experiences imaginable. Not only were these children abused by the very people who should have protected them, the exploitation extended to figures in privileged positions, who should have upheld the morals and values of our society. Liam's attempts to reveal what was happening had only led to further suffering. Since then, legal proceedings have taken place and he has received compensation, but this did nothing to ease or lessen his suffering such as his recurring nightmares and flashbacks. He feared sleep, as sleep reawakened the suffering, exploitation and cruelty of his childhood.

Since the age of fifteen, Liam had made several suicide attempts. To his knowledge, twelve men from that children's home have committed suicide. Two years before I saw him, his brother became one of those twelve. From the age of fifteen, Liam's life revolved around alcohol, drugs and thefts to pay for this lifestyle. He acknowledged that, as a young man, he had been impulsive and violent throughout his detention, and this had increased the length of his sentence. It seemed that the emotional deprivation and harshness of prison life had come to mirror much of the bleakness of his early years.

When we first met I was taken aback by his exceptionally handsome features. At around six feet, four inches, he had a superb physique, olive skin and a mane of dark hair which contrasted with his clear blue eyes. He was from Ireland and as his words rolled together his soft accent could be quite mesmerising. In spite of the extreme deprivation in his life he held a sort of refreshing raw naivety that came through in his openness and a quality of compassion that I would discover.

From the beginning, Liam could be quite challenging about when our sessions should end, and often wanted to extend our time together. I discussed this dilemma with my supervisor, who suggested that Liam was "controlling, demanding and manipulative". I felt disappointed in myself; I felt that I had failed to convey the endearing qualities I perceived in him. Liam could well have some or all of the suggested traits but there also seemed within him to be a gentle tenderness and passion, which revealed itself in his compassion for others and for the injustices of the world. My supervisor remarked on Liam's accounts of what he thought he could see in my eyes. Little did I know then that for Liam my eyes would become the focus of much attention and that he would often comment on what he thought he saw in them. When my supervisor suggested, "Liam could fall in love with you", I swiftly dismissed this as an assumption that patients will fall in love with their therapists. I considered the dependency the therapeutic relationship may create, but "falling in love" seemed far too extreme.

In one of our sessions, Liam told me about a violent riot that he had been involved in. He described in a very visual manner the chaos of the prisoners' upheaval, in which he was badly beaten and thrown naked in a cell. After that he spent six months in segregation. He blamed himself for the incident—as he blamed himself for his child-hood abuse. I had been listening very intensely when Liam's gaze upon my face became puzzled and concerned. He leaned forward and said, "There's a tear on your cheek." I had been so engrossed in his story that I had lost sight of my responses. Embarrassed and hurriedly I wiped my cheek. Over the next few days I experienced what I can only describe as intrusive disturbing images of the last scene in Liam's story about the riots, in which I saw his naked beaten body in the segregation cell, curled up like a frightened animal. These images of his life came from nowhere and without warning, and left me feeling confused and worried that they could remain with me.

After these unsettling experiences, I was worried that Liam's disclosures might have troubled him through the week, as they had me. But, much to my bewilderment, in the following session he reported that he had felt uplifted during the week. The nightmares seemed to have lessened, and he talked very openly about how important I had become to him. My supervisor became concerned that Liam had the ability to project his own emotions into me so that I was left feeling them.

The next time we met, as Liam was talking about himself as a child in a self-loathing, deprecating manner, when he suddenly stopped, looked at me with puzzlement and said, "Don't look so sad."

"I do feel saddened by the hostility you express for yourself as a child. I wondered why you seem to forgive the people who harmed you, but not yourself?" Liam chose not to answer my inquiry, instead he turned his attention back to my eyes and asked, "Why is it, when I look in your eyes, I can see pain and suffering? You are the only person to have shown me such compassion and I think it is because you too have been hurt. But I don't want to hurt you."

"Hurt me?" I repeated in a surprised tone. Once more Liam did not follow my signal. Instead, he made his way over to the window and stared out at the rain. The heavy downpour seemed to fill the silence in the room. "Is it ever going to stop raining?" he asked in a dreamy voice. Then he whispered, "They say the mountains back home are washed away by it all . . . Look at the rain. There are my tears. Think of me when you're at home tonight and you hear the rain pelting against your window. Think 'There are Liam's tears . . . God is crying for Liam.'" That night as I drove home, the windscreen wipers fought hard to clear the heavy rainfall. I could not help but think of Liam's powerful metaphor of God's tears for him. I was overwhelmed, as I had no control over the tears I wept for Liam, just as I had no control over the rain outside.

There were occasions when Liam talked of longing to weep for his suffering. He would say he could feel the tears behind his eyes, but he feared letting them fall. He said his tears could push him over the edge. He had not had a visitor for over three years, as their parting sorrow was too painful for him to bear. In contrast, both in and outside our sessions, I had no difficulty in feeling deeply moved by his suffering. There were times when I would think of him and I felt a great sadness.

During these early sessions, there were a couple of occasions when our interactions were extremely intense, yet lively. In this period I experienced a wealth of different emotions, from deep despair and sadness to light-hearted humour. Thoughtful reflections were replaced by an active spontaneity from us both. It felt healthy and I thought much progress and movement was occurring in the therapeutic process. After such sessions I felt quite light-headed and dizzy and had to work hard to compose myself.

When the possibility arose that Liam would be moved to another prison. I felt I had to say to him that our sessions would be coming to an end. When I brought this up, Liam moved closer, slowly shook his head, smiled and reminded me that once I had suggested the importance of being open and honest in our relationship. I acknowledged I had said this. His gaze remained fixed on my face and I knew he was monitoring every expression. "Well," he continued, "The truth is I've fallen in love with you and I think you know it too."

"Know it too?", I gasped. I was both confused and surprised by his statement but he was not discouraged by my reaction. "You know there's something powerful between us—and it does not have to end."

I struggled to compose myself but felt the need to be firm about the boundaries of our relationship.

"We need to be very clear about this. We will never have any contact outside of these sessions."

"You don't understand," pleaded Liam, "I could go to an open prison for eighteen months and then we could get together. We could get married. I have money, you would never want for anything. Do you believe in love at first sight? Well, I know it's true. From the first time I saw you, I knew you where the one. And you knew it too. I saw it in your eyes. What do you think? Remember, "openness and honesty"?"

I called for Liam to think about the possibility of having hopes and wishes, and of wanting them so much that it's possible to believe others want them too. As much as I did not want to take away from what was occurring in the room, I needed to stress that we had to be clear that this was very different from our lives outside—that part of the therapeutic process was to manage our feelings about the ending of the relationship.

"You mean you've set me up," snapped Liam.

"Come on Liam. Let's think about who's setting this up?" I replied.

"It takes two to tango," Liam said. "Can you honestly look me in the eyes and tell me you don't care for me?"

During this stage of my training, I had gained some understanding of theoretical ideas that gave meaning to what was happening between us. I wondered whether Liam, unknowingly, was trying to seduce me into a situation where I too could abuse him, as others had, and in so doing, could confirm his mistrust of professionals. But theories failed to explain my own feelings in all of this. You see, Liam had become important to me. Often I thought of him outside of our sessions, much more than I did of my other patients. I really enjoyed being with him, and I looked forward to being with him.

His words "It takes two to tango" made me think about my own role. After all, there were two people in the room. I had to think about my own reactions and, as uncomfortable as this was, to admit they were implicated in this process. I searched within myself and questioned myself. Was I acting out some unconscious wish? Was this the result of some longing within me? Or should I push aside the theories and accept that Liam and I were just two people whose lives had crossed with mutual resonance? But all I felt was more confusion. Although the ethical part of me was aware that under no circumstances could there be a relationship outside of our sessions, there was also a part of me that was drawn.

I knew there was a price to pay for this as I began to feel as though Liam was taking energy from other parts of my life. At times, those close to me remarked that I seemed withdrawn and it was then that I would be thinking about him. His wish for us to be united outside the sessions continued to thrive. Although he seemed to accept my reasons for the impossibility of this dream, it kept resurfacing and it was clear that he still held hope that his desires would come true. He had an incredible sensitivity and was finely attuned to my overall being. The idea that someone could know me so well was attractive, even though at times this felt quite eerie and awkward. Liam attributed my avoidance of talking about his wishes for a continued relationship to my fear of intimacy. He suggested that I filled my life so no one could get near to me. He assumed that I had been hurt like he had, and for that reason was rejecting his wish for intimacy beyond the therapeutic relationship.

Initially, I felt too embarrassed to talk to anyone about my feelings regarding Liam, as I was concerned that it might lead to the recommendation that I should stop working with him. I did not want to consider this, as I felt a loyalty. If I withdrew now I would be yet another person turning away from him. I feared that others would see my practice as immature if I shared my feelings. But, eventually, I did talk of my feelings in supervision and to my relief my supervisor was very supportive. We came to the conclusion that above all this was an opportunity to offer Liam a different experience of relationship, compared to the negative experiences he had undergone. We also considered that he had mistaken my empathy for him as his own desires—that through me he was able to get some sense of the emotional pain that he was unable to bear himself.

I wondered whether it would be appropriate to share my feelings with Liam, rather than keeping them to myself. I argued that by acknowledging my feelings of attraction I could define clearer boundaries. I felt that our relationship had to be genuine in order for me to help him to find reality in himself. Throughout his life there had been so many who had deceived him through their disguises. I did not want to become yet another person who misled him. My genuine regard for him helped me feel secure in the fact that I would not act on my feelings but my supervisor did not support this idea:

she found my reasoning valid, but stressed that this could only be the case if the patient respected the therapist's separateness. Eventually we decided that Liam was not yet ready to do so.

The responses from my fellow trainees were also extremely helpful. Rather than the criticism I feared, I found genuine interest, concern and support. It struck me that the more openly I discussed my feelings, the weaker they became. I was told was that my strengths lay in my ability to empathise and be open. However, these same qualities were also seen as a weakness; I may have over-empathised and been too open. Yet, I myself did not feel as if I was being any less or any more open to him that other patients. So why was he affecting me so deeply? In time, these questions became clearer within the process of my own personal therapy. I discovered how the deprivation of his childhood and his longing for intimacy had awoken similar desires within me. My own story of longings and desires had become woven into our therapeutic relationship.

As our sessions continued, our spontaneous responses became replaced with more thoughtful reflections. Gently I told him that it felt intrusive when he imposed on me what I felt and thought, even if his perception was close. I began to speak about all the differences between us. I noted that, whenever he felt uncomfortable, he moved the focus onto our relationship. I started to feel with relief a sense of separateness between us. Liam on the other hand bridled at these changes and could at times be quite prickly and angry. Although our relationship transformed I still felt very fond of him but these feelings no longer engulfed me; rather I became more able to accept and manage them. He struggled with these changes and, at times, it was difficult to stay with his distress. I also felt a sense of loss, but was unable to decipher its meaning. In time I came to realise that my loss was in sacrificing my fantasy of him and what he had come to represent in the aspirations of his dreams.

Then one day Liam came to one session looking terrible. His golden skin was ashen and he had dark shadows under his eyes. He told me that he had slept very little, his nightmares had been so powerful that he had vomited throughout the night. Soon he became very tearful, then was heaving sobs. He talked about his abusers and how they were still destroying his life through nightmares and flashbacks. He angrily paced the room, at one point kicking the footstool. He was raging and, at last, it felt as though this anger was directed towards his abusers, not at himself or me. After forty minutes he asked for the session to end. Before being escorted to his wing he stood in the corridor sobbing his eyes out. His cries seemed to echo around the building and I longed to offer some comfort.

The following week he was in much lighter sprits. He had brought with him four Polaroid photos of himself, and talked about each one in depth. The photos where taken in prison, but they held happier memories, such as Christmas parties and working in the gardens. Upon leaving, he put a photo on the table and said, "I want you to have this." I hesitated, as I knew the photo was precious to him, but our session was closing and there was no time to discuss why he wanted me to have it. As he walked out of the door, he turned and faced me. His eyes glistened with tears as he said, "I will never forget you." Then, as I watched him walk away, it suddenly struck me . . . Liam was saying goodbye.

He did not come to our next three appointments, and while I waited for him each week, I experienced very mixed emotions. I was annoyed that I had not seen the photo as a parting gift; I regretted that I had never had the opportunity to say goodbye to him. I mulled over his words about how I fill every space in my life. Is this what I would do now? Fill Liam's space with the next patient? I remembered his parting words to his departing father, "I will never forget you," and I wondered what he had been trying to convey to me as he repeated those words. Did he feel I had abandoned him like his father had done? But now it was Liam who left me. Did he want to put me in the position of the little boy who watched his dad leave? In the third week I wrote to him. I said that I would understand if he did not want to continue, but that I would hold his session open for a given time and the following week he attended.

When he arrived he appeared anxious and agitated. He was due to have a parole board meeting in a couple of weeks and was trying to hurry along reports from solicitors, psychologists, probation, psychiatrists.

"Do you feel that you have been let down?" I asked.

"That question makes me realise that you are the only person who has not let me down," he replied. "I am sorry if I have hurt you by not attending. I thought it would be easier to cut my losses and end the relationship before it had to end."

"And you have returned," I added.

Liam then told me that throughout our meetings he had kept a diary and had reread it several times over the last few weeks. It had then occurred to him that much of what he had written about me was in fact what he himself had been feeling. When he had talked of my fear of anyone getting too close, he explained, it was because he feared that I was getting too close to him—but then he had thought about what he was giving up. "And what are you giving up?" I enquired.

"The chance to trust someone . . . I trust you . . . Do you know why I trust you? Because you're brave," he continued. "Brave?" I repeated with some surprise. "Yeah, I thought about you, and the times I've seen you laugh and cry, look happy, look sad. It felt really genuine and that takes courage, especially in a place like this. It shows you trusted me enough to show me your feelings . . . and that's why I trust you with mine. You know everyone I've trusted has hurt me."

Gently as I could I reminded him that when our time would come to part, there might be some hurt feelings and he might feel let down by this relationship too. He sat back and smiled. "That's an understatement if ever there was one. It will be one of the saddest days ever for me. But you know, in a way you will always be with me. You see, you have a place in my heart alongside my brother and no one can take that away from me. So I'll have two good people inside me always."

As our sessions carried on, Liam very gradually started to feel safe enough to express his emotional pain. He described events in which he had felt shame, guilt, fear, total helplessness and anger at the injustices that had been done unto him as a child. Within this, he was able to reflect on the suffering he had caused to others. During these distressing periods, I tried to stay as emotionally close to him as I could. It felt important that he should know that I too could bear the enormousness of his distress. What aided me through these periods was my clear knowledge that this was Liam's suffering— not mine—and that all I could hope for was to be near to him.

As our time progressed, I often thought back to our early meetings, when difficult and painful feelings from my own past had been awakened. Yet now I knew that, within the bigger story, this experience had been helpful for, although I had felt uncomfortable and embarrassed about my feelings for him, somehow they had shown me that I must be no more or no less than myself if I hoped to give him the freedom to be himself. I felt humbled and thankful to have met this remarkable man. What's more, I knew that when the time came for us to part, I too would feel a parting sorrow. I was comforted by his belief that I would hold a place in his heart and even though I was unable to tell him, he too would hold a place in mine. I felt sure he would know this.

The next week as I walked through the prison I was greeted by an officer who cheerfully informed me, "You've got one less today." When I reached the clinic, I was informed that Liam had been transferred in the night, without forewarning. "Ghosted" is the term used in the prison when a prisoner is no longer there the next day. The reason for this procedure is that escapes cannot be planned nor the transfers sabotaged. After the initial shock I descended into a state of grief that touched my own painful past losses. I seriously contemplated my suitability to become a psychotherapist and I vowed to myself that I would never again become so emotionally involved with a patient. Then one night I had a dream. I stood weeping by a nameless grave. I bent down to place a rose on the grave and leant forward to stroke the blank headstone. Gradually, the words 'Thank God I Knew Him' became visible on the headstone. I was reminded of a time when Liam had thought suicide was his only escape, and had dreamed about his death and his funeral. He told me that he had seen me crying alone by his graveside. He said that if this ever came true then I should consider that, even though he was gone, he would know I was there. Even though my dream was heart-rending, it also held some comfort and helped me to conclude that, if I could turn back time, given all I knew now, I would still want to meet this brave man, Liam.

The Case of Anna F.

Maggie Murray

Ifirst came across Gerti Hartmann in the early 1960s. I was a
hospital visitor at Broadmoor. She was in her late seventies and
had lived on one of the wards since she was forty-nine. Her grave
is still in the grounds if you know where to look.

It's a tough enough institution today, but then it was a mausoleum
for the half-dead—dimly-lit corridors echoing with muffled shouts,
dingy communal areas and undecorated individual rooms as narrow
as coffins. One of the other older women whispered to me that Gerti
was famous. She didn't take shit from anyone and in the 1940s she
had made a run for it. Later on I learnt that, God only knows how,
she got to the top of the wall. It must be thirty foot high—weaving
for several miles around a patch of best stockbroker-belt Berkshire
like a snake disturbed in the grass. When she dropped down on the
other side she broke both legs.

One day I was playing cards with a patient at the day-room table.
Pale sunlight slanted through the narrow windows into the thick fug
of cigarette smoke and dust. A smell of pine disinfectant masked the
taint of urine and stale sweat. In the background women lounged
on sagging armchairs in front of the flickering black and white TV.
A nurse, as the guards are always called, sat the regulation three feet
away from us. "Have you ever read Freud's case history of Dora?"
my partner asked as she melded a perfect Canasta. She was a clever
woman and knew of my interest in turn-of-the-century feminism.
At her words Gerti Hartmann, who was lying on her usual sofa
nearby, sat bolt upright—skinny and rigid, eyes glittering.

"All wrong," she said in her lightly accented and still erotic
voice—shades of Marlene in those cavernous Berlin nightclubs
portrayed in 1940s films. She flicked back her long grey hair and

pulled her sagging black cardigan around her as if it was a fabulous, bejewelled and imperial robe. "And the other one about a woman—all wrong. I knew him, you see, during and after the war—first war, that is. Sweet man, loved a joke, but an unreliable storyteller."

The nurse raised her eyes to the ceiling. "Him and Joan of Arc get on together, do they?" she sneered.

Gerti windmilled her arms around in a wild and frightening way. "You leave Jeanne out of this," she shouted, "She's voices. Doctor Freud was in the world." My card-playing partner looked at me. "Ignore her for a moment," she said, dealing especially carefully, "She's a bit of a romancer some of the time—but as solid as a rock when the voices aren't on her."

Several years later the woman I visited moved on and Gerti put in a request for me to come to see her instead. She didn't play cards, but talked incessantly and chain-smoked Golden Virginia roll-ups the whole time I was there. She had a wicked sense of humour and hinted at a disreputable early life, but her fund of stories only related to her time in England. She had arrived as a refugee in 1937 and had never really got used to her changed circumstances and what she called our 'English double reserve'. It was a phrase she swore she'd read on a bottle of sherry and it always made her laugh. After some months we were allowed the privilege of meeting in the Central Hall where the less volatile patients had tea with their visitors.

A dozen small tables were scattered round the large space. Narrow iron columns of Doric ancestry supported the high ceiling. The ornate cornices and carved woodwork were original 19th century and perfectly preserved. The paintwork was peeling and over the stage area the paintings by a former patient looked as if they needed dusting. Nevertheless, it was an impressive room. Gerti said that at Christmas and on other special occasions it did duty as a dance hall or concert venue. The thought of those closed events, where the male and female patients mixed with the staff, filled me with excitement and unease. I fantasised about wangling an invitation for myself and I imagined Gerti seizing me round the waist and waltzing me off to the strains of *The Blue Danube*.

On visiting days four or five duty nurses in navy uniforms sat round the edge of the room—bored and watchful. We would take a table in the middle. It meant we had some privacy. We could also go to the shop together. "Such rubbish these pastries," Gerti would say, peering at three or four flaccid pastries under a plastic dome, "In Vienna we would have fed them to dogs." But she always ate at least one. "So sweet of you to buy them for me, darling girl." Her thin eyebrow would lift and I could see for sure how charming and seductive she had been as a young woman. Even in her late seventies she was pretty devastating.

At that time I was working on my Masters—obsessively according to most of my ex-friends. I had picked up on a 1960s lecture that Firestone gave about Freudianism and feminism growing 'from the same soil'. I urgently needed new material and it was proving difficult to find. One day I asked Gerti if it was true she'd met Freud. I told her I was researching the background of some of his case histories. "Which ones?" she asked in a very superior tone. "Dora," I replied a little sheepishly. It seemed too obvious a choice, "and the case of homosexuality in a woman." I had her attention. She stared at me and lit another cigarette. "So . . . Doctor Freud's nameless little lesbian," she said.

I was taken aback. Most people haven't heard of her. They certainly don't know any details, such as the fact the client, unlike in all the other case histories, is given no name. I said nothing, but I guess I looked expectant. She pouted her lips at me and raised her chin, "I'll tell you about her next time, darling. When you bring me a real *millefeuille*."

I got the authentic version easily enough from Patisserie Valerie in Soho—four in a tastefully decorated box. The assistant who served me was agog to hear where they were going and very helpful. Getting them through the security procedures was another matter altogether. They were too small to contain a metal file of any useful size, so I suppose they were worried I'd laced them with dope or heroin. I was so innocent in those days that the possibility hadn't even occurred to me. The staff scrutinised the till receipt minutely. They poked into the pastries with a knitting needle and questioned me closely. Finally they got tired and waved me through with my prize. It did the trick. Heroin or no heroin Gerti was ecstatic.

"Liebling," she said easing back the cardboard lid with practiced fingers, "That you should spoil me so—and all on account of a little pupil." At this point I didn't know what she was talking about so I simply watched her bite delicately into the impeccable pastry. The cream squashed out sideways. She scooped a bit off with her little finger and licked it slowly. To say that I felt she was toying with me would be an understatement. I tried to slow my breathing and said nothing.

"What a strange, cruel, open child she was. And as an adolescent—such romantic and electrifying fantasies." She glanced at me slyly, "I saw her on-and-off throughout our lives. The last time she was a middle-aged woman. Still 'other-worldly' . . . but sharp. She came to visit me here with the faithful Dorothy. In the fifties I think it was. Freshly ground mocha coffee they brought me. Delicious. I can't tell you how much I enjoyed it."

I made a mental note of what to bring next time. My heart thumped. "Anna Freud and Dorothy Burlingham were here?"

"I wrote to her, she wrote back to me. She came on a visit. We talked of the past. But the case you are interested in she couldn't bring herself to mention." Something clicked in my head. Could it be? The words were out before I could stop them. "You . . . are you . . . the case? The homosexual woman?" Her laughter peeled across the stained tabletops and grubby linoleum floor. People turned to stare. A duty nurse set out towards us.

"No, no, Liebling," she coo-ed as she was led away, "I'm the bisexual with the big house and the married lady-friend, who carried on promiscuous affairs with a number of men. Ha ha."

It was weeks until I sat with her in the Central Hall again. It worried me that they might have increased her medication. I did write, but she would never reply with more than a single line on a post card—confirming a visit or thanking me for a gift. I could hardly wait to see her again and rehearsed questions I could ask.

"So," I said as I sat down at the table and held out my hands to let her smell them, "A packet of freshly-ground mocha has gone to your ward in a security box. You'll get it later." She stroked my fingers in a very sexual way and bent over them inhaling deeply. "Ah . . . such pleasure. Your Dr Freud would have loved that—with one of his best cigars." I was desperate to get to the point. "Who was the homosexual woman?"

"Not so fast, Liebling. Let us order some of your dreadful English tea." She signalled to one of the patients whose job it was to wait on the tables. "Gerti, please! Who was she? She must have been a friend of the family—or even a member of the Freud family itself. A cousin, a niece. I've read all his writings and hers. Nothing else fits. What was her name?"

The tea arrived in thick cups. She took a biscuit as well and attentively broke it in two. "I have read them all as well, you may be surprised to hear." I was, but I tried not to show it and kept silent. She never failed catch me off balance. "It is difficult to unravel because Dr Freud, for reasons of medical ethics, or perhaps more likely personal reticence, changed many things in the story." She sounded very precise and rather prim—as if she was quoting from a document or legal deposition. I squirmed like a stupid and gauche schoolgirl. "I know—but who was she?"

Gerti slowly stirred three spoonfuls of sugar into her tea. "His youngest daughter, Anna." My hands shook and my mind raced ahead. Was it possible? I needed to consult my references, the texts, dates. Damnation that I couldn't bring books into the Central Hall! "Gerti," I steeled myself, "You're not having me on?"

"Why should I? I'm an old lady—who cares what I say?"

"Well if Anna's the young woman . . ."

"The lesbian—yah." I hardly dared think about it and rapidly moved on. ". . . the irate father in the case must be Freud himself."

"Yes. Irate is a good word, yes."

"You were . . . intimate?"

"He was . . . yes . . . as he put it, one of a number of men who visited me regularly."

I was hyperventilating by that point, my name already adorning the front page of the *New York Review of Books*. Anna Freud was a lesbian? Her father wrote about it? He had affairs with . . . ? Gerti continued. "He was entrancing and entertaining. All you people with your noses in books—you're so naive. Did you really believe that because he gave up sex with his wife, he gave up sex? Pffaf. He loved it. And he used to confide in me his worries about his daughter. Since I was skilled in the arts of the erotic—as he so flatteringly put it— he thought I might help her. As a cross between a mother and a whore, I think."

"He introduced you . . . to his daughter?"

"He engineered a meeting. We became friends. 'The Psycho-Analyst's Daughter and The Cocotte.' A better title for the case, don't you think?"

A thousand questions welled up in my mind. But Gerti was unstoppable. "You would know, of course, about her fantasies of being beaten and her amorous daydreams. Pfaff. Took all that in his stride—published articles about it. But that she fell in love with me he couldn't bear. He said it wasn't an illness. 'It' meaning homosexuality. He said all sorts of things to explain it—that she was feminist, an intellectual, too intelligent to accept the role of a hausfrau. But he still couldn't bear it. She was only eighteen but he sent her away to stay in Merano for a 'rest cure'."

"When her sister was getting married?"

"Yes. Real little goody-two-shoes that one. Mother's favourite girl."

It was falling into place. I wasn't sure though whether the ferment I was in was purely intellectual. Gerti's eyes were so amused and her silences so inviting. "What about . . . the girl's—Anna's—suicide attempt? . . . jumping over the wall, onto the railway . . . when you— it must have been you! . . . met her father out walking."

"Teenage histrionics. Later she wrote about symptoms like that— behaviour that would be psychotic at any other time being normal in adolescence." I nodded, hungry for more. I had overlooked so much. "She was upset, naturally. It rankled to find she shared me romantically with her father. She adored him. Absolutely no doubt of that. But there was no real suicide bid, no railway line on the other side of the wall—only a patch of scruffy grass. It was he that had a fear of trains, though. After that they sent her away."

"Was it a breakdown?"

"A broken heart, Liebling. She loved him—but worshipped me. Besotted, I think you say in English. He hounded her about it and attempted a 'cure' a couple of years later. Analysed her himself. Outrageous I'd say, but perhaps he was frightened of letting anyone else try. Who knows what would have come out?"

"She never married either . . ."

"She threatened to marry Ernest Jones. Told me that with his reputation he'd do. It was only to annoy her father. He was beside himself with guilt and jealousy. Wanted her all to himself. But he had to put up with Dorothy in the end didn't he? But it seems he liked her."

"And did you . . . did she . . . were you ever . . ." I was ablaze with curiosity.

"Liebling! Please!" She looked offended. "A little discretion. Next time you can ask more. And I'll tell you about dear Dora as well."

There never was a next time. She died in her sleep three days later. I did get a postcard though. She must have sent it the next day, but because of clearance procedures it didn't arrive until after the funeral. "I hope you enjoyed the entertainment," it said. "Thank you for the mocha."

That was all. No signature, no date, no kisses.

I went back through the original sources with a flea-comb trying to corroborate the story. For weeks the *Standard Edition* was never out of my arm's reach. I wanted to believe it and the dates fitted. Many of Freud's comments took on new meanings. Most of all there were parallels and slips I found in different texts. He seemed confused, in conflict.

Gerti left me her possessions. There wasn't much. A silver-backed hairbrush, a small radio and a German translation of *Cyrano de Bergerac*. In the front, copied out in English was the following inscription:

With love—and in praise of 'Altruistic surrender'   Anna (1936)

Author's Note

Although this story is entirely fictional and my own fantasy, most of the facts about Anna and Sigmund Freud are true. I have taken artistic license in allowing Anna's visit to Broadmoor and her inscription in the book. But the play was one of her favourites and she referred to the last act when Dorothy Burlingham, her life-long companion, was dying, according to Elizabeth Young-Bruehl's work Anna Freud.

I feel that my assumption that Sigmund Freud knew the 'cocotte' personally is clear from his own text, Psychogenesis of a Case of Female Homosexuality in Volume 14. *All the dates fit—especially if you allow for changes often introduced in the name of ethics and confidentiality. Anna was certainly sent on a 'rest cure' when she was eighteen and in some distress about her sado-masochistic and masturbatory daydreams—again discussed in Young-Bruehl's book and in Anna's own, clearly autobiographical article,* Beating Fantasies and Daydreams.

As to Anna finally concurring with her father's wishes, her classic work, The Ego and the Mechanisms of Defence *details altruistic surrender as a major defence against the gratification of one's own wishes. She gives* Cyrano de Bergerac *as the supreme example of this 'retiring in favour of others' as Sigmund characterised it. Both Freuds link it to homosexuality.*